Richard L. Evans —

THE MAN AND
THE MESSAGE

Richard L. Evans

Richard L. Evans —

THE MAN
AND THE MESSAGE

by Richards L. Evans, Jr.

BOOKCRAFT INC.
SALT LAKE CITY, UTAH

Library of Congress Catalog Card Number: 73-84591

1st Printing, 1973

LITHOGRAPHED IN U.S.A.

PUBLISHERS PRESS
SALT LAKE CITY, UTAH

Publisher's Foreword

For the publishers, the release of this book is an event of exceptional significance. It symbolizes circumstances for which we are profoundly grateful—the special and close relationship which has existed between Bookcraft and Richard L. Evans and his family since the inception of the company.

Bookcraft has good reason to hold Richard L. Evans in high esteem. It was he who conceived the name *Bookcraft*. In those early days he was a part-owner in the fledgling enterprise, a financial interest which his characteristic integrity and scrupulous honesty later led him to surrender, lest his mounting Church responsibilities should somehow involve him in a conflict of interest.

We greatly miss the pleasant association and valued counsel we continued to receive over the years until he passed on. But there is comfort in the thought that others gain where we lose, that Elder Evans has now renewed pleasant companionships he experienced in mortality. Among others, he is no doubt enjoying the society of two close associates, each a staunch supporter of Bookcraft in its early days, who preceded him into that next world—his "second father" Elder John A. Widtsoe and his trusted friend J. K. Orton, the founder of Bookcraft.

It is fitting that we express our sincere appreciation also to the family of Richard L. Evans—to his four fine sons and his devoted wife and companion Alice. We are grateful not only in general for their continuing happy relationship with Bookcraft but also in particular for their diligence and cooperation in the preparation of this book.

No book could fully capture the character and spirit and accomplishment of Richard L. Evans. Nor does this book even attempt definitiveness. What is hoped is that it will portray the essence of this great man's life, together with a representative selection of the concepts and thoughts he expressed and which essentially made him what he was. In this spirit we take pride in presenting *Richard L. Evans—The Man and the Message.*

MARVIN W. WALLIN
BOOKCRAFT

Preface

If someone had asked me to write a biography of my father—even one of the limited length in this volume—the task would have seemed too awesome for me to attempt. Thus the sketch of his life in Part I—entitled *The Man*—came into being not so much by original design as because one thing led to another.

Marvin Wallin, manager of Bookcraft, conceived the idea and format of this book. When he presented his thinking to our family, I agreed to help by gathering information from family and friends and by research into available written materials. For the sake of clarity, I conveyed most of my "findings" to Bookcraft in writing instead of orally. Eventually I found that, without initially intending to do so, I had written the greater part of the biographical sketch that Bookcraft sought. I am indebted, however, to Bookcraft editor George Bickerstaff and to Hartt Wixom for considerable contributions to the writing of the manuscript. George Bickerstaff also critically reviewed the manuscript and made many helpful suggestions. Without his literary workmanship this book would be much less than it is.

Part II, *The Message,* brings together representative selections from Richard L. Evans' talks and writings. The sections in this part are derived as follows:

Sunday Morning from Temple Square	Mainly from broadcasts of the Spoken Word
To the Church	Talks given at general conferences and to other LDS groups

A Rotarian Speaks   Talks given mainly to Rotary
                                     gatherings

From ". . . the Pen of a   Selections from the King
   Ready Writer"   Features articles mentioned
                                     on page 51

Besides those mentioned above, I feel indebted and express my appreciation to others who helped in the preparation of this book:

To my mother and my three brothers for letting me impose on them for long hours, sometimes through much of the night, to obtain the facts and to review the manuscript at various stages.

To Norma Anderson for assistance in selecting and compiling my father's talks and writings included here.

To Geniel Robbins, Helen Hintze and Lucille Rossiter (my father's secretaries at the time of his passing) and to Paul H. Evans (executive producer of the Tabernacle Choir Broadcast) for their cheerful and ready responses to my requests for information.

Most importantly, I feel deeply grateful for a father who set an extraordinary example for his sons to follow, not in his specific attainments, for they were uniquely his, but in the qualities of spirit and character which pushed him onward. He did not pause to talk much of himself or his work, even to his family. As a result of the research for this book, the significance of his life and achievements may perhaps be even better understood now than before his passing.

Contents

PART I
THE MAN

The Man Behind
The Spoken Word

"...Toiling Upward In The Night"

The Voice Is Stilled

Sunday morning broadcast — Richard Evans awaits cue
from control room

The Man Behind the Spoken Word

The man seated near the microphone looked at a paper in his hand, then pressed it against his knee and crossed something out. Somewhere a voice called out, "Two minutes!" But the man did not look hurried. He seemed deep in thought as he penciled something over the crossed-out lines. Then he arose and moved up to the microphone in time to begin: "Once more we welcome you within these walls, with music and the spoken word, from the Crossroads of the West . . ."

Millions of listeners instantly recognized the deep, reassuring voice. Once again it was Sunday morning, the time for the weekly half-hour broadcast of the Mormon Tabernacle Choir from Temple Square in Salt Lake City. Once more the thrilling strains of the 375-voice choir and the great organ would charm the ear and exalt the heart. But more than that, the first words told the listener that Richard Evans was again at his post at the microphone and that they would hear another inspiring message in his Spoken Word.

That Word lasted only two to three minutes, but for many listeners it was the high point of the broadcast. Here was a message from Milton or Matthew, from Longfellow or Luke, always brought to the context of the listener's life with that deep insight into human nature which Richard Evans had made his own. Here was inspiration and motivation; nothing theoretical or academic, but a piece of practical counsel, not for some vague future time but here and now, today. Here too was a subtle invitation to focus on the thoughts expressed, for the words themselves were delivered so calmly and eloquently and smoothly that listeners tended to think only of the message rather than of the man behind it. And that was just as Richard Evans wanted it.

He wanted something else in his broadcasts too—timeliness. This he achieved partly by a habit which in someone else might have looked like poor organization—the deliberate practice of not preparing the Spoken Word script until two or three days before broadcast time. Having a familiarity with the poets and prophets and the best in literature generally, he could have stockpiled scripts months in advance. But that would have eliminated an ally—pressure. He worked better under last-minute pressure, he told his family. Furthermore, the "feeling in the air" at the time, occasionally in relation to a national event, was more likely to inspire the comment, the nuance of thought appropriate to the occasion, than a leisurely advance preparation could have done.

Hence the late preparation and the last-minute, almost last-second, alterations to the script he had "finalized" just hours before. "There is no use saying a piece of copy is final if you can improve it on or off the air," he would explain. Thus what had been a perfectly clean typewritten page when he entered the Mormon Tabernacle on Sunday morning could soon contain so many crossed-out words and so many scrawled insertions on margins and corners that at the exact moment he was to go on the air only Richard Evans could read it.

Such an approach could hardly be recommended to others as a sure-fire route to success, but it proved to be completely appropriate to the unique talents of the man who for forty-one years wrote, produced, and announced the longest continuing radio program in America and who in the process created over two thousand messages of hope and inspiration which he delivered to millions of listeners.

Not that he perfected the style and format on the first broadcast and never deviated from it after that. Behind the scenes he was constantly analyzing the program and, especially during its early years, he made many changes as a result. Before he joined the Choir broadcast, the musical numbers had been announced in a conventional manner. But he began to weave through the music a moral and spiritual thread of spoken messages which soon became an inseparable part of the program. He evaluated and revised the format for years before arriving at what seemed right to him as regards the length and approach of his "Spoken Word" comment. For nearly twenty years too he changed and refined the wording of the opening "welcome" and the conclusion or "sign-off" portion of the broadcast, finally settling on the phrases that became almost his trademark throughout America: Each week he welcomed listeners with—"Once more we welcome you within these walls with music and the spoken word from the Crossroads of the West." Half an hour later he bade them farewell with—"Again we leave you within the shadows of the everlasting hills. May peace be with you, this day and always."

The wife who tuned in after breakfast, the husband who put down the morning paper at the familiar opening strains— the listeners knew only the inspiring results and not the pressures behind the program. One such pressure, particularly in the early days of radio when the concept of the commercially precious second was new, was broadcasting time. The program must start and stop precisely on time, since every second was earmarked. Once, early in his career, Richard Evans was ten seconds early in concluding the half-hour broadcast. Before he could walk across the street from the Tabernacle to the KSL studio, a telegram had arrived from CBS in New York City inquiring as to the cause of the wasted ten seconds.

Another built-in pressure, always present for a radio announcer, was accentuated in a program carrying the seriousness and dignity of the Spoken Word. Once on the air, the announcer must not cough, sneeze, make a long hesitation, get hiccups, or mispronounce or stutter over a word. At times, when listening to the radio, if Richard would hear an announcer make such a mistake he would comment, full of empathy: "Poor fellow, I know what he's going through." Richard made few such mistakes himself, but the ever-present possibility hung over his head.

Still another source of pressure was that the Choir broadcast is one of the few radio and television programs still carried "live" over a national network instead of being prerecorded, any errors then being spliced out before the broadcast. For all that, the broadcast was not rehearsed in its entirety. Though the organists practiced, the Choir rehearsed and Richard prepared his Spoken Word, these were not all put together until air time. What went out over the network therefore represented the first and only time that the program was put together or timed as a whole.

While Richard almost never felt free from the pressures of the broadcast, tensions mounted just before air time. Only when the broadcast was over could he relax somewhat. How then did he manage to come across to his listeners so calm and deliberate? Only he knew the answer to that question. As smooth and unruffled as was his delivery and his personality, it might seem that doing the program was easy for him. Many people in fact complimented him on being so calm and relaxed during the broadcast. This was ironic to him, for he confided to his family that he had never done the broadcast without feeling great tension, nervousness, even fright— the fear of making a mistake. The pressure churned inside him and increased as Sunday approached, and he had to exercise strict control over his feelings when he approached the microphone for the broadcast.

But the inner rewards and satisfactions made it all more than worth while. Appreciative listeners continually affirmed the powerful influence of his brief observations given each Sunday. Two comments probably best sum up this general reaction. One listener, an active member of another Christian church, wrote that he gave her "more to think about in five minutes than all the rest of the denominations can in their masses, sermons, and devotions." Another said, "He is not so much a voice as a heart."

Both Richard's heart and voice, together with his extra-ordinary qualities of mind and soul, were brought to bear on the matter of capturing the imagination of his listeners and persuading them to set their sights higher. Yet his messages, though frequently based on a quotation from scripture or other literature, were never didactic or preachy. Simply phrased and expressed, they portrayed profound truths in a form universally understandable. They skillfully dramatized old truths, persuasively submitted new ideas, and depicted both as part of the eternal scheme of things. Many listeners had no formal creed or religion, yet the simple power of his messages made them feel closer to God. Beauty of expression was always there, but never that alone. The soft, determined voice was constantly conveying the positive, uplifting ideal: "You *can* change. Do it! Do it now!"

While his Spoken Word comments were geared to the general audience and deliberately avoided missionary-type allusions, listener interest in both the man and his message brought to his office many inquiries about the Church. These he always responded to personally, where appropriate putting the inquirer in touch with LDS missionaries. Many of those who inquired were eventually baptized into the Church, having received from the Spoken Word the initial impetus to investigate its message.

While Richard Evans was best known throughout America for his weekly broadcasts, whose success was widely acclaimed, he fitted much more than that into an intensely busy life. It was "part of the job" of course to travel with the Choir on their tours. He acted as commentator in scores of Choir concerts throughout much of the United States, in Canada and Mexico, and in six European countries. Apart from that, a summary of his attainments and assignments (not in chronological order) would read something as follows:

Filled a mission of nearly three years in Europe for The Church of Jesus Christ of Latter-day Saints, during which he edited the *Millennial Star* and wrote a history of the British Mission. Gained a bachelor's degree in English and a master's in Economics from the University of Utah. Served as a member of the general board of the YMMIA. Served as managing editor of the magazine the *Improvement Era* for fourteen years and a senior editor for twenty-one years. Served as a General Authority of the Church for thirty-three years. Was director of the Temple Square Mission. Was President of the University of Utah Alumni Association. Served for twenty years on the Board of Regents of the University of Utah and for eighteen years on the Board of Trustees of Brigham Young University. Was appointed a member of the first Utah State Board of Higher Education and was on the board of directors of many business and financial enterprises. Served in Rotary for many years, first as president of his local Salt Lake Club, followed by other offices culminating in his election as Rotary's International President for 1966-67; and was also Chairman of the Trustees of the Rotary International Foundation. In Rotary work, visited and spoke in some ninety countries, on every continent. Authored numerous newspaper and magazine articles appearing in *Encyclopedia Britannica, Reader's Digest, Look Magazine,* and many other publications. Served as a circuit speaker for the Knife and Fork Clubs and the Executive Clubs and as a master of ceremonies at numerous civic and university functions. Wrote a regular column for a national newspaper syndicate. Published seventeen books. Managed to squeeze in a happy marriage and the raising of four sons.

Small wonder that in 1938 a newspaper, after giving him a birthday salute, added: "Hobbies, none. Except his sons."

By any standards, even the superficial recital above adds up to a life of great accomplishment. What was there about the man behind the Spoken Word that could produce such outstanding attainment? What qualities of character, what powers of mind and heart, combined to impel Richard Evans to heights of achievement?

The answers are illuminating. They reveal a completely honest man. For the very characteristics which took him to success were the solid, "old-fashioned" qualities he gently advocated over the years in his Spoken Word programs.

Richard Evans was talented, gifted. But so are many who live out lives of mediocrity. His strength lay in the realization that the development of talents is one of the purposes of life; that it is a prerequisite to complete happiness; and that although we properly use our talents in the service of others, as he certainly did, there is nothing selfish *per se* in seeking through all honorable means the satisfaction which achievement brings. To these realizations he added the catalyst many lack—he *acted* upon them.

Manifestly one of his talents was a power of expression, an ability to communicate through the written and the spoken word. In the improvement of this gift he early developed a love for good literature, which he read as widely as time permitted—more extensively in earlier days, more intensively later as time narrowed and perception broadened. The scriptures were always close at hand, to be savored and digested as daily scriptural food. But literature alone might have made him merely bookish. The insights it gave him into human nature were further enhanced by the more important human relationships—family, friends, associates, acquaintances. His close friend and mentor, Elder John A. Widtsoe, summed up this aspect of his development with the words: "Wise reading, extensive travel, and association with worthwhile people have extended his educational horizon."

The habit of the selected experience—the shunning of inferior in favor of superior literature, for example—carried over easily from input to output. During his lifetime he won many awards, from the Junior Chamber of Commerce award at thirty-four years of age as the outstanding young man of the year to honorary doctorate degrees from three universities and numerous other honors. But what really marked his strivings was not quantity but quality. His sights were set high. Hence came that meticulous workmanship which identified Richard Evans and which literally demanded success.

This approach to life, this devotion to the ideal of quality performance, made personal industry an integral part of Richard's being. His early environment had much to do with this. Left fatherless as a baby, he learned the value of work while still a boy. Not only did he do his share of work around the home as one of nine children, but he also started outside, after-school work at an early age. Later he worked hard to earn money to put himself through college.

Talent and interest early led him in the direction of the kind of work he was to excel in. At seventeen he was the editor of the high school newspaper. He won a state championship in debate that earned him a scholarship to college. While serving as editor of the *Millennial Star* in England during a two-year, full-time mission for his Church, he also wrote a history of the British Mission. All this meant hard work— long hours, pressure from deadlines, concentrated mental application in research and writing, exhaustion of brain and body.

As skills and assignments multiplied, he was to increasingly pay this kind of price. But wasn't this part of the work ethic, the concept that had made America great and offered success to her enterprising citizens? And didn't the satisfactions he received more than compensate for the effort? To Richard Evans the hard work was a completely natural and normal part of the total picture. He came to think of it not even as a part of the "opposition in all things," but literally as something to be enjoyed rather than to be endured.

But natural gifts, the unending reach for higher performance, and personal industry may not be adequate alone. Also required is the ability to hold to a predetermined course, to insure stability of purpose. Richard supplied this partly through a rare tenacity of will. Once a well-conceived project was planned, a goal set, an objective established, he did not allow any but the most important of unforeseen considerations to deflect him from the appointed end. Not that he was inflexible—personal goals more than once gave way to a Church calling, for example. But the steel under the calm and courteous exterior simply refused to yield to less than fundamental considerations.

This tenacity was closely related to another sturdy, "old-fashioned" trait of character—a sense of duty. He recalled that in his boyhood his mother would frequently remind her children: "Do your duty, always do your duty." She taught her youngest son well, for he grew up with a strong sense of moral obligation to do whatever duty required and displayed an amazing ability to subordinate his own desires and convenience to whatever he felt to be his obligation at the moment.

Nowhere was this more apparent than in the weekly broadcast. What would have been more natural and reasonable in these days of taped programs than for Richard Evans to prerecord his Spoken Word comments and thus obviate the need for his presence at the broadcast? But that would not do. He was the one responsible. He was the announcer and the producer. To be avoidably absent from the broadcast would in his eyes have constituted a dereliction of duty.

Even the occasional short vacation, which he squeezed in more for the family's benefit than for his own, had to be worked in between Sundays. On one vacation the family took a trip to California, visiting the beach and the wonders of that state. But Richard was back in Salt Lake City in time for his Sunday morning broadcast. In the entire forty-one years he never once willingly missed being personally present at a broadcast from the "Crossroads of the West."

As much as anything it was a sense of duty too which gave him his personal drive. While some equated his success with genius, to him the simpler answer was the correct one— hard work plus good organization. In this he conscientiously applied a primary doctrine of Christ's Church that earth life is given for each to prove himself, to use his agency and powers to make something of his life. If a man truly believed in himself and in what he was doing, he would use his time wisely. And though Richard must supply the initial impetus, a conviction gained through prayer told him that while he was doing things God approved of he could count on divine assistance.

Richard's Spoken Word comments often talked of rising above circumstances, of taking hold of life, of living in the present, of overcoming handicaps. This was no armchair philosopher speaking, for his own life contained its sometimes poignant examples of difficulties surmounted, of stumbling blocks converted into steppingstones. The sadness of being left fatherless was by a mother's wisdom and Richard's diligence transformed into industrious independence. On the other hand, a tragic accident Richard suffered at eleven produced a "handicap" which could have set back a weaker soul for life. But while he was ever afterwards conscious of it, he overcame its potential for personality damage and went on to make it instead a source of human understanding, insight and empathy.

Richard's work with the broadcast, service and civic groups, universities, and the Church he loved, considerably curtailed his activities at home. His dedication to challenging assignments also challenged his wife—Alice Ruth Thornley of Kaysville, Utah, whom he had met while both were students at the University of Utah and who had to be equally as dedicated as he. She realized early that her husband wasn't the kind to spend much time at home changing diapers, preparing formulas, or working on the yard. That early appraisal turned out to be correct.

It was quality rather than quantity time too that Richard spent with his young sons Richard Jr., John, Stephen, and William. As the boys grew older they noticed that even around the house their father was usually involved in work brought home from the office or in reading or writing. But as engrossed as he might be, he was always available for things that mattered. His son Stephen recalls: "We felt free to go to him with personal matters. Sometimes he seemed not to be paying much attention. But we had only to mention the word *problem* and he would drop everything he was doing and help out. As I approached draft age, for example, I told Dad that the military alternatives seemed confusing, that I didn't know which one to choose. Over a period of several days he phoned the draft board and questioned military officials and others until he became an authority on the question I had asked. Then he sat me down and explained all the possibilities so that I could decide how to fulfil my military obligations. He wouldn't dismiss my problem from his mind until I had gotten it solved."

Like the messages for his listeners, which he repeatedly rewrote and revised to make them simple and easily comprehended, Richard Evans' personal life was characterized by a humble simplicity. He liked simple foods rather than fancy dishes. If he began to accumulate too many material possessions, including items of clothing, he would return them to the store, give them away, or otherwise dispose of the surplus, and would let it be known that he wanted no more. His family remembers occasions when some item given as a birthday or Christmas gift was returned to the store. "If he told us he didn't need another shirt, he meant it. In time we learned not to give it to him, for if we did, he would just take it back. Finally we left him to buy his own clothes."

Although never light-minded, and not a joke-teller in the usual sense, Richard Evans often carried a trace of a smile on his countenance. His entire body could quietly explode into humor, and it often did. About 5 feet 10 inches in height, appearing a little thinnish in his face but not his shoulders, and with intense but sparkling brown eyes, he was described in an early radio journal in his younger years as being "spendid in appearance." But he sometimes evoked laughter by jokingly referring to his physical appearance. After traveling for months in his capacity as president of Rotary International, losing sleep and meeting hectic schedules everywhere, he would tell audiences: "I fear I'm beginning to look like my passport picture, and everyone knows that anyone who looks like his passport picture isn't well enough to travel."

His wit made him much in demand as a master of ceremonies at civic and university functions. The humor would surface also while he was acting as commentator for the Tabernacle Choir concerts during their tours. To a large, primarily non-Mormon audience he mentioned that most of the Choir members were married, a few of them to other members of the Choir. After having these married couples stand in their respective places, he commented, "If you are quite quick at counting, you would have noticed that they came out even." He then gave the audience a few seconds to figure out that little Mormon joke.

Dr. Truman Madsen, a member of the faculty of Brigham Young University (who after Richard's death was appointed the first holder of the new "Richard L. Evans Chair of Christian Understanding"), once asked him: "How do you account for your composure, your serenity of soul, under the frenetic schedule you must keep?" Richard's answer came back without hesitation: "Exhaustion!"

This was not only typical humor but typical modesty. He would never have admitted to greatness, though that was the appraisal of many friends and admirers. They saw in him not only a gifted being who worked hard and conscientiously to achieve, but a humble person whose life was shaped by such Christian virtues as honesty, integrity, compassion, and kindness—a gracious, charming gentleman. That is the way he came over in his weekly broadcasts. That was the true character of the man behind the Spoken Word.

" . . . Toiling Upward in the Night"

A legacy of family tradition was handed down to Richard Louis Evans at his birth in Salt Lake City on March 23, 1906. His maternal great-grandparents and his paternal great-grandmother had heard the inspiring message of Mormon missionaries in England, believed it, and desired to gather to Utah with the saints, as converts were encouraged to do. It meant leaving all that was familiar, forsaking the known for the unknown, but they did it. For Mary Wooley Evans the price proved heavy. She died on the overland trek to the Salt Lake Valley, and was buried near Florence, Nebraska.

Her eldest son David took care of the motherless youngsters as he sought a livelihood in the new land of Utah. David himself died at the early age of forty-three. His son John Alldridge Evans, father of Richard, understandably learned the value of hard work early. Starting as an errand boy at the *Deseret News,* in time he earned the position of general manager of that newspaper. He taught his family much about the rewards of energetic effort, but was never permitted to directly teach the ninth child, Richard, who was but ten weeks old when his father met a tragic death in the early summer of 1906.

Precise details of the accident are not known, for even after John A. Evans regained consciousness—during the remaining month that he lived—he was not able to reconstruct exactly how the accident occurred. What is known is that, in

Richard's parents John Alldridge Evans and Florence Neslen Evans

Florence Evans and her nine children several years after her
husband's death (Richard at center of front row)

going home late at night, he got off a streetcar just before it
reached a full stop on South Temple Street. He had done
this many times before but this time he was struck by the
streetcar. He was found unconscious and taken to the hospital
with deep cuts and bruises over most of his body. Even then
his family did not think the painful injuries would prove fatal.
He appeared to be recovering, when suddenly his restorative
powers failed. Despite all hopes and prayers, he died.

Left behind was a widow with nine children, the oldest
eighteen years old. Up to that time the family had received a
modest but sufficient income. Now, as Richard later put it,
his mother took a firm and gentle hand. "With a meager
and unreliable income, she immediately sent my eldest brother
on a mission. Such faith as that in the home in which I was
reared could produce only one result, and the result is that
all of my brothers and sisters have come up through the program of the Church to be a credit to my mother and to all
that this Church stands for."

Richard himself nearly passed away during the first
winter after his birth. He contracted membranous croup and
almost choked to death on several occasions. But the Lord had
work for him to do in mortality, and he survived in good
health.

While it was now their mother whose training prepared
them for the difficulties and adversities of life, the children
recognized that John Alldridge Evans was not entirely missing
from the home. Richard later explained that he and his
brothers and sisters were raised with their father "still standing in his rightful place as head of the household." There
was frequent reminder of this as the mother asked such questions as, "Would your father approve of that?" or commended
with the words, "Your father is very proud of you for this."

To provide for the family, the mother had to spend most
of her time taking care of domestic chores while all family
members who could obtained outside employment. As Richard
grew into a young boy he took his place beside his brothers
and sisters in working to help support the family. He kept

Richard in childhood and early youth

himself employed during the school year as well as during the summer. He later mentioned that he could scarcely remember ever attending school without having a job to go to after school hours. From the early years of grade school to the time when he left on a mission at twenty years of age, he worked in a variety of jobs including: delivering newspapers; selling magazines; raising and selling flowers; washing dishes and working behind a soda fountain in a cafe; working in an ice cream factory; making confectioner's syrup and performing various other tasks in the confectionery business; collecting bills; driving trucks; working on a railroad surveying crew; working with an advertising and printing firm; and selling clothing as a traveling salesman. In short, he did anything honorable he found to do which would make time plus effort equal money. This necessity of working hard in those early years impressed on his soul the importance of always being purposefully busy.

From his earliest years his mother taught him to pay one-tenth of his income to the Church, no matter how small his earnings. It was years later, when called to be one of the General Authorities of the Church, that he traced the beginnings of his spiritual convictions to those youthful days at his mother's knee when he was taught to pay his first few pennies in tithing.

It was in his loving Latter-day Saint family, under the guidance of his mother, that he gradually developed too the rudiments of the industry, integrity, honesty, and devotion to duty which characterized his later ministry. Taught and encouraged in the gospel, he found that Church practices became second nature to him. He attended auxiliary meetings, later his priesthood meetings, participated in such activities as Boy Scout, youthful quorum leadership, and later as Sunday School teacher, YMMIA officer, and other local callings from which he gained experience in Church practices and procedures.

Richard displayed an adventurous spirit as a youngster, and it sometimes caused consternation to those around him.

For instance, at the age of eight, too young to realize the concern he was causing others, he "borrowed" the horse of a well-to-do neighbor and rode it far above the family home on the "Avenues" into City Creek Canyon. While one family sought the missing horse, another family sought their missing boy. Gone most of the day, Richard found himself in "hot water" when he finally returned. Years later, he joked about having "started out in life as a horse thief."

When Richard was eleven years old, life dealt him a staggering blow. It was the year 1917, and World War I soldiers were firing at one another in trenches over in Europe. One day Richard and other local boys were playing "war" in neighborhood "trenches" with toy guns. Unknown to Richard, one of the boys had a loaded BB gun. As they were playing, the boy raised up out of his trench and fired in Richard's direction. The pellet struck him in his left eye. Running home in pain, he met his sister. She saw the damaged eye and burst into tears. "Don't cry, Sis," Richard said, "Just pray." But Richard's prayer on this occasion was not answered exactly as he and his family had wanted it. The eyeball was removed that same day in the doctor's office.

For a time he could not accept the permanence of what happened, and he implored the Lord to restore his eye. He anguished too over what effect the loss would have on his life. There were instances later in which, when he was seeking employment, others referred to his being "handicapped." Whether such comments were made directly to him is not known, but it was a sensitive point to him, this possibility that his loss of an eye would prevent him from being or doing anything he might choose. Years later, in speaking at a funeral involving tragic circumstances of death, he referred to his own earlier misfortune and disappointment: "I recall an accident that came into my own life as a young lad. I had been taught to pray and have faith, and I found myself praying and asking my Father in heaven to make it so that this accident had never happened. But it had happened, and I came to realize that I was asking my Father in heaven too much. But I grew in faith that he could overrule it for good."

He chose not to talk about the loss of his eye except in speaking to people who had suffered similar misfortunes and who had sought, or whose families had sought, his guidance and encouragement. Even many of his friends were not aware that he had lost an eye. The remarkable fullness and accomplishments of his life would indicate that the loss was ultimately not a significant hindrance to him in the more important areas, since he could hardly have worked harder or given more effectively of himself even if he had been spared that disappointment. Certainly he did not let his handicap become a barrier to growth or an excuse for poor performance.

Actually his accident may well have sparked a spiritual growth he could otherwise have lacked. He was naturally gifted with keen intellect and unusual powers of oral and written expression. At twenty-one he wrote in his diary that, though he had always had to work hard and under handicaps, he had always been able to come out on top in school or in any other desired endeavor, and he confessed that he found it hard at times to be as humble as he knew he ought to be. The loss of his eye undoubtedly helped him to develop greater humility before God and greater compassion and understanding for people, a deeper empathy for others who needed strength to overcome their sorrow or discouragement. Oppressed by various burdens, many of his broadcast listeners sensed that here was someone who had also carried a load and had learned how to do it without complaint.

It is interesting that in maturity he quoted frequently from Emerson's essay on Compensation, including the statement that "a certain compensation balances every gift and every defect." Richard eventually found the compensating strength. In doing so, he perhaps accepted another thought of Emerson's: "There is a time in every man's education when he arrives at the conviction that envy is ignorance; that imitation is suicide; that he must take himself for better or worse as his portion . . . . that though the wide universe is full of good, no kernel of corn can come to him but through his toil bestowed on that plot of ground which is given to him to till . . ."

Ten years after the accident, in connection with a problem he faced as a missionary, he expressed in his own words his belief in a principle that apparently he now applied to his own earlier misfortune: "We need the bitter for the sweet to be appreciated, the pains for joys, losses for victories, experience for wisdom, and everything for our good, although we may not see it now. No harm can come from anything we are big enough to overcome."

At the age of sixteen Richard received his patriarchal blessing. There is no indication that the elderly patriarch knew much about Richard, yet he was inspired to say that the boy had a "bright career" ahead of him, and to predict many things then unforeseen which would later come to pass. He told Richard that he would "stand in holy places and mingle with many of the best men and women upon the earth"; that he would serve as a missionary and as such "be called into distant lands, travel much and see many wonderful things"; and that he would be "especially favored with the spirit and power of blessing and perform many administrations amongst the sick, and witness the power of God wonderfully made manifest in miraculous healings." Significantly too one paragraph reads: "Thy tongue will be loosened and become as the pen of a ready writer in dispensing the word of God and in preaching the gospel to thy fellow men. Thou wilt have courage to face and overcome difficulties that may lie in thy pathway."

Speaking through the Spirit, no doubt without any comprehension of the tremendous accomplishments Richard's life would register, the patriarch had clearly designated the young man as a youth of promise. But fulfillment was another matter. That depended on Richard's use of his agency, his choices in life. At sixteen he did not even yet know the type of career he would pursue.

Meantime he was a leading student at the LDS High School in Salt Lake City, where he won recognition for high scholarship and was heavily involved in school activities. Following a natural bent, he took up debate. His logical thinking, his cogent arguments, and his strivings to find the exactly appropriate word rapidly gave him confidence before an audience. Already language was beginning to intrigue him. In his junior year, besides working on the school newspaper, he won state championship honors as a member of the debating team. In his senior year, while continuing his debating activities, he was named editor of the school newspaper. Upon graduation from the LDS High School, he was presented with the Heber J. Grant Award for distinguished service to his school.

Even at this youthful period Richard's drive and zeal were apparent. His pattern of working the long hours necessary to excel both in the classroom and in school activities, and to keep up his ever-needed outside employment, did not go unnoticed by his friends. Upon his graduation, one of his classmates wrote to him: "I'm not going to write anything funny, Dick, but something I believe with my whole heart, that the world will hear from you some day. You will make a name for yourself." Appropriately the yearbook staff selected this verse from Longfellow to appear by his graduation picture:

> The heights by great men reached and kept
> Were not attained by sudden flight,
> But they, while their companions slept,
> Were toiling upward in the night.

Richard registered in the fall of 1924 at the University of Utah on a scholarship won in his high school debating activities.

Desirous of serving as a missionary for his Church, as young LDS men are encouraged to do, he was conscious of the financial problem. Unless he could save much of the money required for his support in the mission field, he would be a financial burden to his family. So toward the end of his second year at the University, at twenty years of age, he looked for a good-paying summer job. His search took him to the Utah Woolen Mills, for whom he agreed to travel to the Pacific Northwest to sell their warm, heavy-duty clothing to the lumberjacks. Payment would be on a commission basis only. He was unfamiliar with the big and boisterous lumber camps, but no new experience had been overwhelming to him in the past, and he felt at ease in meeting people. So he left Salt Lake in an old Model-T Ford with his clothing samples and another salesman who was to accompany him.

After several weeks in the lumber camps of Washington and Oregon, the two salesmen became completely discouraged. They had had no success in selling and were broke. They decided to head for home. Having reached Boise, Idaho, Richard phoned his family to let them know he was coming home.

His older brother Dave listened carefully to the story. When his response came it jolted Richard: he had set out to do a job and he ought to complete it. As Richard later explained, "It was made clear that my family would not accept me returning as a failure."

This experience provided one of the great lessons of his life. Even though surprised and disheartened at his family's reaction and though the other salesman continued on home, Richard turned his Model-T around and headed back toward the lumber camps. During the next three months he worked tenaciously, ignoring the jibes about his boyish appearance and his courteous rather than rough manner. It didn't matter as long as he sold shirts. He ended up selling more clothing than he had hoped for. As a result, he was able to drive home to Salt Lake City in October having made what in those days was a lot of money for a young man and feeling the satisfaction that comes from hanging on and finally succeeding in an assignment that had initially been difficult and unpleasant.

Richard's life might have been very different had he returned home a failure at that impressionable age.

At one point during his subsequent mission in England he reflected on the experience with obvious relish, as he concluded in his journal: "I find that I made about $750 between the middle of June and the last of September, over $400 of which I saved, and this in spite of traveling over 15,000 miles in my own car, clear up into British Columbia and the Pacific Northwest, living in hotels and working on straight commission." Four hundred dollars then was of course worth several times what it is now.

Within several weeks after returning from this sales trip, he received a call from the Church to serve in the British Mission, whose headquarters were in Liverpool, England. He left Salt Lake City on November 5, 1926; and after a stormy Atlantic crossing that brought him a four-day siege of seasickness, the boat docked at Liverpool on November 21.

Assigned after two days to Lowestoft, a city in eastern England, he quickly had his first taste of "tracting"—going door-to-door or striking up conversations in the streets in attempting to distribute pamphlets and to interest someone in his message.

For nearly six months he worked in the "Norwich District," in the cities of Lowestoft, Norwich and Peterborough. His journal speaks of doing extensive tracting, much of it in cold, rainy or snowy weather, with virtually no success in arousing interest in the message. He studied hard, visited members of the Church, attended the weekly Church meetings —and tracted and tracted and tracted. He observed, "People are always in a hurry to close doors, indifferent, and have no time to discuss religion."

As the weeks passed, he became concerned about his lack of visible success: "I am often worried about my labors here. . . . I pray to be guided to know how to be a good missionary. I hope I shall soon be comforted and have that assurance."

The next day he added: "I am a little discouraged tonight because I cannot see that I am doing any good and I don't see how to do any more than I am doing. I hope and pray that I may be the means of bringing someone to the knowledge of the truth, as the instrument of the Lord."

Three and a half months after beginning his work as a missionary, he recorded: "This has been the most discouraging day I have yet experienced. In four hours' tracting, I didn't sell a pamphlet, did not have a satisfactory gospel conversation, was ordered off property, called names of all kinds, and had doors slammed in my face. Other matters haven't helped any; my stomach has been upset; my eyes give way and ache and blur and refuse to work in study; and altogether the prospects look rather dark this evening."

Despite disheartening times, he continued to put in long hours of work on most days and soon discovered that discouragement more often came not from lack of success but from not working up to his full strength and ability: "The lesson I learn more each day of my life is the old lesson that is so much stressed as to become seemingly commonplace— 'do it now.' I find that I am infinitely more happy and content when found in the line of my duty, putting job after job behind me, than while thinking and wishing it were done and idling precious moments away. The flesh is weak, and slothful habits prevail often, but it can be done with effort. . . . The indifference of the people is maddening. But regardless of how they receive the message, I feel much better out tracting with a feeling that I am doing my duty to the best of my knowledge so that I may be able to interest them and at least tell them what we have to offer. Whether or not they receive it is, of course, up to them."

Four months after Richard began his mission, the missionaries and local members of the Church gathered for a district conference. Here for the first time Richard met his mission president—Elder James E. Talmage of the Council of the Twelve, who had come down from Liverpool for the conference.

Dr. Talmage, who had been born in England, was a geologist by training, a distinguished scholar, a past president of the University of Utah, and a fellow of several British Royal Societies including the Royal Society of Edinburgh. He was remarkably gifted and accomplished in the use of the English language and had already written two books that are classics in Mormon literature—*A Study of the Articles of Faith* and *Jesus the Christ*.

During the two-day conference, President Talmage interviewed Richard as he did each of the other missionaries. Richard wrote: "He did his usual cross-examining for which he is noted. He asked me much about my schooling, experience and age, family, etc." Before the conference concluded, Elder Talmage asked Richard to write an article for the *Millennial Star*, the British Mission magazine Elder Talmage edited, the oldest periodical in the Church then still in publication.

After this conference, Richard was one of seven missionaries working in the Norwich District. The other six were assigned in pairs, as is the custom, to work in other cities in the district while Richard was left to work alone in Norwich. He wrote: "President Talmage suggested the arrangements and no doubt he could see that I was no favorite with the Norwich girls, hence my appointment. . . . I feel very humble and very happy to think that I have been trusted."

Sixteen days after the conference, having still not written the required article, he took a day off from his missionary labors and finished it. One month later a letter came from Elder Talmage commending him for his article and asking him to write another one. The letter also asked Richard to proofread some enclosed galley sheets of the *Star*.

Four days later, another letter arrived from the mission president asking Richard to get the second article to him "tomorrow." Richard reports that two days after that a telegram came from President Talmage "telling me to come to Liverpool at my earliest convenience after making my necessary visits. I sent by return mail the schedule I planned and notified him that I would be in Liverpool a week from tomorrow." The next day, before Richard could visit any "interested" contacts, another telegram came saying: "Curtail visits. Come earliest possible day. Wire." Richard wrote in his journal: "I grabbed a dictionary and looked up 'curtail,' so I knew he meant to cut out that visit stuff. I wired that I would come tomorrow and then packed my trunk."

In Liverpool, President Talmage told Richard he wanted him to work hard on the *Star* and that if he "showed the stuff" he would be made the associate editor. He quickly found Elder Talmage to be a fair but rigorous taskmaster who expected Richard to achieve the kind of excellence in his work that the president demanded of himself. Through his meticulous criticism of Richard's writing, he taught the young missionary much about the precise use of the English language. Richard recalled rewriting one editorial nine times before President Talmage would accept it. It must have been a sobering experience to the former debater and high-school newspaper editor who had felt he was pretty good with the "King's English."

Richard acknowledged in his journal: "The *Star* is more of a job than I thought it was going to be." But he also added: "I enjoy my work immensely; I have never been so contented in my life."

Richard obviously "passed the test," for on July 21, 1927, exactly two months after he started work on the *Star* he was officially informed by Elder Talmage that he was the new associate editor. Several years after his mission, Richard looked back with gratitude upon his days under Elder Talmage: "Under his tutelage, I found myself squirming at times, but nevertheless greatly benefited by his rigid scrutiny and exacting requirements. It was a good experience. And I love and honor the memory of the man who so painstakingly troubled himself to train me in ways of precision and exactitude, when oft times it would have been much less trouble for him to have done the task in hand himself."

His high opinion of Elder Talmage is amusingly reflected in an otherwise insignificant entry in Richard's missionary journal: "Had a wild ride to the depot in a cab with the President on Saturday when he had to catch a train in ten minutes. We would have wrecked for sure if it had been anyone but James E. Talmage."

On Christmas Eve 1927, Elder John A. Widtsoe of the Council of the Twelve, with Mrs. Widtsoe and their daughter Eudora, arrived in Liverpool to replace Elder Talmage as president of the British and European Missions.

Elder Widtsoe was born in Norway, emigrated to Utah when eleven years old with his mother and brother, trained as a chemist, graduated from Harvard with highest honors, and then obtained his doctorate at the University in Goetingen, Germany. He achieved eminence for his work in soil chemistry and on life-giving irrigation projects that made great areas of arid land productive. He served as president of two universities before being called by the Church as a member of the Quorum of the Twelve Apostles.

President Widtsoe continued Richard as associate editor of the *Star* and also asked him to undertake a book or research project for the British Mission. The subject matter of that project was left open for a time.

Several months later, in May 1928, Richard had to do considerable research for an article in the *Star* entitled "Brigham Young in England." In the process he became interested in the history of the Church's missionary work in Britain, and it was agreed that that could be the subject of his project. Many years later, Richard recalled the travels and research that the project required:

"The assignment took me, in a Model-T Ford, through the British Isles, finding places that had long been forgotten, such as the pool of water on the old John Benbow farm where a whole congregation was converted through the work and witness of Wilford Woodruff almost overnight."

"I went conscientiously from cross-roads to cross-roads, on assignment, finding such places and documenting and photographing and writing about them. I dug deeply into the journals of those early brethren of the British Mission. . . ."

As he wrote the history of the British Mission it was published in installments in the *Star,* beginning in July 1928. Several years later, Richard updated the manuscript, added several chapters, and published it in 1937—the one-hundredth anniversary of the founding of the British Mission—as a book entitled *A Century of Mormonism in Great Britain.*

Within several months after the Widtsoes' arrival in Britain, they began to have Richard drive the car for them in their travels through England and Scotland as they would hold conferences with the missionaries and members of the Church and perform other official duties. A bond of great trust and affection soon developed between Richard and the Widtsoe family. Richard wrote in his journal of the deep love and respect he felt for them.

His early travels with the Widtsoes included an eleven-day, twelve-hundred-mile trip through Scotland. Soon after this Richard recorded: "I have been given full charge of the car by President Widtsoe and travel a great deal now."

In personal attributes, Elder John A. Widtsoe was everything that Richard felt a person could ever hope to be. He was highly educated and brilliant of mind, yet humble, down-to-earth and easy-going. He worked hard and long hours and with amazing speed and had a remarkable habit that fascinated Richard of managing to read, memorize, write and otherwise work even during the few seconds of in-between times that almost everyone wastes—while waiting perhaps for an appointment, or a train; yet he would readily and happily drop his work to enjoy and give full attention to his family or to others who sought his company. He was a man of great

Missionary Richard Evans, 1927

Richard, President and Mrs.
Widtsoe, and the Ford

President and Mrs. Widtsoe, their daughter Eudora, Richard
Evans and other missionaries at a conference in
Sunderland, England

physical strength and energy; he lived honorably by the high standards he believed in; and he had great faith and a great heart that was full of love and kindness and compassion for people.

In trying to describe his trips with President and Sister Widtsoe, Richard, in his journal, stumbles with superlatives like "glorious," "most thoroughly enjoyable," "most worth-while," etc. Why the Widtsoes opened their arms to him as they did is not known. In part, perhaps, it was that Elder Widtsoe had special empathy for Richard, for as a six-year-old boy the president had lost his own father, and he and his widowed mother and younger brother had had to struggle to make ends meet. Additionally President and Mrs. Widtsoe had lost five of their own seven children in death, their last surviving son having died at twenty-four years of age only a few months before Elder Widtsoe's assignment to England as mission president. Whatever the reasons for the Widtsoes' pulling Richard into their family, it is impossible to calculate the extent of the influence upon his life that came from his intimate association with these choice people.

Though the frequent trips with the Widtsoes were exhilarating, joyous, and precious occasions for Richard, they greatly increased the burden of putting out an issue of the *Millennial Star* each week in addition to his other assignment of researching and writing a history of the Mission. The work simply piled up while he was away. His efforts in trying to keep several balls in the air at the same time are illustrated by an occasion when he drove Mrs. Widtsoe approximately three hundred miles from Liverpool to Dover (in a car and on roads that would be considered "ancient" and inadequate today) for her to catch a boat for the Continent, where she was to meet her husband. Of what happened after getting her safely to Dover, he wrote:

"I felt that I had to get back to London that night, for I had more than 220 miles to travel the next day and the *Star* was waiting for me in Liverpool. Every time I leave, I have to work ahead and then work doubly hard after returning because there is no one here to help with the literary work.

"That parting was hard. I love Sister Widtsoe almost as a mother and have learned to look upon her as such in the mission field. To leave her for more than a month, to drive about 300 miles alone, to go back to Durham House—left me in no light mood. . . .

"I arrived home at about 8:00 P.M. the next day and found the proofs of an entire *Star* waiting to be read and two or three pages waiting to be written. It had to be done so I did it, in spite of my sleepless week of travel and my long day of driving. It was beginning to get light when I finished."

It was not unusual during that period for Richard to work around the clock in that manner. As a result his weight dropped from 160 to 135 pounds and he became very run-down physically.

As Richard's length of missionary service approached the customary two years, Elder Widtsoe explored with him the possibility of his staying longer. Richard was anxious to do so, subject to the feelings of his mother and brothers and sisters, for theirs would be the financal burden of supporting him.

Richard wrote to his family and quickly received their reply: They not only urged him to stay in the mission field as long as he "was accomplishing good and was needed" but also told him that they had not even used his savings he had left them for his support, that they had instead been contributing monthly themselves to a "family fund" to support him. Money had never been plentiful since his father's death, and Richard was deeply moved at his family's sacrifice.

This response having been received, Elder Widtsoe released Richard from his *Millennial Star* responsibilities and called him to be secretary of the European Mission. But he gave Richard several weeks of rest for him to regain his full health and strength.

During the course of his new calling, Richard purchased a car in Paris, obtained an international driver's license, and accompanied the Widtsoes on a four-month trip through eleven countries of Europe from the Mediterranean up to beyond the Arctic Circle. Richard drove the car over most of the distance, handled business details relating to travel and accommodations, and filled speaking engagements and other assignments under President Widtsoe's direction relating to the work of the Church's missions in Europe.

This trip marked the completion of Richard's duties as mission secretary. Toward the end of the trip, in Germany, Richard and President Widtsoe said goodbye to each other. The president had to take a train to Czechoslovakia, while Richard drove Mrs. Widtsoe and her daughter back to Paris, where he sold the car. He then crossed the Channel to England, where he boarded a ship for the United States. Of the parting from Elder Widtsoe, he wrote:

"This morning I parted company with the best man I have ever known. President Widtsoe left on the 11:36 train for Prague. Before we parted, he gave me the most wonderful blessing I have ever had and promised long, full service, health and achievement and told me in certain terms that the Lord was pleased with my labors.

"We put our arms around each other and parted as father and son. Sister Widtsoe joined in the blessing. I hated to break the wonderful 1½-year association—but it will be renewed."

Richard arrived home in Salt Lake City on September 1, 1929, having been away from his family just two months short of three years.

When the Widtsoes returned from Europe several years later, Richard's association with them was renewed. The mutual affection deepened with time. It was not difficult for the Widtsoes to take this sensitive and dedicated young man to their hearts. They counseled with him, watched his pro-

gress with interest, and rejoiced in his successes. He became
as a son to them. To him it was always a treasured relationship.
The Widtsoes even gave Richard a key to their home, which
he made frequent use of, dropping in on them, often spon-
taneously, at any hour of the day or evening until the death
of Elder Widtsoe in 1952 and Mrs. Widtsoe in 1965. Even
after their passing he continued to carry that house key in his
pocket until the day he died, as a symbol of what the Widtsoes
had meant to him.

He hoped that he had been able over the years to return
even a small part of their kindness to him. Close to Richard's
desk, after his own passing, was found one of Elder John A.
Widtsoe's books, *Evidences and Reconciliations,* inscribed as
follows:

"Dear Richard: This book has been made possible by
your suggestion and labor. Its mechanical beauty of type,
paper, arrangement, cover and jacket reveal your innate feeling for and sense of the beautiful in thought, word and form.

"To me this volume is another evidence of your goodness
to me. No son could do more than you have done for me in
our association together. This I appreciate beyond ordinary
expression. I recognize your gifts, service to the world and
to your people; and rejoice in the abundant share of your
affections bestowed on me.

"Before you lies a long, increasingly distinguished career,
in which your inborn and trained powers and your unusual
wisdom will have full play. Your every attainment gives me
gladness.

"Thank you again. The Lord bless you. Affectionately,
John A. Widtsoe."

Although Richard had given some thought in the mission
field to pursuing his college education away from Salt Lake
City, the nearly three years on the mission was long enough to
be away from home. He decided to resume his studies at the
University of Utah.

He registered for a full academic load at the University and also began to look for full-time employment on a schedule that would permit him to attend his school classes. At this point a possible career in radio had not entered his mind. One day he saw an advertisement that an announcer was required at KSL. He applied for the position, and within just a few weeks after his return from a mission he had a full-time job as a radio announcer.

KSL, along with the radio industry generally, was still in its infancy. The fact that consequently no one had had much experience either as announcers or as executives in that business did not prevent one of the officials at the station from making an interesting prediction. Though consenting to Richard's having a try at the job, he remarked, "Dick will never make it as a radio announcer because his voice is too deep."

Richard soon fell in love with radio. Not only was it especially suited to his abilities but the industry was new enough that there still prevailed the sense of wonder at the miracle of being able to reach hundreds of thousands of people with one's voice.

Although this was the year 1929, and the Great Depression had begun which was to rock the economic foundations of America, apparently Richard felt little affected by it. If things were difficult in working full-time and attending school full-time as well, things had been difficult before. And unlike countless others in the country at that time, he could be grateful that he even had a job.

He did script-writing as well as announcing. He became involved also in the business aspects of the station, soon serving as Supervisor of Announcers, Director of Publicity, and then Production Manager. Several years later, the radio station's own "in-house" newspaper the *KSL News* carried a brief article on him:

"For upwards of four years Mr. Evans has carried the responsibility of production at KSL. Only broadcasters realize the vast amount of work—continuity writing, episode building, choosing of personnel, time checking, developing of sound effects, rehearsing and auditioning—that goes into radio production. It doesn't just happen that great radio features begin and end on a split second, or that they are well balanced and that one feature is appropriately juxtaposed against the other.

"That is the work of the production department.

"Mr. Evans has now prepared a large volume of continuities which have been presented over both national networks from coast to coast. The program directors of these great radio organizations have been enthusiastic in their praise of his work."

For over six years Richard worked full-time for KSL while also continuing his education at the University. Two years after returning from his mission, he graduated with an A.B. degree in English. A year later he received a master's degree in Economics. Both degrees were awarded with honors. He then commenced work in his "spare time" toward a doctorate.

In the spring of 1930, only about seven months after he began working at KSL and while still working toward his bachelor's degree at the University, he was given a new assignment as part of his responsibilities at the station—announcing the weekly nationwide Tabernacle Choir radio program which had begun broadcasting over the NBC network only about ten months earlier. (The program continued with NBC for two more years and then switched to the CBS network, where it has remained ever since.) He was then twenty-four years old. Richard continued at this weekly assignment as the writer, producer, and announcer for the Tabernacle Choir broadcast until the time of his death, more than forty-one years later.

Many other radio presentations of the Church also went through his hands, including a series of twenty-three gospel discourses he wrote and which he delivered from the Tabernacle each Sunday evening during the winter and spring when he was twenty-eight years old. During that period of time, in speaking of the Choir broadcast and of these other Church presentations, he wrote in a letter: "The greatest constructive joy I have in life is the writing, production and presentation of the radio programs for the Church. It is this contribution that I am able to make that makes my long and tedious hours of routine work here at the radio station bearable."

His work with the Choir broadcast soon attracted nation-wide attention and in January 1934, two months before his twenty-eighth birthday, he received a national award from *Radio Engineering,* a nationally distributed Bryan-Davis publication in New York City, as the best radio announcer for 1933. Notice of the award was carried in most of the leading newspapers and radio magazines of the country. The *Los Angeles Examiner* observed that it was "perhaps the first time that an announcer from the far west has been so singled out for honors by a far eastern publication."

While at KSL, Richard handled other major microphone assignments of national interest for the CBS network, including coverage of the Utah Repeal Convention, the 1932 Campaign Address of Franklin D. Roosevelt from the Mormon Tabernacle, and the International Automobile Speed Runs at the Bonneville Salt Flats. The Speed Runs must have been exciting, although considerably different from the Spoken Word. His report of the assault on the land speed record took place at the scene on the Salt Flats some one hundred miles west of Salt Lake City. It must have been a challenging assignment not only for Richard but for the entire radio staff. Much field equipment had to be set up to make on-the-spot news coverage and interviews possible in those days.

Richard's unusual capacity for work characterized those years at KSL. At one time he gave an account of his activities at the radio station in a letter to Elder Widtsoe, whom he continued to look upon as a father. He wrote: "I spend a full seventy hours a week working here. I never have a day off, not excepting Sundays or holidays. At one time I went two

Early days of broadcasting: Giving the Spoken Word from the
Mormon Tabernacle, and covering the International Automobile
Speed Runs at Bonneville Salt Flats

years without a vacation or a single day off, except one day spent in bed under doctor's orders." This was said not as a complaint but matter-of-factly. Indeed, in a letter he wrote to someone else he commented that the "phrase from Livingstone, 'fear God, and work hard' is a great prescription. I believe that a man cannot watch a clock or serve his own convenience or pleasure and accomplish very much in any endeavor."

It is evident that Richard had not only an intense drive to excel but also a bulldog tenacity. The latter quality was not apparent to many who knew him, who were more conscious of his gentle soft-spoken manner, his usual gracious and charming demeanor, and his ready wit. But once he took hold of an idea, an assignment, a project, a cause, he rarely let go.

It was these qualities of driving to excel and "hanging on" that enabled him to develop an unusual capacity for sustained work and concentration. Marion D. Hanks, who was closely associated with Richard for several years in the Temple Square Mission, commented:

"The one thing I would extract from his life is his unusual —his unique—aptitude and capacity for work, his commitment to the best he could produce. For a generation I have watched him labor seven days a week, all day long and into the night. . . .

"Richard Evans' capacity for work is prodigious. I have watched him turn away shyly as people have said that he is the only religion they have ever known or believed in, he is the only church they ever attend—in these broadcasts for forty-two years. I have heard so many say, 'Oh, you don't have to worry; it just rolls out of you.' This morning I would just remark on my knowledge of how the stuffing process occurs before the rolling out begins.

"I have watched him labor in anguish and anxiety all week to get those three minutes ready. He only had a few minutes here and there, but he had great wisdom. Richard knows that sharpening pencils, arranging a desk, and getting the lights just right are easy. But that does not get anything done. So early each week he dictates a thought out of his heart and head—some idea. This is typed triple-spaced on yellow paper by a great secretary. He has begun. . . . He is into the job and he does the work."[1]

In the same vein, Elder Hanks wrote: "When others spoke of his genius, those who knew Richard Evans nodded in agreement, but those who knew him well recognized the working garments in which the genius was clothed."[2]

Somehow, on August 9, 1933, Richard found time to get married.

Actually it is amazing to Alice Ruth Thornley, in looking back on it, that Richard stood still long enough for the two of them to be introduced in the basement lobby of the Park Administration Building. The area—nicknamed "the pump" after the water fountain in the center of the lobby—served as the informal meeting-ground for University of Utah students. It was here that a mutual friend of both, who was one of Richard's fraternity brothers, introduced Richard Evans to Alice Thornley. Richard was twenty-three and had been home from his mission about a month. Alice, from Kaysville, Utah, was nineteen and was just beginning her second year at the university.

Alice's first meeting with the man who was to become her husband as well as the man behind the Spoken Word was not particularly auspicious. "It was not love at first sight," Alice relates. Richard asked her a few days later if she would like to take a ride with him, in a car she later learned was borrowed from a friend. During their ride she caught a rather humorous glimpse of the concentration and total involvement in what he was doing that was so typical of him, for "he became," she says, "so engrossed in driving the car, swinging around the corners, watching the road, etc., that he seemed

---

[1]Marion D. Hanks, Brigham Young University Devotional Assembly, October 26, 1971 (Provo, Utah: Brigham Young University Press), pp. 5, 6.
[2]Marion D. Hanks, "Elder Richard L. Evans, Apostle of the Lord, 1906-1971," *Ensign,* December 1971, p. 7.

hardly aware that I was there. There was little conversation, and I thought afterwards that I might as well not even have been along."

As they continued to date occasionally, however, their feelings slowly developed toward each other. During their courtship Richard may have felt at a disadvantage in competing with other fellows for Alice's time, since he was occupied nearly every evening with his job at the radio station. He found ingenious ways to compensate for this disadvantage and to turn her attention in his direction, no matter who else she might be going out with.

An example is what he contrived to make out of the occasion when Alice, who loved to dance, and her date won a ballroom dancing contest one evening out at the old Saltair Resort on the Great Salt Lake. As usual, Richard was stuck that night at the radio station. Hearing of her first-place prize, the next day during a radio program of recorded music in which he was the disc jockey he announced on the air with great flourish that Alice Ruth Thornley of Kaysville, Utah, had won the "important" dance contest. He conspicuously omitted any mention of her escort, but following his announcement he played on the air a rather ridiculous old record that he had dug out of the music files. The title of the record just happened to be the last name of Alice's date of the night before.

Alice's friends who heard the program thought it was hilariously funny and just had to check with Alice to see if she had heard it. Thus during the next several weeks Alice was reminded over and over again of "what Richard had done." Considering how little time Richard had for courting, it seems that he did remarkably well at keeping himself in Alice's thoughts.

Even though theirs was not the rapid kind of romance often pictured between boy and girl, Richard and Alice became engaged about fifteen months later, on New Year's Eve 1930. But it was two and a half years after that before they were married. Richard was then twenty-seven years old.

Richard and Alice at approximately the time of their marriage

Alice loved music, played the violin, and had a beautiful voice. She also liked to cook, and at first she concocted many gastronomical innovations. But she found that her husband preferred more simple things. The "banquet circuit" more than satisfied what little taste he had for fancy dishes. He was content to see in front of him a little meat and potatoes, a tossed green salad, and a glass of buttermilk.

He did have a taste for sour foods, which he attributed in part to his access to the "pickle barrel" when he was a boy working behind a soda fountain, and in part to his travels with Elder and Mrs. Widtsoe, especially through the Scandinavian countries (Elder Widtsoe being a native of Norway). There Richard acquired a fondness for yogurt, buttermilk, strong cheeses, raw salmon, and pickled herring. He could finish a good evening meal with a dish of ice cream, for example (which seemed normal enough to his wife), but then would cap off the ice cream with a dill pickle!

He was not especially fond of cooked vegetables. At one time after his four sons were grown, he made a declaration at the dinner table: "I am announcing that from now on I am not going to eat vegetables to impress my children!"

About the time he got married, Richard was giving serious consideration to leaving Salt Lake City to pursue more earnestly the work on his doctorate and to take advantage of the greater financial opportunities available in radio in the larger eastern cities. He had ties in New York City, Washington, D.C., and Boston with people who knew of his talents and of his performance at KSL. Some contacts were made in his behalf and several job opportunities opened up to him.

By this time, through his work on the Choir broadcast, he had developed a close relationship with Heber J. Grant, President of the Church, and decided to talk to him about the possible move. He reported that when he did so President Grant looked at him with a twinkle in his eye and said, "I think I'd stick around if I were you."

Richard would have liked to know more of President Grant's thinking, of why he said what he did, but the President was not inclined to elaborate. Richard later remarked that he knew he had no obligation to ask for advice in the first place, but having asked for it, and gotten it—from a man he accepted as the prophet of the Lord—he felt it would be foolish to disregard it. So stick around he did.

At twenty-nine, with nearly six years behind him at the radio station, Richard was approached by President Heber J. Grant, Elder John A. Widtsoe and others as to his willingness to leave KSL and take over the editorship of the *Improvement Era*. This monthly magazine, the official organ of The Church of Jesus Christ of Latter-day Saints, had hundreds of thousands of readers around the world. Elder Widtsoe would later explain that Richard had been chosen partly because of the fine literary judgment and craftsmanship he had earlier revealed as editor of the *Millennial Star* in England.

Richard loved his radio work and dreaded the thought of leaving it. Hence he resisted the gentle persuasions of these good men for several months before finally yielding and once again becoming an editor. He later gave this brief account: "I struggled with myself for more than six months from the time the Presidency first called me over and suggested that I take the editorship of this magazine, until the time that it was actually undertaken. They did not make the request in the nature of a call. They left it entirely to my judgment, and it took me six months to reach the conclusion that they would not have called me over there if they had not wanted me to do it; but this realization finally settled upon my consciousness and I made the change—for what reason I did not know at the time."

He became the managing editor of the *Improvement Era* shortly before his thirtieth birthday and continued in that capacity for fourteen years, then becoming a senior editor for an additional twenty-one years. Though editorship of the *Era* was a full-time job, he continued on a part-time basis with

KSL as its Director of Public Events and Special Features, and he continued to write, produce, and announce the weekly Tabernacle Choir broadcast.

Two years and nine months after he accepted the editorship of the *Era*, Richard was called by President Heber J. Grant to become a member of the First Council of Seventy, filling the vacancy occasioned by the death of J. Golden Kimball. If the request to head the *Era* had surprised him, this new call left him bewildered and shaken.

He was thirty-two years of age, the youngest man called as a General Authority of the Church in more than thirty years. The average age of the other six members of the First Council of Seventy at that time was sixty-five, the youngest being fifty-seven years old. His wife says she never saw him so depressed and forlorn as during the several days after this call came from President Grant. For one thing, he felt unprepared for the role and responsibility of a General Authority. Members of the Church, including local Church officials of much greater age and experience than he, would now be looking to him for decisions, help and advice. He had difficulty in seeing himself adequately filling the role.

There was an additional reason for his low spirits—the sacrificing of cherished goals. Presidents Widtsoe and Talmage had each exerted great influence on him in the mission field and had become ideals to him. He sought to emulate them, not in the sense of becoming a Church authority but in pursuing his education, obtaining his doctorate, then growing and contributing and succeeding, as they had done, in whatever field he chose. Richard knew that his call to the high Church office meant a virtual end to further schooling and to professional pursuits.

Elder Widtsoe, who knew of the turmoil Richard felt as he desperately tried to reorient his life during those early days after the call came, wrote of Richard in the November 1938 *Era*: "The call was unexpected and unsought, as all calls to service in the Church should be. Office-seeking has no place

1938 picture of Richard with other First Council of Seventy members (l. to r.) John H. Taylor, Antoine R. Ivins, Rulon S. Wells, Levi Edgar Young, Samuel O. Bennion (Rufus K. Hardy absent when photo was taken)

in the Church. We know that Brother Evans stood in fear and trembling before the new opportunities for service and the accompanying heavy responsibilities to a great people."

The call came from President Grant on a Thursday night. The next day Richard was "presented" to the eight thousand members of the Church assembled in the Salt Lake Tabernacle in general conference. Richard's widowed mother was sitting in the congregation when her son's name was announced. She thought, "I can't have heard it right." She turned to the stranger sitting next to her and asked whose name had been read. Then she knew that her youngest child was now a General Authority of the Church.

The following day, Saturday, Richard stood before the conference and said:

"I spent a sleepless night Thursday night, burning old bridges and building new ones. I think that perhaps this call would have come easier to me a little later in life, after I had had a better opportunity to make substance of more of my dreams, but perhaps this is not so. Perhaps I must just exchange old dreams for new dreams. . . .

"Those who were close to my feelings yesterday morning, before the announcement of my appointment to the First Council of Seventy was made at this conference, were aware that if there had been any way to turn back in honor I would have done so, but I do not know to what point I would have turned back, and I realize keenly that there was no turning back—that turning back would have been turning away.

"If I had been of a mind to turn back, I should have done it at my mother's knee. I should have done it before she taught me to pay out my first few pennies in tithing. I should have done it before her firm and gentle hand directed my steps into the ways of truth."

While serving on the First Council of Seventy, Richard continued his work with the Choir broadcast and his editorship of the *Improvement Era*. Thus a busy man became even busier.

It is difficult to see how Richard could have successfully carried out his increased responsibilities without the full cooperation and sustaining strength of his wife Alice. In conversations with his sons over the years, he frequently paid tribute to their mother for her support and for the freedom to work that she had made possible. He would say that a man could not get anywhere by working only forty hours a week or by "watching the clock," that it was not enough simply to put in the hours, but that jobs had to be completed and put behind you. He occasionally quoted Winston Churchill— "It is no use saying 'We are doing our best'; you have got to succeed in doing what is required." He acknowledged that he would not have been able to work as he did without his exceptional wife. It took a very special woman not to become annoyed or feel slighted at not knowing what time each night to expect her husband home, for he would stay at the office until the project at hand was finished, whatever time that might be. Especially during the early years of their marriage, a lot of evening meals got cold and ended up being eaten alone. As he grew older, he began more often to keep early hours instead of late ones, often rising between three and five o'clock in the morning to work several hours before going to the office.

As his four sons got old enough to know what vacations and outings are and to want and appreciate them, he would occasionally take some time off for that purpose. His family has precious memories of two trips to Yellowstone National Park, one to the National Parks in southern Utah, one to southern California, and a pack trip in the high Uinta mountains in eastern Utah. Of course any vacation had to be taken during the week so that Richard could be back in time for his Sunday morning broadcast.

That pack trip was a glorious occasion for Richard's two oldest boys, Richard Jr. and John, then about fourteen and eleven years old respectively. Their father took them on horses up north of Roosevelt, Utah, along the Uinta River into the Chain Lakes and the High Uintas Primitive Area. "My brother and I had the time of our lives, catching fish, and enjoying the outdoors," John relates. "But our father didn't seem so interested in fishing as in doing the work—taking care of the horses, cleaning the fish, preparing the meals, doing the dishes, and keeping the camp in order. We realized later that this was partly because he wanted us to have as much free time as possible, but also because it was his nature to keep purposefully busy."

There was however one form of recreation which Richard learned to enjoy without reservation. When his sons became involved in athletics and other activities in high school, he delighted in watching them participate. This, in addition to his serving for a time on the University of Utah Athletic Board as one of his assignments as a member of the University's Board of Regents, sparked in him an interest in athletics which never diminished. He enjoyed going with his sons to football and basketball games on a regular basis at the University of Utah near his home and occasionally at Brigham Young University forty-five miles away, where he also served as a member of the Board of Trustees.

He appreciated nature and the outdoors, especially in the mountains, but permitted himself little time to spend in it. He enjoyed a horseback ride occasionally but found more satisfaction in owning and keeping horses for the use of his boys, which he did from the time his oldest boy was three or four years old.

The family's opportunities for recreation in Utah's mountains were enhanced by the proceeds of a writing assignment Richard undertook when he was forty years old. At that time he was invited by the late William Randolph Hearst to write for Mr. Hearst's King Features Syndicate out of New York City. For more than five years, until after Mr. Hearst's death, Richard wrote a weekly, nationally syndicated newspaper column that was circulated to millions of homes in the United States. (While writing this weekly article he of course continued his usual work with the *Improvement Era* and the

Richard and son John near family cabin

Choir broadcast and with his Church responsibilities as a member of the First Council of Seventy.)

The extra income received from his weekly newspaper articles was much welcomed. Much of the money saved from this endeavor was used when his four boys were between the ages of seven and sixteen to build a comfortable summer cabin for the family in a beautiful mountain meadow on the upper Weber River sixty miles east of the family home in Salt Lake City. This mountain retreat became, and still remains, a choice gathering-place for the family and their friends and has served as one of the means of keeping Richard and Alice, their four children, and later their grandchildren together in a close companionship. Though the area offers fishing, hunting, swimming, hiking, tubing in the river, horseback riding and other activities, if you dropped in at the cabin on a summer weekend when the Evans family happened to be there, you would usually find them either in the cabin or close by, simply enjoying each other's company "without the telephone ringing."

Richard nearly always worked a seven-day week, with Sunday, the "day of rest," ironically producing the greatest pressures—from the broadcast and from his assignments as a General Authority. He once commented that ever since starting to produce radio programs for the Church at KSL when twenty-four years of age, he had not known much else but a seven-day week, and that having lived that way so long he did not really mind not having a day off. After the family cabin was built, however, he found relief and great renewal in "leaving it all" every second or third weekend in the summer for a Saturday at the cabin with his family.

Even at the cabin however, although he enjoyed an occasional volleyball game or a ride on a horse, during most of the day he would "putter around"—repairing leaky plumbing, applying linseed oil to the outside walls of the cabin, and doing a dozen other jobs—pausing occasionally to watch his boys gallop on the horses across the pasture or to cheer on the underdogs in a family volleyball game. His fun came more from watching his family have fun and in just being with them than from his own participation in recreational activities.

Much has been said about Richard's industrious working habits. It might encourage some homeowners to know that there were some things he couldn't—or wouldn't—work into his schedule, one of them being yard work at home. At least, he didn't spend much time at it.

Once during a family outing on a Saturday (a day when the next morning's broadcast was usually very much on his mind) he left early for home so that he would have time, before working on the radio script, to keep his promise to his wife to apply a large bag of peat moss to the garden. As gardeners know, this requires making an even application and then mixing the peat moss into the soil. As it happened, shortly after he had left the family, the party "broke up" and everyone else also headed for home.

When Alice reached their home, perhaps fifteen minutes after Richard's arrival, she found him in the house engrossed in the following morning's radio script. She inquired about the garden, and he informed her, "Oh, it's all done." Going outside, she got a laugh at what she saw. Peat moss was scattered helter-skelter around the garden, lying on top of the soil and mostly in large piles. It was obvious that, in his anxiety about the script and his haste to get at it, he had just grabbed the peat-moss bag and flung its contents in the general direction of the garden! Perhaps this kind of thing shows that even in his "perfectionist" approach he was properly selective —time being valuable, he concentrated on the things that he judged to be most significant.

He was in fact remarkably skillful with his hands, at carpentry, plumbing, and other skills that are needed around the house. For instance, he personally installed the sprinkling system in the front and back yards of his home. Usually, however, because of his time pressures, his simple response to a plumbing problem, for example, was, "Call a plumber."

Even in reading, which was one of the joys of his life, he used time to the best advantage. He would "skim" through books. He told his family that if he could glean "just one or two great thoughts" from an entire book, he felt the time "to be well spent." He would remind his sons: "There are millions of books. You can't possibly read them all, or even a significant number of them, so don't waste your time with any but the best." He read only from the "best books," and from those he "skimmed off" the best thoughts and writing. This reading was generally done after the long day's work.

When his sons entered their teen-age years, Richard made more consistent efforts than formerly to get home from the office in time for dinner, which was usually scheduled relatively late to suit the time of his arrival. The dinner table was the main place of family gathering as well as of family conversation both amusing and serious. His sons had a standing joke that the two best ways to get to talk to Dad were to call his secretary at the office for an appointment or to catch him at the dinner table.

After dinner, he would often linger around the table for a few minutes to continue in family conversation. If he had no outside appointment that evening, he would then skim the newspaper and settle down to the work he had brought from the office and to some reading.

When Richard Evans was forty-three he was elected president of his local Salt Lake Rotary Club, and this began his extensive involvement in civic affairs. A year later he was elected president of the University of Utah Alumni Association, serving three successive one-year terms in that position. At about the time he stepped down as Alumni President he was elected president of the Salt Lake Bonneville Knife and Fork Club.

Each year, as Alumni President, he was asked to give a short talk at the University's commencement exercises, to briefly greet the graduates and welcome them into the Alumni Association. This gave him the opportunity for a little humor, as his opening comments in one of those talks shows:

"I think I know what some of you are thinking.

"You're thinking that this is called commencement because it seems to have no end.

"But some of you have been waiting for this a long time—and we shouldn't want you to think we were shortening the ceremonies. Besides, after what some of you have been through, a few minutes more or less now won't too much matter. (And with 47 percent of you married, as indicated by Dr. Olpin, waiting should by now be one of your cultivated virtues!)"

Referring to a talk he had just given in Evansville, Indiana, he continued: "I have a thoughtful brother who insists that I was invited to Evansville only because my name is Evans. My answer to him, if he deserves one, is that I know of some people by that name who were not invited to Evansville!"

Because humor would have been inappropriate in the dignified and sacred atmosphere in which the Tabernacle Choir broadcast was presented, those who knew Richard only as listeners of the broadcast would have been surprised to know the extent to which wit and a sense of humor were part of his makeup. Even in normal conversation he could not help showing his gift for repartee. One of his close associates on the *Improvement Era* staff described it as a "dry wit that is sometimes explosive in its effect."

As Richard became more involved in community affairs, his quick and penetrating humor became more widely known, and because he blended it so remarkably with simple yet eloquent expressions of fundamental thoughts and feelings, he quickly became in great demand as a master of ceremonies and as a speaker in civic and university functions. He could "let his hair down" and have a great time emceeing a homecoming "skits and quartets" night for the students and alumni at the University of Utah, yet feel equally at home delivering a major address before a convention of the American Medical Association. His appearances as a speaker at these "non-Church" functions at home and throughout the country reached into the hundreds.

As president of the University of Utah's Alumni Association, he was an ex officio member of the University's Board of Regents. At the conclusion of his third year as president, he was appointed by the governor of Utah to a "regular" four-year term on the Board. Each fourth year thereafter until 1969 he was reappointed, by three successive governors, to a renewal term, thus spending a total of nineteen years as a regent.

In 1969, when the Utah State Board of Higher Education was created by the Utah Legislature to govern the state's universities and colleges, he was appointed as one of the fifteen original members of that board, where he served until his death two years later.

Richard also felt very much at home in the business world. His business acumen stemmed originally from the variety of jobs he had had as a boy, his heavy involvement as European Mission Secretary in the business and administrative details of the Mission, his obtaining a master's degree in Economics, and his work as a young man in the business end of KSL as well as in the "creation" and announcing of programs.

His membership in the Salt Lake Rotary Club and with the Chamber of Commerce brought him into wide association with the business community and he served as a member of the board of directors for several business corporations in the fields of banking, radio and television, public relations and advertising, and livestock.

Richard Evans served in the First Council of Seventy for fifteen years. When he was forty-seven years old, another summons came from his Church. President David O. McKay called him to be a member of the Quorum of the Twelve Apostles.

After Richard's name was announced to a general conference of the Church convened in the Tabernacle on Temple Square in October 1953, he rose to respond to the call. He began:

"I pray that I may be given utterance in that which I should briefly say.

"I have frequented these beloved walls for a period now approaching a quarter century in many situations and assignments. But this is the most difficult thing I have here had to do. It seems that this chapter was not in the script which I had written for myself.

"In the brief, but in some respects too long a time since first I became aware of this possibility, I have measured the full measure of my life many times over. There are those here who know much better than I the weight of this work. There is none here who knows better than I my own limitations, inadequacies, and imperfections, and the feeling of smallness which I have. But if you and my Father in heaven will accept me as I am, with your help and his I shall earnestly endeavor to be better than I am or have ever been."

He had now received one of the greatest honors that can come to any man—to be an apostle of the Lord Jesus Christ. It is also a calling heavy with duties and responsibilities. Full-time in the service of the kingdom of God, Elder Evans was caught up in a round of new and demanding activities— even more challenging office responsibilities, increased counseling with Church members, more committee assignments, heavier duties in relation to the stakes and wards of the Church. The demands on his time as a public speaker, already considerable, increased with his new calling.

As a member of the Council of the Twelve, Elder Evans would serve on committees relating to the Church magazines; Temple Square activities; world fair exhibits and other Church information centers; the Tabernacle Choir and the Choir broadcast; general conference broadcasts; Hill Cumorah Pageant; Nauvoo and other Church historical sites; management of Church communications, public relations, publications, translation and distribution; the Church educational system, Church correlation, temple ceremonies, and others.

A review of Elder Evans' calendar of appointments during the last year of his life discloses a relentless round of Church activities and assignments that would be typical also of others of the General Authorities. These include attending stake conferences on assignment, counseling with stake leaders, extensive interviewing of members in connection with installing new stake officers, and performing ordinations and settings apart; attending committee meetings and conferring with Church administrative officials relating to his particular areas of responsibility; attending meetings of the General Authorities; hosting out-of-state and foreign dignitaries visiting the Church headquarters; preparing for speaking assignments; interviewing and setting apart missionaries; counseling those who came to his office and home to receive guidance and

Richard Evans when called to be an apostle

Richard and Alice with sons (l. to r.) Richard, Jr., John, Stephen, and William (front) at time of Richard's call to apostleship

Quorum of the Twelve Apostles in 1953: l. to r. (seated) Joseph Fielding Smith, Harold B. Lee, Spencer W. Kimball, Ezra Taft Benson, Mark E. Petersen, Matthew Cowley, (standing) Henry D. Moyle, Delbert L. Stapley, Marion G. Romney, LeGrand Richards, Adam S. Bennion, Richard L. Evans (newest member)

comfort; visiting and administering to those who were ill; performing temple marriages and occasionally sealings; visiting missions of the Church, interviewing missionaries and counseling with mission leaders; and numerous other activities. He carried in addition a heavy correspondence and other "office" load requiring three secretaries, and filled during that last year over two hundred speaking appointments.

This whirlwind of activity required long hours and frequent travel and was carried on in an often urgent atmosphere with the telephone ringing and people waiting in the "outer office" to see him. One can begin to sense the meaning in Richard's occasional casual comment that "my life is not my own." One also begins to understand more fully Elder Mark E. Petersen's words at Richard's funeral as he described the devotion of the men in the Council of the Twelve:

"Like their associates in this great ministry, the Twelve know what it is to be devoted completely to the cause of Christ.

"Daily they go the extra mile. Daily they serve their Master with might and heart and soul, never counting the cost, willingly sacrificing even of their health and well-being as necessary, but always seeking to build the kingdom of God with an eye single to his glory."

For Elder Evans too there was always the weekly broadcast. The pressure under which the script for that broadcast was prepared has been briefly referred to earlier. His two- to three-minute Spoken Word messages—which listeners sometimes referred to as "Sermonettes" or "Comments"—were rarely prepared far ahead of time. When he was going to be out of town the latter part of a week, he would often dictate a first draft on Monday or Tuesday. Generally, however, he began on Thursday or Friday—only two or three days before broadcast time the following Sunday morning. The preparation consisted of dictating his thoughts, having them transcribed, dictating a revised version, boiling them down. He repeated the process as often as necessary to compress the material to three minutes of air time or somewhat less. He would vary the length of the Spoken Word somewhere between two and three minutes until he felt it expressed exactly what he desired to say.

His wife, who saw and partially felt the tenseness as he ran down to the wire each week, occasionally suggested that he get a dozen or so scripts prepared in advance so as to avoid always facing a deadline. He replied that he had little time to prepare for the broadcast and that he worked better and quicker under pressure. So he purposely kept the pressure on.

He would often have his latest draft retyped late Saturday night. Regardless of when he began to prepare his Spoken Word comment, he continued to revise and edit it right up to broadcast time.

In the more than forty-one years of announcing the Choir broadcast, Richard was absent from the microphone on Sunday morning only two or three times because of illness, and even those absences were due only to a "cold" that had resulted in some laryngitis—a remarkable record of health.

There were, however, other occasions when Church or Rotary assignments away from Salt Lake City made it impossible for him to fly back in time to be in the Tabernacle on Sunday morning. On those occasions, though another announcer would have to be at the Tabernacle to announce the musical numbers, Richard's three-minute Spoken Word message would still be delivered in his own voice at the appropriate time during the half-hour program by one of two means: by his having left a prerecorded message or by his delivering the Spoken Word "live" from wherever he happened to be.

Whenever possible, Richard preferred the latter method because, as he would say, "there is something about a live performance, the reality of it, that brings out the best everyone has." In this preference there emerges again his feelings, not always understood by others, that it was better to "keep the pressure on."

Photos symbolize the weekly Choir broadcast cycle: (a) Preparing
Spoken Word script (b) Delivering Spoken Word, stopwatch in hand
(c) Leaving the Tabernacle after a broadcast

To give the Spoken Word "live" when away, Richard would either go to the studio of a local CBS-affiliated radio station wherever he happened to be or he would work from his own hotel room using a microphone brought from the Tabernacle, which he would attach to the telephone line. To this line, which would have been reserved through to the Tabernacle in Salt Lake City by prior arrangement with the telephone company, radio engineers would attach their high-fidelity equipment. On Sunday morning Richard, through earphones, would monitor the broadcast as it was in progress from Salt Lake City, and then on cue from the Tabernacle would deliver his Spoken Word with split-second timing.

For the layman familiar with only the receiving end of the Choir broadcast, it staggers the imagination to think of his broadcasting live to the nation his traditional Sunday morning message, from New York or Europe for example, thousands of miles away from the Choir and while sitting on a chair in his hotel room.

But these instances, though fascinating as an example of what can be done with electronics, are far from being the most remarkable part of the Spoken Word story. What is truly astounding when contemplated is the almost incredible level of commitment and dedication which Richard Evans put into this broadcast. In the midst of a grinding schedule of other responsibilities, to also prepare weekly a talk of moral and spiritual substance and deliver it over nationwide radio each week, with no vacation, no "two weeks off" each year, no stand-ins, no ghost writers—to do this week after week, month after month, year after year for over forty-one years is surely a kind of heroism rarely manifest.

As to the content of his broadcast comments, Richard gave this explanation on authorship:

"Many listeners have inquired as to their source, their procurability, their originality. As to originality—that is, of course, a relative term. The words and phrases belong to the author insofar as he is aware—except where there has been a borrowing from [another written source], in which case the debt is acknowledged. As to originality of thought—well, they represent the author's convictions, the source of which is that common heritage of truth available to all who will be partakers of it."

The Spoken Word comments covered, with minimal repetion, virtually every topic touching on character, human relationships, and life in general. They were particularly concerned with encouraging positive values in life. Many messages or excerpts might be reproduced as "typical." Here is one:

"Life is not a thing that begins and ends at two definable points. It is an eternal journey, to an endless destination; and the highest reward is for consistency of performance—not merely for occasional flashes of brilliance, or isolated acts of goodness, or brief periods of dependability. It is still true, as it was when it was anciently spoken, that he that endureth to the end has the greatest assurance of success and the greatest promise of having the labors of his life pronounced 'Well done!' "

By the time Elder Evans was called to be an apostle, of course, the Tabernacle Choir broadcast had become something of a national institution, the Choir's occasional tours serving to popularize it further. The gifted announcer and commentator continued to add lustre to that program with down-to-earth yet uplifting and stimulating expressions, all delivered with a quiet graciousness for which he was well known.

Richard Evans continued to receive praise, both for the weekly broadcast and for his announcements and comments at Choir concerts. Of a concert in Montreal, Frances Goltman wrote in the *Gazette*: "In the intermission period, Richard Evans gave an illuminating address and had the audience in stitches with some of his witty comments." Two days later Elliot Norton commented in the Boston *Record American*: "Good concert? It was more than that. Thanks largely to Richard L. Evans, who acted as commentator, it was also a good show. The singers made it a memorable musical; he introduced notes of his own that were generally genial and often humorous. In his own modest way, he is as capable as they, and just as polished."

A 1954 editorial in *Life Magazine* said:

"Before the H-bomb, before the atomic age, before World War II, before the 'long presidency,' before the Great Depression and even before the Wall Street crash, long, long ago, on July 15, 1929, a great 375-voice choir began broadcasting coast-to-coast from the Salt Lake City Tabernacle. . . .

"Those who know this program . . . need no arguments for listening to it, or no introduction to its producer and commentator, Richard L. Evans. . . ."

For the new apostle, the new time-pressures seemed scarcely a difference in degree, let alone in kind. To say that he had long been called upon to squeeze the most out of every minute would be only slight exaggeration. Half in fun, he raised the corner of the curtain on the kind of scheduling this could sometimes result in when he gave a short talk at the University of Utah commencement exercises on Tuesday, June 9, 1953. He said in part:

"Following the Baccalaureate held here Sunday, I left at 1:00 A.M. yesterday morning for a commencement talk in Indiana. . . . Now, two sleepless nights later, after a cyclone, a milk train, and a crippled airplane, I am back—and have been since thirty seconds before the academic procession started."

Even with his increased responsibilities as an apostle, it is doubtful that he could have squeezed much more than this out of the "unforgiving minute."

No sketch of Richard Evans' life would be valid without some reference to his association with Rotary International, which was to culminate in his holding the highest office in that organization during the time he was an apostle.

The object of Rotary is to encourage and foster high ethical standards in business and professions, the giving of service in personal, business and community life, and the advancement of international good will through a world fellowship of business and professional men united in the ideal of service. Richard's first impressions of Rotary came in 1919 when Rotary held its world convention in Salt Lake City. Richard, a Boy Scout of thirteen, served as a messenger boy. He was impressed by the Rotarians he met and felt that he would like some day to be one of them.

He became a member of the Salt Lake Rotary Club on July 5, 1938, when he was thirty-two years old. He had already become well known in the community for his work on the Choir broadcast and with the Church magazine, and at the weekly Rotary meeting when Richard's name was announced and he arose to receive his welcome as a new member, one table of Rotarians stood up and gave him a rousing chorus of "Jesus Wants Me for a Sunbeam." That was one of the few times in his life when he was at a loss for words.

At forty-three, he was elected by the Salt Lake club as its president. Of his home club, Dr. G. Homer Durham wrote:

"It is a joy to attend Richard's home Rotary Club in Salt Lake City, Utah. Serving as club president in 1949, Richard continued and enriched a tradition for excellence of expression by club officers. I have attended meetings at many different clubs on several continents. None, to my critical ears as a university president, carries a higher quality of discourse than Richard's home club—yet they have fun and fellowship as well."

In 1954, Richard was elected District Governor over Rotary District 165 (now District 542), which included approximately forty-two Rotary clubs in the states of Utah, Idaho and Wyoming. In this capacity he, together with other newly elected district governors from throughout the world, attended Rotary's annual leadership "Assembly" in Lake Placid, New York. Richard was impressed with the integrity, ability and achievements of these leaders of Rotary International and quickly formed strong friendships with many of them.

He was invited back to the Assembly the following year, this time to act as an instructor and counselor to the then incoming district governors.

Some of his friends in Rotary International then began to encourage and support him and to "talk him up" for higher positions of leadership in the organization. He could see the possibilities of Rotary's soon taking large amounts of his time unless he were to turn away from further opportunities in the organization. He counseled with Church President David O. McKay, who encouraged him then and several times thereafter to accept leadership responsibilities within Rotary if they became available.

One thing led to another and he found himself elected as one of the twelve Directors, then as a Third Vice President, then as President of Rotary International, an organization consisting in June 1966, when his one-year term of presidency began, of approximately 12,450 local clubs with a worldwide membership of 590,000 scattered in one hundred and thirty-three countries and geographical regions.

In his acceptance speech he said:

"My life is not as long in looking ahead as it once was— nor is yours—and I have to examine what I do with every day. Not only would I not give a year to Rotary, but I would not give even an hour, if I did not feel that it could and does perform a service exceedingly significant.

"Regretfully, Alice and I will miss the pleasure of visiting *all* of you. No one has; no one can. We shall go as far as we can by every means we can, with as much time as we can, and still keep up the other obligations of the trust you have placed upon us."

During the next year he did go "as far as he could," not even sparing his own strength or health. He and his wife drove themselves through a relentless schedule of travel, public

Richard, Alice, sons, and daughters-in-law at 1966 Denver Convention at which Richard was inaugurated President of Rotary International

Rotary President Richard Evans with President Lyndon B. Johnson

Lake Placid, New York — Rotary leaders from every continent at
annual International Assembly, 1966

With Dr. Antonio Coggiano, Archbishop of Buenos Aires, Argentina

Greeting the Governor of the
State of Gujerat, India, 1962

Richard and Alice photographed
with Chinese children in Taiwan,
March 1966

Visiting a Rotary-sponsored diabetic clinic in Dakar, Senegal,
November 1966

With West Berlin mayor Willy
Brandt, August 1966

At the Berlin Wall, with Branden-
burg Gate in background,
August 1966

Meeting the King and Queen and
Queen Mother of Greece,
September 1966

With Prince Rainier and Princess
Grace at reception in palace at
Monaco, May 1969

appearances, and speaking appointments. In a talk Richard gave before a Rotary gathering in Singapore in March, 1967, when there remained only about three months of his one-year term as president, he gave a glimpse of his life-style for that year:

"Now for a moment, I think perhaps we owe you a brief report of Rotary and our discharge of the trust that you have placed upon us this year. Alice and I have been moving fast and far. We have visited more than 50 countries out of 134 countries that comprise Rotary International. We haven't taken time for sightseeing; just a few days ago we were in Sapporo in Hokkaido, Japan, in the morning, spoke to the Tokyo club at noon, and attended and spoke at a large inner-city meeting at Osaka in the evening. We were at a meeting similar to this in Hong Kong last evening. We've been getting about everything we want, except sleep—and very little of that."

Their pattern was to travel by plane, sometimes at night but usually the first flight out in the morning, in order to spend each afternoon and evening in a different city. It was during this period of time that Richard began to make comments to his audiences like the following:

"We have found ourselves up late at functions and getting up for early planes the next morning. I come from a long series of pioneer forbears and was told once that they didn't think anything at all of getting up at 4:00 or 5:00 in the morning. I want to say to you that Alice and I don't think much of it either."

At each city they would be met at the airport by Rotary officials, often by local leaders of the Church, and by the press. There would follow press conferences, luncheons, interviews, meetings, receptions, and banquets, with Richard giving a talk at one or more of these functions. Then they would go back to the hotel late to grab a few hours of sleep before hurrying back to the airport at the crack of dawn for the first flight out to the next city.

When the year was ended, Richard and Alice had visited

and spoken in sixty countries on every continent, and in six provinces in Canada and twenty-five states in the U.S. (Other countries visited on assignment by Rotary before and after that one year brought the total to some ninety countries abroad.)

His one-year presidency saw its culmination in Rotary's annual world convention in May 1967, for which Richard was responsible. That year it was held at Nice on the French Riviera. The July 1967 *Rotarian* described the five-day event:

"The élite Garde Republicaine came down from Paris— 70 men, 45 horses, golden helmets, resplendent uniforms, drums, trumpets—1,000 kilometers by special train. An unprecedented honor!

"The aircraft carrier *Clemenceau,* France's largest, dropped anchor in the harbor and invited all aboard—another exceptional compliment!

"On the Place before the Palais des Expositions rose more than 100 saplings 40 feet tall cut in and hauled from the forest in the east of France and painted purest white. On these flew the brilliant banners of the countries of Rotary.

"Onto the crossarms of streetlamps all along the Riviera went 16,000 flags—the tricolor of Frances and the blue and gold of Rotary; in shop windows and on facades in every part of Nice and its sister towns appeared golden, cogged wheels, 6,000 in wood, another 3,000 in plastic.

"And then—after 10,000 more things went up and in and around, and when all was ready, the people came.

"They came in such numbers and in such spirit as to cause their leader, quiet-spoken Richard L. Evans, to term the 1967 Convention of Rotary International, as he brought the final plenary session to a close this afternoon here in the Palais, 'an almost unbelievable event.'

" 'Unbelievable' how?

"—Veteran Convention planners at first thought 12,000 might come; optimistic Nicoise thought several thousand more. The final registration figures showed 19,362. . . .

"—With Rotarians and guests signing in from 101 countries and geographical regions, this was the 'most international' in Rotary's 58 years of Conventions. . . .

"How these thousands came to Nice is, of course, the story. On the parking lot fronting the Palais we espy three families of the 'U.K.' who came by caravan, complete with range, refrigerator, shower, and tea cups. . . . In the harbor are yachts that brought folks from as far as the Thames. . . . Out at Nice-Cannes airport is a small, twin-engined private plane which brought a Rotary couple all the way from the Iowa cornfields. They flew it.

"—And this is also, sans doute, the most amiable commingling of nationalities, tongues, cultures, customs and viewpoints held anywhere in a long while."

Somehow Richard kept up that year with the Tabernacle Choir broadcasts, preparing his usual Spoken Word message each week and either flying back to Salt Lake for Sunday morning or, if that were impossible, either providing a prerecorded message before he left or broadcasting his Spoken Word comment live from wherever he happened to be. He also filled many Church assignments during the year, including conducting interviews and holding meetings in many of the areas of the world where his Rotary work took him.

Although his Church activities were necessarily somewhat limited during that year, he found that his Church position conspicuously followed him wherever he went. The following is excerpted from a letter he wrote to President David O. McKay during his Rotary presidency:

"In almost every Rotary function I have been in worldwide, I have been introduced as a member of the Council of the Twelve, Church of Jesus Christ of Latter-day Saints, and in almost every press clipping, in every one of 133 countries worldwide where notices have been published, the word "Mormon" or the name of the Church has appeared, whether in Arabic, Greek, Japanese, or whatever the language may be.

"Local Church officers are nearly always invited to these official Rotary functions.

"Thanks for your confidence and encouragement."

When the convention in Nice was through, Richard came home. His sons were shocked that he was so exhausted and had aged so much during the year. And though his strength returned in time, he never regained the physical condition he had been in before his term as president of Rotary.

It was in many ways, however, a wonderful and glorious year. He and Alice had found that nearly everywhere the Rotary leaders who hosted them were leading figures also in their businesses and professions and communities and were people not only of great integrity, high morals, and temperate habits but of great sincerity and warmth. Elder Evans counted this all as part of the fulfillment of the patriarch's blessing on his head as a youth, that he would "mingle with many of the best men and women upon the earth." Alice continues to feel a great affection for these approximately one thousand choice Rotary families worldwide and maintains some contact with them as time permits.

Richard had been received also by the political leaders of many of the cities and countries he visited—mayors, presidents, prime ministers, governors, chancellors, kings, etc.

At the close of his presidency, the Rotary Board of Directors paid a tribute to him, part of which reads:

"You have been a guiding star and a tower of strength to the Rotary world at a time in Rotary's history when your great personal attributes of devotion, integrity, and humility were most urgently needed. As Chairman of the Board of Directors, you have at all times exemplified to 'your team' a patient, impartial leadership, which has served to bring together the members of the Board from far-reaching areas of the world, representing diverse backgrounds, professions, occupations, and interests, into a unified team for the year. In all Board meetings over which you have presided, you have done so in a friendly manner which has made participation in deliberations a delight and a personal privilege and pleasure for each member of the Board.

"It is with heartfelt gratitude that we also express our sincere indebtedness to Alice for sharing you with us this year, and to you for allowing us to share in Alice's radiant love for all mankind, a quality which is self-evident in her devotion to you, to your family, and to Rotary."

It is perhaps fitting that, though a Church official by calling, his work with the Tabernacle Choir and with Rotary oriented him in a special way toward those who were not of his faith and for whom he felt great love and respect. An *Improvement Era* article written about him in 1954 observed:

"One of his greatest satisfactions is the esteem in which he is held by his fellow Rotarians and by Chamber of Commerce and other business and professional friends who are not Mormons. Without compromising the religious principles or practices for which his Church stands, Brother Evans seems able, in an unusual way, to win the confidence of men of all faiths and walks of life and return friendship and understanding in kind, as indicated by the non-Mormon press when he was named to the Council of the Twelve."[3]

No wonder that friends and family occasionally kidded him that for his time he seemed to be "the Apostle to the Gentiles!" It was also said of him: "In many nations, men proudly call Richard Evans friend, and give deference to others of us because we are his friends. In this community, he was a bridge of strongest stature across the streams of differences and lack of understanding."[4]

Richard Evans was sixty-five years old on March 23, 1971. His day was spent working as usual. He celebrated his birthday at home that evening with a family dinner attended by his sons and their wives and children.

---

[3]Marba C. Josephson, "Richard L. Evans of the Council of the Twelve," *Improvement Era*, February 1954, p. 106.

[4]Marion D. Hanks, address given at funeral service for Richard L. Evans, November 4, 1971.

At this point Elder Evans was at the pinnacle of achievement. First and foremost, he and his capable and devoted wife had raised their four sons and seen them grow into manhood and seek careers which required more than the average amount of preparation. Rick, John, and Bill were attorneys, while Steve had received a master's degree in business administration and was completing studies toward his doctorate. All four sons had served Church missions abroad and remained steadfast in the faith of their parents. Richard and Alice had invested quality time with their boys with the aim of imparting strength for life's battles. Now they could collect some dividends on their investment.

Elder Evans had put in a lot of quality time too in service to others outside his family. Aside from all the meetings, committee memberships, assignments filled and projects completed, both in and out of the Church, he had touched people's lives for good in more direct ways. At sixty-five he could look back on the fulfillment of that fifty-year-old patriarchal blessing in the hospitals he had visited, the healings in which he was the instrument, the strength he had brought to the suffering. If he had stopped to think, he could have recalled the gratitude of the mother whose young son had lost an eye in an accident and the visit Elder Evans made to his hospital room to cheer and encourage him and impress on him with unusual empathy that the future was still very much in his own hands. This was quality time invested indeed.

"Thy tongue will be loosened and become as the pen of a ready writer in dispensing the word of God and in preaching the gospel to thy fellow men," the patriarch had also said. Elder Evans' talented and dedicated exertions over three decades of General Authority service had brought this promise to brilliant realization. In that time he had given thousands of addresses at general and stake conferences and ward sacrament meetings—warning youth, parents and others of the burgeoning temptations in the modern world, depicting their often insidious nature, and indicating ways to combat them.

At hundreds of funeral services his calm, kind voice and demeanor had brought comfort and consolation to the bereaved and reminded the mourners of the need we all have for the gospel anchor. He had given of himself selflessly also to speak words of counsel and encouragement to scores of groups of Church members of all ages at firesides and other gatherings. Wherever he went too his presence and personality taught along with his words. Observing him, for example, Church members recognized a humble man. Listening, they found good reason to practice that principle. As he expressed it: "None of us can create a worm. And if we cannot create a worm, that ought to make us pretty humble." He had certainly preached the gospel to his fellow men.

Nor was this by any means all—there was also more than two thousand Spoken Word comments. Deliberately these messages did not portray peculiarly LDS concepts and doctrines, but they nonetheless depicted simply but with superlative appeal gospel principles all believers in Christ (and other good people without specific religious beliefs) could and did relate to—the importance of the family, courage to face life's difficulties, comfort in bereavement, love and consideration for others, the fleeting nature of mortality and hence the wise use of time, the assurance of a life hereafter, and many more. Of the millions who listened weekly, no one knows how many were moved to improve their lives. Many wrote letters of appreciation. Many inquired further concerning the speaker's church and, having been initially attracted to the concepts expressed, went on to learn of and accept the restored gospel of Jesus Christ.

Richard Evans' office received thousands of letters each year relating to the broadcast. Many of these were routine requests for a copy of a particular sermonette, and to these requests his secretaries responded. But many of the letters required consideration and a written response from Elder Evans. He answered these personally with a response fitting the individual correspondent.

The benefits coming to the Church through the Spoken

Word could never be properly assessed, but certainly it won many friends and admirers for the Church. Countless instances have been reported of people even claiming membership in "Richard Evans' church." LDS missionaries thus sometimes found that Elder Evans meant the difference between being able to present the missionary message and not.

As an example, one missionary said: "We had been explaining the Book of Mormon, but the woman said she 'just wasn't interested.' The only religion she could believe, she told us, was the one taught by the man from Salt Lake City on Sunday mornings. When we told her he was an apostle in the Church we represented, she suddenly became interested."

At sixty-five, Elder Evans could look back not only on value given but on value received. He had of course enjoyed communion with LDS people, those who held dear the same faith and convictions that he had. But both at home and in his travels throughout the world he met good people who were responsive to principles and ideals he had espoused and from whose examples he in turn could learn. Many of his friends and close associates were in fact active, dedicated members of other churches or belonged to no organized religious group.

There were other satisfactions he might have pondered too. His love for good literature, which had deepened with the years, had enhanced his powers of expression, which in turn had made possible the success of such things as the Spoken Word programs. It had also made possible the King Features Syndicate articles, the books Elder Evans had written, and other projects which, together with wise investment, had improved income to the point where the family was much more comfortable financially than in the early years. Yes, there were financial satisfactions too.

None of it had come easily. He had not only worked hard, but had surmounted the worry and disadvantage occasioned by the loss of his eye; for especially since he was engrossed in literary pursuits, he could never be entirely free of concern about potential damage or deterioration to the remaining eye. But he had overcome. How well he had done so had been expressed in a letter from a former neighbor in the area where he grew up and who remembered the accident to young Richard's eye:

"How well I remember that tragic accident of yours and how so many hoped and prayed for your recovery. It could have been fatal. How courageously you have adjusted these many years. How few ever stop today to realize what a handicap it has been.

"How heroically you have measured up to every assignment, how gallantly you have met every challenge. . . ."[5]

Yes, there were many satisfactions Richard Evans might have pondered on his sixty-fifth birthday. But there was no particular reason to think in retrospect. He was surrounded by the love of his family, the friendly banter of the dinner table, the chatter of grandchildren—all the lovely sounds of home. Early tomorrow he would again be immersed in labor he loved, working with associates in an atmosphere of mutual esteem and brotherhood. There was neither time nor inclination to look back with any sense of deliberation, but only to look ahead.

Neither Elder Evans nor his family could then suspect that he would not see another birthday anniversary.

[5]Letter from Bertha Kleinman.

The Voice Is Stilled

On Richard Evans' sixty-fifth birthday there was no hint even of impending health difficulties. Despite his grinding, relentless schedule, he was remarkably blessed with good health. Until the illness he died from, he had never been a patient in a hospital; and as noted earlier, he had missed only two or three Sunday morning broadcasts for health reasons in more than forty-one years—and those merely for laryngitis.

Another seven months went by before he became ill. During the weekend of October 16-17, 1971, he filled one of his usual assignments for the Church in presiding at a stake conference. It was held in Spokane, Washington. He had been tired from other duties when he left for Spokane and the conference there turned out to be unusually taxing. He was required to divide the stake, creating two stakes out of one, which necessitated extensive interviewing and the selection of new stake officers.

He flew to Spokane Friday afternoon, interviewed stake leaders during the early evening, and then drove the 120-mile round trip to Coeur d' Alene, Idaho, to speak to a gathering of about four hundred students from thirteen universities and colleges.

Saturday was spent in a full day of interviewing Church leaders in relation to the division of the stake, and in two meetings at which he presided and spoke, the last one ending about 9:00 P.M. He then spoke at a third meeting, a special gathering of youth from twelve to eighteen years of age.

Early the following morning, Sunday, he engaged in further consultations on new stake officers, spoke briefly to four different Junior Sunday Schools, and presided and spoke at the stake conference of about 2,200 people where he also divided the stake.

He afterwards participated in about seventy-five ordinations and settings apart, in thirty-six of which he acted as voice. He then flew back to Salt Lake City at approximately 10:30 that night—exhausted.

He had been dead tired before, frequently enough, in fact, for it to be almost routine. But this time he could not shake it off. Mrs. Geniel Robbins, his devoted secretary for more than twenty-seven years, relates that she had never seen him as tired as he was the next morning at the office. He continued to work for four more days. On Thursday night he became ill with what seemed like a flu. Two days later he began to have difficulty in speaking, which greatly alarmed his family. He was taken to the hospital and was found to have a viral infection in the central nervous system.

The next morning—Sunday—in the hospital, he could not speak and appeared to be only partially rational, yet he kept looking at his watch. Around nine o'clock he began checking his watch almost every few seconds. About 9:15 he tried to get up. His wife and a nurse gently but firmly restrained him and assured him that arrangements had been made for another announcer to be at the Tabernacle for the 9:30 broadcast.

Despite their attempts to reassure him, he kept looking at his watch and attempting to rise. In frustration at not being permitted to get up, he went into convulsions at 9:20. This was repeated again at 9:40, near the time at which he would have been delivering his Spoken Word message over the air, and again at 10:00 when the broadcast went off the air. It appears that his extraordinary sense of duty and his habitual weekly pattern was subconsciously impelling him toward his place at the microphone at the appointed time.

After that, he made no further effort to get up. His condition deteriorated and he died eight days later, just after midnight on Monday morning, November 1, 1971. Even while he lay in his hospital bed near the end, it was his voice that the listeners heard on the broadcast, recorded in an earlier program and now repeated. He might almost have been speaking to his family in consolation for their anxiety and their impending loss:

"There is a short sentence from Vergil that says: 'Endure, and keep yourselves for days of happiness.' There are times when we feel that we can't endure—that we can't face what's ahead of us; that we can't live with the disappointments, the problems; that we can't carry the heavy load. But these times come and go, as our strength and courage and circumstances run in cycles—from high to low to high—and in the low times we have to endure; we have to hold on until the shadows brighten, until the load lifts. . . . We do wonder if we can take it at times—but there are built-in safety factors, and we find that the human soul—the spirit, the body, the mind of man—are resilient. There is more built-in strength in all of us than we sometimes suppose. And what once we said we couldn't do or couldn't live with or couldn't carry, we find ourselves somehow doing and enduring, as time, reappraisal, readjustment, and sometimes sheer necessity, modify our sense of values and our attitudes, and we find strength and endurance and hidden resources within ourselves."

Those subconscious Sunday-morning urgings, impelling him from the hospital bed toward the microphone, reflect the very special feeling he had always had for the Tabernacle Choir broadcast, even though other responsibilities and honors crowded increasingly into his life over the years. There was almost never adequate time each week to prepare his script for the Spoken Word. But though the broadcast was a small part of his total week in terms of time spent, it remained in some ways central to his life's work; his devotion to that assignment never diminished.

On one occasion, about five years before his death, his wife gently suggested to him that the demands of his worldwide work in the Church and as an officer in Rotary International might at some time require him to give up the broadcast, and that he also face the fact that "advancing years" might eventually make it impossible to keep up with radio and television's rigid demands for quick thinking, perfect timing, and crisp and unfaltering speech. His response to this suggestion was a look of almost unbelief. To give his wife an idea of how difficult it would be for him to step down from that assignment, he retorted: "How would you feel if someone asked you to give up one of your children?"

The implications of this conversation have helped his family to be reconciled to his death. He was taken before the declining years could interfere with his usual activities. "For him it was only autumn, as we think of it," said President Harold B. Lee at his funeral service. "Age had hardly begun to take its toll."

On November 1, 1972, one year after his passing, at Brigham Young University the announcement was made that the "Richard L. Evans Chair of Christian Understanding," had been established. This endowed chair is to be occupied by a distinguished scholar at BYU who will promote, as Elder Evans had done, "understanding among people of differing religious faiths through teaching and other activities centered in Jesus Christ and his teachings." On the occasion of the announcement, Elder Marion G. Romney, a close associate of Elder Evans in the Council of the Twelve, gave the following insight into his passing:

"A year ago today, on Monday the first of November, 1971, while in Hong Kong, I was advised by telephone of the passing of my beloved friend Richard L. Evans. I was saddened, of course, by the message but I was not surprised.

"Thursday afternoon, on the twenty-first of October, ten days earlier, the last day that Richard was at the Church administration building, he came into my office late in the day. We were completing arrangements for showing some Japanese dignitaries through Temple Square. He was to conduct them through the Square and the Tabernacle and the Visitors' Center.

"As I accompanied him to the door that night to say goodnight, I remarked: 'Richard, you should get some rest; you look tired.' His response was: 'I am tired; I'm worn out.'

"The next morning, needing to check some last-minute details, I called and, not finding him in his office, I called his home. Alice said he was sleeping (it was very unusual for him at that time of day), and she did not wish to disturb him.

"He never came back to the office.

"The next and last time I saw him alive was a few days later at the LDS Hospital. A group of his associates, the General Authorities and his family, stood around his bed. We had come there to administer to him. President Lee asked me to seal the anointing.

"As I spoke a prayer and a blessing, I was advised by the voice of the Spirit that he would not get well, that his work was finished here on this earth and he was needed for a greater service on the other side.

"That is why I was not surprised when I received the word a week later way over in Hong Kong."

Many were the expressions of regret at Elder Evans' passing. Friends from far and near sent messages of condolence. Some expressed appreciation for personal help he had given them at some time—a letter, a thought which touched their heart, a lift in their life. All expressed a sense of loss.

Speakers at memorial services gave articulation to the unexpressed thoughts and feelings of thousands of friends and admirers. At the Brigham Young University Memorial Service, Lorin Wheelwright summed up Richard Evans' power of expression as shown in the Spoken Word program:

"He captured the essence of universal truth and magnified its meaning to reach millions—not by multiplication of words but by their compression. His text had the cutting edge of the laser beam—finely focused, penetrating, able to reach an infinite distance and countless people."[1]

At the same services, Heber G. Wolsey offered another perspective:

"To millions of Americans, however, he was not the executive, the educator, the writer, but a personal friend who dropped in Sunday mornings to introduce the selections to be performed by the Mormon Tabernacle Choir and organ and to share his short, inspirational messages. Many people throughout the world have claimed membership in Richard L. Evans' church . . . Their only 'religion,' an enjoyable half-hour weekly with 'Music and the Spoken Word.' "[2]

One tribute at the same service, given by Lowell Berry, underlined the fellowship which many people not members of his Church felt for Richard Evans:

"I first heard Richard Evans, as many of you have, in his program, 'From the Crossroads of the West,' on Sunday morning, October 3, 1954. I awoke to hear the words of Richard Evans in a talk he gave at that time on the 'Church of the Air' entitled, 'We Are Not Alone in Life.' It was one of the most profound, touching, and moving messages that it has ever been my privilege to hear. I think it will go down in the history of literature, particularly Christian literature, as a message of faith and strength and renewing of belief by us all.

"Subsequently, I journeyed to Salt Lake from my home in Oakland to become acquainted with the man who had given this message. I had never met him before. I found that he was indeed a friendly and fine person. We visited for some time in his office, and we found that we had much in common. For instance, our Rotary friendship—I had been president of

[1]*Memorial Services for Richard L. Evans,* November 2, 1971, pamphlet published by Brigham Young University Press, p. 9. Copyright 1971 by BYU Press.
[2]*Ibid.,* p. 3.

the Oakland Rotary Club and he, of the Salt Lake Club, and there seemed to be a kindred fellowship in this.

"I think maybe he took a special favor for me. Perhaps it was because I was a fertilizer man. That was my business. I do not know whether that amused him a little or not to start with, but we grew to be the dearest of friends, in spite of the fact that we were miles apart in our homes and in our businesses and I was not of his church. But we were Christians, both of us, and I have never met, nor do I ever expect to meet, a man who has touched my heart so warmly."[3]

Elder Evans' funeral service was held in the Salt Lake Tabernacle on November 4, 1971, where tributes were paid by several of the General Authorities of the Church. Significant were the words of President Joseph Fielding Smith in relation to Elder Evans' having been taken by death to another area of service:

"Brother Evans has been taken by the Lord to another field of labor, where his great talents will be multiplied a hundredfold; where he will continue to use them in the furtherance of the Lord's work; and where they are now needed even more than they were here among us.

"And may I say for the consolation of those who mourn, and for the comfort and guidance of all of us, that no righteous man is ever taken before his time. In the case of the faithful saints, they are simply transferred to other fields of labor. The Lord's work goes on in this life, in the world of spirits, and in the kingdoms of glory where men go after their resurrection. . . .

"The Church on earth has lost the services of one of its most able and competent leaders who was endowed with special talents and abilities which are seldom equaled. But the same Church, which has an even more perfect and effective organization among the righteous dead, has gained another pillar of strength to use in the great labors that are performed there."

---

[3]*Ibid.,* p. 7.

President Harold B. Lee, first counselor in the First Presidency of the Church, impressively capsuled Elder Evans' impetus to accomplishment:

"By the time his widowed mother had completed her earthly mission when her last-born child was now ready to take on the responsibilities of life, he had climbed to the summit of his career. As Karl G. Maeser, that great pioneer teacher said it, "There is a Mount Sinai for every child of God if he only knows where to find it.' Richard found his Mount Sinai and climbed it to its summit. . . .

"As I searched for a simple phrase to describe how this man reached the heights of his career, I found it in two simple words: 'Give me love and work, these two only.' 'We have too many men who live without working, and we have altogether too many who work without living.' (Charles E. Hughes)

"Richard L. Evans loved his work. He lived joyously, courageously while he worked, because he loved with all his heart the work in which he was engaged."

Elder Evans' friend and associate in the Council of the Twelve, Elder Mark E. Petersen, spoke some eloquent words on the highest of Richard's many mortal assignments, his calling as an apostle of the Lord Jesus Christ:

"In the Council of the Twelve, men are bound together in a great brotherhood which can hardly be equalled anywhere else in the world. These men—these Twelve—have a special and distinctive calling from the Lord. They are chosen for one great purpose—to testify of Christ and teach his word. And this they do.

"One in their divine commission, one in a great effort to waken the world to its true opportunity to find peace and the abundant life, these men are united in heart and hand.

"They move as one. They work as one. They feel as one, and today, they sorrow as one at the passing of one of the great servants of Almighty God who has given his all for the work. . . .

"Greatly talented, brilliant of mind, charming of personality, humble of heart, he never rested from his task. Of his
own free will he sought constantly to teach the word on a
wide front and in many and varied fields of endeavor."

Reading the words of Elder Marion D. Hanks, Assistant
to the Twelve and long-time friend of Richard L. Evans, one
can almost feel the setting of that service in the Tabernacle:

"It is so appropriate that we meet here today in this
building on this, his 'beloved ten acres,' with this choir singing,
and with his cherished associates nearby. Early and late
through the years of his service he has been in this place,
within these walls, at the Crossroads of the West, and here his
voice will ring and his memory live while time shall last."

"A suitable memorial to the life of Richard Evans would
require, to do him justice, the wisdom and power of the voice
and pen of a Richard Evans. But there is and ever will be
only one of his mold, and the voice and pen are stilled for a
time, and we are left, with our limitations, to try to express our
appreciation and our love. . . .

"For all those years he lived under intense pressures,
always fighting deadlines, always meeting schedules, always
facing tasks bigger than most men ever undertake, and always
performing every assignment in his special, choice way. His
efforts have been incredible, his output remarkable. Over a
broad scale of manifold talents, he gave himself without consideration for himself, generously sharing the richness of his
gifts and of his love. . . .

"And finally I mention his love for the Lord and His
Church, love which undergirded and overarched all of his life
and all that he did. . . .

"We shall miss him, oh, how much we shall miss him!
We shall miss the light he brought into the room, his wit, his
quiet question, his eloquent prayer. We shall miss going into
his office with his books and papers and mementoes, and the
letters and talks coming and going."

Yes, he is greatly missed. But his loved ones, friends and associates are comforted as they look beyond this life and visualize his joy in his continued service. For Richard Evans knew with his whole soul that he and all men would have purposeful existence after the death of the body. Accordingly there are perhaps no more appropriate words to apply to him and bring to a close this sketch of his life than those words he himself spoke at the death of his beloved friend John A. Widtsoe:

"He is still himself, and should we ever come within reach of so high a place as where he is, we should like to take his outstretched hand and resume our talk where last we left it.

"Almost to the last time he talked to us, he was earnestly anticipating other activities, and I doubt not that already he is engaged in them.

"There are walls that will listen for sounds that are silenced. There are places and people that will be lonelier than they have been. But somewhere . . . there has been a glorious reunion, and the sweet sounds that have faded from our ears are somewhere heard in a heavenly setting.

"For what he was, for what he has done, for what he has meant to many—and for what he is—God bless his memory; and may the peace that passes understanding be with all of us, and especially with those who shall miss him most."

PART II

THE MESSAGE

Sunday Morning From
Temple Square

A Lesson from Huckleberry Finn

Concerning this matter of a supposed emancipation from morality, may we forthrightly face and reaffirm this fundamental fact: that unhappiness, frustration, and impairment of the minds and lives of young and old alike, come with failure to keep the commandments.

Explain it any way you will, in technical or in commonplace terms, or in the jargon of those who want to rid themselves of all restraint, yet it all adds up to an overwhelming evidence that in this we are dealing with eternal truths, and that men cannot escape the consequences of their own conduct—that, indeed they pay a heavy price when they degrade their bodies, minds, and morals.

Well, we cannot leave it there. There has to be an answer—and there is: The answer is the simple, honest process of repentance. But to be relieved of any burden at all, a person's repentance must go deep beyond the surface— a repentance that is honestly sincere—an actual change of heart, of life; a real and literal departure from the errors of the past. And those who try to lift the load in any other way will *not* find the peace they so much seek.

This point is made by Mark Twain as, in ungrammatical language, this simple, honest message comes from Huckleberry Finn: "It made me shiver," he said. "And I about made up my mind to pray and see if I couldn't try to quit being the kind of boy I was and be better. So I kneeled down. But the words wouldn't come. Why wouldn't they? It warn't no use to try and hide it from Him. . . . I knowed very well why they wouldn't come. It was because my heart warn't right, it was because I warn't square, it was because I was playing double. . . . I was trying to make my mouth *say* I would do the right thing and the clean thing, . . . but deep down in me I knowed it was a lie, and He knowed it. You can't pray a lie —I found that out."[1]

So much for a lesson learned by Huckleberry Finn— a lesson all of us must sometime learn.

If We Treat a Person As He Ought to Be . . .

"If you treat a man as he ought to be," said Goethe, "he will become what he ought to be." What is true of a man is equally or more true of a child. In an atmosphere of encouragement and confidence much more is accomplished than in an atmosphere of criticism. Countless children tragically have become much less than they could have become because they have been discouraged, made to feel unimportant, unpromising, unappreciated.

A performer rises to the expectation of the audience. Unheard or unappreciated performances are not likely to be the best. We tend to try to become what others give us reason to feel we should and can become. President McKay used to cite the words of a faithful wife standing by and saying, "You can; you must; you will."

An understanding and encouraging wife, a kind and encouraging husband, can make the difference between unhappiness at work and at home, or a feeling of happy service and success.

It is so with children, as parents and teachers patiently encourage—and care—and convince them they can—and so

---

[1]Mark Twain, *Huckleberry Finn: You Can't Pray a Lie,* ch. 31.

they often do. More trust, more love, more effort, more output come by telling them how they can improve rather than how poorly they perform. And one tragic way to have a child—or anyone—feel that he is a failure, is to expect nothing of him, or fail to give him an awareness of what he can become.

In many other ways the love and loyalty of family play a vitally important part. Many a young person has resisted temptation because he knew what his parents and family expected of him, and because he knew if he disappointed them, the hurt would be deep in their hearts. Such family love and loyalty have proved to be the safety and salvation of countless young people—letting them know that their loved ones believe in them.

Overall, the world will be better if we treat people as if they are or could be what they ought to be—and give them confidence and encouragement. If we treat a person as he ought to be, he will tend to become what he ought to be.

"The Desire to Be Appreciated"

"The deepest hunger in human beings," said William James, "is the desire to be appreciated."

A wife, a mother, can put up with faults and imperfections—with inadequate income, disappointments, difficult conditions, if there is kindness, consideration, appreciation. A father can work and worry, meet problems, debts, discouragement, and face the world, if there is kindness, consideration, appreciation. A teacher can try harder to teach and labor patiently and long, if there is willingness to learn—and appreciation. A worker can work longer and do better if there is encouragement and appreciation.

We can be driven by others only so far, but we can drive ourselves much farther, if we feel there is fairness and appreciation. This is true in marriage, in the home, between parents and children, in business, and in all relationships of life. Hearts are broken, lives are blighted with unkindness. Talents and creative gifts are squelched and stifled without encouragement and appreciation. Children can be made to feel as nothing, and go nowhere and learn little, and young people never fulfill their possibilities, except for encouragement and praise and appreciation.

A person can drive, extort, intimidate, threaten, yet never realize the results that fairness and appreciation will produce. It isn't the *work* of life that so much wears us away as the frictions and frustrations—not being noticed, not being recognized, not being appreciated, not being kindly considered. Men shrink with fear, withdraw from coldness, and with unkindness harden or break their hearts—but with kindness, encouragement, appreciation there can be peace and blessing in the home, satisfaction in service, and happiness in the heart.

In this time of frustrations and too many tensions, let there be a renewal of appreciation for people, with loved ones coming closer, with families caring and encouraging, and with kindness, encouragement, appreciation for all that others do to lighten and lift the load of life. "The deepest hunger in human beings is the desire to be appreciated."

If Everyone Must Watch Everyone . . .

There is a simple, old-fashioned subject that is urgently essential, and it is this: simple honesty. There is no credit, no contract, no transaction, no situation that is safe without the element of honesty.

If no one does what he says he will do, no one could count on anything. If everyone has to worry about every property, every possession—watch it, guard it, almost sit on it in a sense, in trying to hold what he has—the world wouldn't run, and life would approach the impossible.

Nobody can watch *everybody* all the time. Nobody can watch *anybody* all the time. No one can stay awake all the time. No one has the time, the strength, the ability to protect himself against all forms of deception and deceit.

No one can know enough in all things always to make safe decisions. We have to trust the physician for his prescription, the pharmacist who fills it, the person who makes things, who sells things and certifies that they are of a certain kind and quality. Few of us, for example, could buy a diamond and know what it was worth. We have to trust someone.

If we can't find a package where we put it; if goods disappear from the shelves; if a car on the street isn't safe; if expense accounts are padded; if we can't leave a piece of equipment with someone to repair, and know he will do only what is needed, and charge only what is fair; if people increasingly deal in deception, there will be less and less peace and progress.

Beyond the boldness of robbery, of burglary and embezzlement, any deception is dishonest: overcharging, getting paid for what we haven't done, taking what isn't ours, saying what isn't so, pretending what we aren't, reporting what we haven't done. In short, if everyone must watch everyone, if no one can trust anyone, there is no safety, no assurance.

If it isn't true, don't say it. If it isn't right, don't do it. If it isn't yours, don't take it. If it belongs to someone else, return it. Honesty is not only the best policy, but a principle, and an absolute essential for the good and happy living of life.

"Character Is What You Are in the Dark"

From Dwight L. Moody we turn to a strong, short, challenging sentence: "Character is what you are in the dark."[2] Every man is two things at least—what he seems to be (what others see), and what he is inside. Both are important, but what he is unseen inside is the measure of the man, and can, in part, be appraised by the answer to a series of questions such as these (and many more):

What would he do with uncounted money? What would he do if he found that which belonged to someone else—something no one knew he had found? What would he do if he were in a position to take unfair advantage of anyone? How would he work when he is paid by someone without being checked on or watched? What does he think when he is alone—and doesn't have to think? How faithfully and considerately does he live with his loved ones? How would he act away from home where he thought he was not known?

There is much cynicism concerning integrity in high and low, in public and private places, and if we can only count on laws and locks, if we can only count on physical force; if we can't count on honor, if we can't count on character, there isn't much we can count on.

There is such a thing as eloquent duplicity, such a thing as words that were made to conceal what is inside, words that were made to cover up true intent. But the words won't finally cover the flaws, and a surface politeness will not make anyone safe from anyone who is not sincere.

What a man thinks of himself—what he really sincerely knows himself to be—is as important as what others think of him. Self-respect is as important as the respect of others, and this world will be safe only as we live so that we can respect

2Dwight L. Moody, *Sermons: Character.*

ourselves sincerely. We know; God knows; and we ought to keep straight with ourselves and with him.

But finally, no doubt, we shall judge ourselves. This is one of the frightening facts that awaits us all: that we shall, in fact, see and know ourselves inside, and that we shall ultimately not be able to deceive even ourselves. And so, the impact of this challenging, eight-word sentence: "Character is what you are in the dark."

"Nothing Comes from Nothing"

This, from a song that is sung is one of the most important lessons of life: "Nothing comes from nothing. Nothing ever could."[3] All the world, and all of us—or any who expect the most from the least amount of effort, or who expect everything from little or nothing—must face the fact that nothing comes from nothing, that nothing ever could.

All the elements there are always existed. All the components of creation always were. Truth is eternal, but knowledge, invention, improvement, production, character, talent, ability—all have to be developed by thought, effort, work, practice, performance; by putting *in* whatever we expect to get *out*.

If we have friends that we can count on, it is largely because we have made friends. Some may ride along on the friends of their families, the friends of their friends, or suppose that friendship will simply show itself. But someone, sometime, had to make the effort and give evidence of the attitude that fosters friendship.

Some *things* we inherit. Some *things* are passed to us from others. But this doesn't make of *us* anything we aren't. We may enjoy the talents of others, but this doesn't develop

---
[3]Richard Rodgers, "The Sound of Music."

our own. We do not suddenly become what we do not cooperate in becoming. We do not learn well what we are not willing to learn.

In indifference, some things may remain in our minds, some things may attach themselves to us. But generally what we are, what we do, what we become is because we were willing to put in for what we want to get out.

Basically we always were. And what we shall be is what we are, plus what we add to it—always and forever. And there would be no better time than now to decide to learn, to do, to develop, to work, to improve, to produce, to increase our competence, to extend ourselves in service.

"The darkest day in life," said Allen Shawn, "is the one in which we expect something for nothing."[4] "Nothing comes from nothing. Nothing ever could."

The Poetry of the Commonplace

The eminent Sir William Osler expressed a thought that brings routine functions into focus. The "poetry of the commonplace," he called it. "Nothing will sustain you more potently," he said, "than the power to recognize in your humdrum routine, . . . the true poetry of life—the poetry of the commonplace, of the ordinary man, of the plain, toilworn woman, with their love and their joys, their sorrows and their griefs."

We often glamorize the unusual, the exaggerated, the artificial, but the world goes on, day to day, by the honest, enduring effort of ordinary, faithful people, facing their problems, meeting debts, caring for children, for the sick, caring for each other, performing essential functions, doing their work well, and keeping going against discouragement. And

---

[4]Allen Shawn, copyright 1966 by *Post Script*.

without these wonderful daily doers of what has to be done, this wouldn't be much of a world.

Machines can never altogether take the place of thinking, conscientious, faithfully performing people. Glamor or leisure can never take the place of the solid work of the world, of doing what needs to be done today. "If you do your work with complete faithfulness . . ." said Phillips Brooks, "you are making just as genuine a contribution to the . . . universal good as is the most brilliant worker . . . Oh, go take up your work and do it . . . with cheerfulness and love . . . profoundly devoted to [*your*] work and yet . . . profoundly thankful for the work which other men are doing . . . that everything should reach its best, that every man should do his best in his own line, . . ."[5] To know what has to be done, and then to do it, is not only essential, but often heroic in its own way.

Thank God for sincere and wonderful men, women, children, who do well and honestly what they have to do each day, despite difficulties and disappointments—for faithful people—for simple things—for routine duties—for work well done—for "the poetry of the commonplace."

"Don't Ever Take a Fence Down . . . Until . . ."

"Don't ever take a fence down," said G. K. Chesterton, "until you know the reason it was put up." Too many people in too many places tend to remove time-honored safeguards, the reasons for which they do not know.

Change is inevitable; fashions will be made and unmade as far as we can foresee. But there are extremists and exhibitionists who flagrantly defy standards, principles, law, morals, modesty.

---

[5]Phillips Brooks, *The Light of the World and Other Sermons: Identity and Variety.*

There is, among other things, good taste to be considered. As Alexander Pope said it: "Be not the first by whom the new are tried, nor yet the last to lay the old aside."[6] But the crux is the difference between what is a principle and what is merely a preference.

There are some foundations that are firmly fixed. If not, there is nothing that one can measure by or count on, except his own preference, his own mood of the moment, and that, of course, is chaos. There are some foundational principles, some standards, some basic qualities of character without which there is no progress, no assurance, without which no society or no person is safe: Honesty, morality, respect for law —such things don't go out of force even if, with some, they seem to go out of fashion. It is so easy to tear down; so easy to reject, so easy to discredit, but the commandments are still there. Cause and consequences are still there, and if we tamper irresponsibly, ignorantly, or even innocently, with the basic laws of life, we shall find to our sorrow why the fence was put up in the first place.

As to modesty, morality, chastity, honesty and honor, one cannot break from the basic foundations and have assurance for the future. Paul said it in a strong, short sentence: "Let all things be done decently, and in order,"[7] "Don't ever take a fence down until you know the reason why it was put up."

"A New Crop of Fools Comes On . . ."

This message was once sent to a president of the United States by a group of concerned young people: "We stand for preservation of our heritage through obedience to law."[8]

Without law, respect for it, living by it, upholding it, we would have no heritage. Law sustains life. Law keeps the

---

[6]Alexander Pope, *Essays on Criticism.*
[7]1 Corinthians 14:40.
[8]M-Men - Gleaners MIA youth organization, 1929. The Church of Jesus Christ of Latter-day Saints.

universe in its course. Law assures that orderly processes will lead to known results. Without law there would be no safety, no standards, no assurance, no guidelines in life. Without law men, nature, life, would be in complete chaos. Then why, Oh why should there be looseness pertaining to law, failure to uphold it?

Frank Crane once gave some terse sentences on this subject: "Every generation a new crop of fools comes on," he said. "They think they can beat the orderly universe. They conceive themselves to be more clever than the eternal laws. They snatch goods from Nature's store, and run. . . . And one by one they all come back to Nature's counter, and pay— pay in tears, in agony, in despair; pay as fools before them have paid. . . . Nature keeps books pitilessly. Your credit with her is good, but she collects; there is no land you can flee to and escape her bailiffs. . . . She never forgets; she sees to it that you pay her every cent you owe, with interest."[9]

Thank God for law, for those who respect it, live by it, help to sustain it: for the laws of health; for the renewal of the air and water of the earth—for seeds that produce what was planted, for the succession of the seasons, for everything that leads to a known result, and sustains life, and makes peace and orderly purpose possible.

Everything we have, everything we may ever expect to have, everything we can count on would be lacking without law. Everything that we *can* count on comes with living and working with law. "We stand for the preservation of our heritage through obedience to law."

It All Adds Up . . .

We have become increasingly aware lately of the so-called exact sciences—of mathematical formulas, for example, from which can be forecast the forces of the inner atom and the orbiting of outer areas.

---

[9]Dr. Frank Crane, *Four Minute Essays: Pay, Pay, Pay!*

Order is evident in all of this—order, and the mind of an Infinite Administrator. But he whose infinite orderliness is everywhere in evidence has not left his children without laws of life that lead to results as sure, as certain as the laws pertaining to physical phenomena—laws of health, moral laws, counsel, and commandments.

There has been a tendency by some to say that this age-old counsel on conduct may have served a purpose in the past, but is no longer essential to human happiness. But it simply is not so. There is no evidence that loose thinking or lax living or so-called emancipation from morals and manners has brought peace or happiness or progress to anyone—ever. And the Father of us all, in his love and wisdom pertaining to his children, hasn't said "Thou shalt" and "Thou shalt not" for no particular purpose.

As Emerson said: "The world looks like a multiplication table or a mathematical equation, which, turn it how you will, balances itself. . . . You cannot do wrong without suffering wrong. . . . A man cannot speak but he judges himself. . . . Every secret is told, every wrong redressed, in silence and certainty. . . . The thief steals from himself. The swindler swindles himself. . . . Men suffer all their life long, under the foolish superstition that they can be cheated. But it is . . . impossible for a man to be cheated by anyone but himself. . . . What will you have? quoth God; pay for it and take it . . . thou shalt be paid exactly for what thou hast done, no more, no less."[10] To use the mathematical vernacular: It all adds up.

As William James worded it: "Every smallest stroke of virtue or of vice leaves its never so little scar."[11] Every thought and act and utterance is being counted "among the molecules and nerve cells and fibers. Nothing we ever do is in strict scientific literalness wiped out."[11]

No amount of rationalizing can cancel out the fact that peace and quiet come with keeping clean, with keeping the commandments, and no amount of rationalizing can save us

---

[10]Emerson, *Compensation.*
[11]William James, *The Laws of Habits.*

from the consequences of misconduct. We are the sum of the thoughts we think, of the habits we have, of all we do and have done. We are the sum of all our actions and attitudes and utterances, of all things stored in body and mind and memory.

The laws given by a loving Father are always in force and always effective. His advice is worth taking, his commandments worth keeping. It all adds up.

"*. . . That Is All There Is to You . . .*"

There is a line from Emerson which somewhat summarizes life's purpose in one short sentence: "Make the most of yourself," he said, "for that is all there is to you."

Each man is always and forever inseparably himself. Each one of us is always himself. We are constantly in our own company. We are a combination of mind, of spirit, of physical faculties, which we use, or fail to use, in one way or another. Either we learn—or we don't know; either we practice—or we don't improve. Either we commit ourselves to the wholesome opportunities of life—or we slip to something less than we could have become.

We build the record of what we are; we build the very substance of ourselves by the choices and decisions of every hour, of each instant. We can become much more, or we can become much less, but we never get away from ourselves.

Sometimes young people drift along in school, in work, or in not much of anything at all, thinking they don't need to put out much effort—just getting by, just loafing along, doing as little as possible. While this may be disappointing to others, ultimately it is damaging principally to one person— to him who doesn't learn and work and produce and prepare himself. As Emerson said it, ultimately and actually, "It is impossible for a man to be cheated by anyone but himself."[12]

Who would be so shortsighted as to be indifferent to the opportunity to learn—or to take the low road, or choose to break the law—so shortsighted as to partake of things that would lower the morals, or injure the body or mind or spirit of any man?

Life is forever, and the pursuit of excellence must be forever: learning, developing, making ourselves more serviceable, living so as to have a clear, quiet conscience, in cleanliness, in honor, in health, in happiness—becoming the best we can become, with reverence and respect.

"Make the most of yourself, for that is all there is to you." To do less would be foolishly, stupidly shortsighted.

"School Thy Feelings . . . "

Much of life and of love, of home and of happiness, is less than it might be because of tensions and tempers, resentments and feelings of offense that separate loved ones, that keep people apart, that drive away the hallowed spirit of home and the peace of the heart.

Sometimes we feel wronged. Sometimes we know we have wronged others. We all say things we wish we hadn't said, and do things we wish we hadn't done, yet often let stubbornness and pride keep us from apologizing, from clearing misunderstandings—and can't quite seem to humble ourselves to face the facts, to clear the air from feelings of offense. And so we sometimes rationalize—blaming others, absolving ourselves—frequently forgetting, or not admitting, that there are two sides to most misunderstandings.

---

[12]Emerson, *Compensation.*

The seasons pass so swiftly that we ought not to let any of life be lived in coldness and unkindness when we could so often clear up offenses if we would—*and we should,* not only for the sake of others but for ourselves, because every lingering resentment we carry around with us is a kind of slow-eating acid that cuts and corrodes and takes from us the full enjoyment of life and loved ones.

Let those who are married talk things out and come closer, and find again in each other what they once found. There must be forgiving. There must be forgetting. There must be honest effort to make amends—not just a gesture, but attitudes and actions that prove we are sincere. Let children and parents come closer, and friends and neighbors, and let life be lived, not with quick tempers and lingering resentments, but with the understanding that knows there are two sides to most subjects.

Admit errors; make apologies; clear up the brooding clouds at home and in the heart that keep us from enjoying life and loved ones, and from being at peace with ourselves inside—all somewhat summarized in an old song:

> School thy feelings, O my brother;
> Train thy warm impulsive soul;
> Do not its emotions smother,
> But let wisdom's voice control.
> School thy feelings; there is power
> In the cool, collected mind;
> Passion shatters reason's tower,
> Makes the clearest vision blind.[13]

Manners in Marriage

It has been some two and a half centuries since Richard Steele, English essayist, wrote: "Two persons who have chosen each other out of all the species, . . . to be each other's mutual

---

[13]Charles W. Penrose, Hymn: "School Thy Feelings."

comfort and entertainment, have in that action bound themselves to be good-humored, affable, discreet, forgiving, patient
and joyful, with respect for each other's frailties and imperfections." It is a good summary—or at least a good beginning—
of what one might make or expect of marriage.

Marriage isn't a matter of shallow considerations—nor
should it be. It isn't a matter of quick decision—nor should
it be. It requires durable qualities of character—devotion to
duty—facing up to facts—solving problems, working—sol-
vency—honest ambition—making a home, teaching children,
adjusting to life, to people, to disappointments. Day after
day, it is a relationship that requires resourcefulness of mind,
resilience of spirit, and an absolute honesty. And yes, there
must be manners in a marriage—manners, kindness, courtesy.

Strangers we can see, and back away from as we want to;
friends we can see from time to time; but marriage is among
the most constant relationships of life. And how important
that those who marry have common convictions, common purposes, common interests and ideals, and in unity teach their
children, and avoid the tragedy of two parents pulling their
children in different directions, sometimes confusing, sometimes destroying faith, and pulling the family apart.

It would be difficult to conceive of a more far-reaching
decision than marriage, remembering that the family was
meant to be forever. And it would be difficult to think of a
better place than home to be at our best. No place in all this
world should we be more kind, more courteous, more honest,
more honorable. No place should we be more clean, more
considerate. No place more than at home should we show
the better side of ourselves.

"Think Not, the Husband Gained, That All Is Done"

There is ever and always this matter of marriage—a subject that suggests quoting an old couplet: "Think not, the husband gained, that all is done./The prize of happiness must still be won."[14] This parallel also could be added: Think not, the *wife* gained, that all is done; the prize of happiness must still be won.

Happiness in marriage, happiness at home, must always be won—over and over again, with kindness and consideration, with honor and honesty, in this most sensitive relationship of life, a relationship that affects not only two people, but children, family, friends, the community and the whole structure of society, and one that never should be entered into lightly. And always to be remembered is that marriage is a relationship of two imperfect people. Any of us, perhaps, could get along with perfect people, but where on earth would we find them!

"A great proportion of the wretchedness which has embittered married life, has originated in a negligence of trifles. . . . It is a sensitive plant, which will not bear even the *touch* of unkindness; a delicate flower, which indifference will chill and suspicion blast. It must be watered by the showers of tender affection, . . . of kindness, and guarded by the . . . barrier of unshaken confidence. Thus matured, it will bloom . . . in every season of life, and sweeten even the loneliness of declining years."[15]

God bless you who are married to make a respectful and enduring and satisfying association—and bless you who are not, to approach marriage thoughtfully, prayerfully, with clean morals, good manners, and the qualities of kindness and

---

[14]Lord Lyttleton, English author.
[15]Thomas Sprat, English author.

consideration that will make a respectful, satisfying companionship.

"Think not, the husband gained, [the wife gained,] that all is done./The prize of happiness must still be won."

"You Two . . .
Build Your Own Quiet World"

All things need watching, working at, caring for, and marriage is no exception. Marriage is not something to be indifferently treated or abused, or something that simply takes care of itself. Nothing neglected will remain as it was or is, or will fail to deteriorate. All things need attention, care and concern, and especially so in this most sensitive of all relationships of life.

It isn't difficult to prove that we are none of us perfect. When we seek to find fault there is much fault to find. And in marriage as in all else, unkind faultfinding can be destructive.

"In the first solitary hour . . ." said an unknown writer, "promise each other sacredly never, not even in jest, to wrangle with each other, never . . . indulge in the least ill-humor. . . . Next, promise each other sincerely and solemnly never to keep a secret from each other, under whatever pretext, and whatever excuse it might be. You must continually, and every moment, see clearly into each other's [hearts]. Even when one of you has committed a fault . . . confess it. And as you keep nothing from each other, so, on the contrary, preserve the privacies of your house . . . [your] marriage . . . [your] heart, from . . . [all others], from all the world. You two, with God's help, build your own quiet world. . . . [Let no] party stand between you two. . . . Promise this to each other. . . . Your souls will grow, . . . to each other, and at last will become as one."[16]

---

[16]Quoted by President David O. McKay.

Remember to build each other up, to strengthen and sustain, to keep companionship lovely and alive. Remember dignity and respect; understanding; not expecting perfection; a sense of humor and a sense of what is sacred and serious; common purposes, common convictions, and the character to stay with a bargain, to keep a covenant—in these are the making of a good and solid marriage.

Remember "patience, persuasion, gentleness, kindness and love unfeigned; without hypocrisy and without guile, that you may know that thy faithfulness is stronger than the cords of death."[17] Every marriage has a right to this. "You two, with God's help, build your own quiet world."

"... Any Who Love You ..."

"We are most of us very lonely in this world; you who have any who love you, cling to them and thank God."

These words from an unknown source suggests something of the searching of soul that comes when we ask ourselves how much we mean to others, how much they mean to us; how much our presence or absence means to anyone, how much difference it would make if we were in or out of the world, how much we would be missed.

Whatever the findings of this line of thought, it leads us to look at loved ones, at those we belong to, those who belong to us, and leads us to know the deep importance of family love and loyalty.

How blessed to be able to turn homeward when we are tired or ill or discouraged, or just plain weary of the ways of the world—of small talk, impersonal people, and the endless round of routine. How blessed to belong, and how much we

---

[17]See Doctrine and Covenants 121:41-44.

owe those who are there, just for the blessing of belonging, just for a place in the family circle.

We may become bored or irritable at times with home and family surroundings. All this may seem unglamorous, with a sense of sameness, and other places may sometimes seem more exciting. But when we have sampled much and wandered far and seen how fleeting and sometimes superficial some other things are, our gratitude grows for the privilege of being part of something we can count on—home and family and the loyalty of loved ones.

Friends enrich life, and the days would be poor and emptier without them. Professional people are appreciated, and add much of service and assurance, but more and more we come to know how much it means to be bound together by duty, by respect, by belonging and nothing can fully take the place of the basic relationship of family life.

"A man travels the world over in search of what he needs," said George Moore, "and returns home to find it."[18] "We are most of us very lonely in this world; you who have any who love you, cling to them and thank God."

Take Time to Listen

Besides *seeking* counsel, which all of us need, there is another side of the subject: taking time to listen so that we can *give* counsel sincerely and sensibly.

"Lately I have thought a lot about 'listening,'" said Hannie Struve. "How often you hear a little child complain . . . 'you're not *listening!*' And how easily the mother replies, 'What do you *want?*' And mostly the child does not really 'want' anything, only to communicate."[19]

Take time to listen—to children—young people—others! Sometimes they are reluctant to ask because they receive

[18]George Moore, *The Brook Kerish,* ch. 11.
[19]Hannie Struve, *Sunrise Magazine,* July 1967.

impatient answers. "Why do we parents so often say, 'I'm busy now' . . ." asked one thoughtful father. "Why do we . . . not realize that a child is like a sunbeam—here for a moment and then gone somewhere else."[20]

Talking—listening—patience, willingness to learn enough before jumping to quick conclusions. Sometimes in just letting them talk and using us for listening, they will come safely to their own conclusions. But when two people both talk at once, when they interrupt each other or when they don't talk at all, there aren't likely to be any helpful answers.

Yes, it takes time to listen, but it takes more time to correct mistakes once they have been made. "Dear Lord, make me a better parent," pleaded Gary Cleveland Myers. "Teach me to understand my children, to listen patiently to what they have to say and to answer all their questions kindly. Keep me from interrupting them, talking back to them, and contradicting them. Make me as courteous to them as I would have them to be to me."[21]

With too many misjudging others, and with too few taking time to listen, counsel cannot seem as satisfactory as it should. "The key is communication," said a thoughtful source. " 'Can't you see I'm busy?' . . . ought to be banned [by parents]. 'Listen' ought to be [implanted] over every parent's heart."[22] If only we could feel we have been heard! If only we would listen when we should!

. . . For the Family Is Forever

Lord, behold our family here assembled.
We thank Thee for this place in which we dwell;
for the love that unites us;

---

[20]Robert M. Neal, "I get to KNOW my boy," *Parents' Magazine*, February 1946.
[21]Gary Cleveland Myers, *A Parent's Prayer*.
[22]*Time* Essay: "On Being an American Parent," December 15, 1967.

for the peace accorded us this day;
for the hope with which we expect the morrow.

These thoughtful lines from Robert Louis Stevenson turn
our hearts to home, to fathers, mothers, family, remembering
that we move in and out of many other things—but the family
is the foundation of society. When the family is broken the
strongest bond is broken, and there is nothing left to take its
place with such permanence, or safety, or assurance.

The strength and hope and peace and purpose of life are
set essentially within the walls we call our home, with children
there to live, to learn, then soon to leave to make their way
in the world. But "they are not made of . . . plastic and
plywood," said one observer on the subject. "You can't stack
them up in a corner to await your own good time to put
together the parts. . . ."[23]

There's a time beyond which some things cannot so well
be done. Our opportunities with children are so perishable,
so precious. And so we come to parents with a plea to listen.
Listen—so we'll know their needs. Listen. Keep the lines
open. And never cease the patient waiting until all are
accounted for. It may be a long wait, but a wait that is
worth it.

And to you, our children: Remember that a father, a
mother who cares enough to worry and to wait—who cares
enough to counsel and to be concerned—is among the greatest
blessings God has given. Keep close. Communicate—fathers,
mothers, families: keep close, with respect and kindness and
consideration—for truth and decency, law and order, peace
and happiness are somehow set and summarized in family
love and loyalty, and the things that could break up a home
are all too hazardous to tamper with.

Oh, "thou who wouldst give," said Carlyle, "give quickly.
In the grave thy loved ones can receive no kindness."[24] Fathers
—mothers—children—open your hearts this day and always—
for the family is forever.

---

[23]Cited in *Pasadena School Revue,* author unknown.
[24]Thomas Carlyle, *Reminiscences: James Carlyle.*

Take Time for Your Children

In these swift-passing scenes and seasons there seems to come—insistently, almost above all else—this compelling cry: Take time for your children.

More and more, professional people are telling us that children are shaped and molded at a very early age—so early that it is a sobering fact to face. Home, parents, early impressions set the pattern for the future—and the evidence is overwhelming that nothing in this world is ever going to take the place of wholesome, happy homes. And there is more to this than food, shelter, and physical sustenance. There is the shaping of attitudes, of minds, of morals; opening avenues of interest and activity; instilling honesty, respect, reverence; prayers at a mother's knee; correction with fairness and firmness "showing . . . afterwards an increase of love"[25] and kindness. All this we cannot be, all this we cannot do, by not being there, by living separate lives, by an overabsorption in outside interests. Take time for your children. They are so soon grown, so soon gone.

"Is mother home?" "Where is mother?" are the questions asked when they come home from anywhere. Oh, let them have the blessing of your being there. Take time for open arms; for talking, for reading, for family prayer: for home evenings and hours. As one discerning poet put it: "Richer than I you can never be—I had a mother who read to me."[26] Take time for making memories; for fixing sure foundations that will last long after less essential things are far forgotten.

Mothers need to be home. A mother, a father, waiting is a source of safety and assurance. Parents need to give their children wholesomeness and wholeness by the very lives they live. Oh, the blessedness of coming home and finding mother there, with love and kindness and encouragement.

---

[25]Doctrine and Covenants, 121:43.
[26]Strickland Gillilan, *The Reading Mother.*

Life goes quickly. Don't brush them off and turn them over to others. Take time for your children—before they're grown, before they're gone. Oh, take time for your children.

As Parents and Children Come to Common Ground

It is an odd thing, in a way, how each generation seems to feel that each preceding generation is somewhat old-fashioned—how each generation listens impatiently to the lessons of the last.

Youth is so sure the rules have changed. Age is sure they haven't. Youth feels it knows how far it can go. Age is deeply aware of the danger. Youth feels it can always apply the brakes in time to save itself. Age knows it isn't always so.

And so parents frequently find themselves groping, reaching, pleading, trying to say what should be said, in a way that will not be misunderstood, in a way that will not seem meddlesome. And always there is great need for parents and children to come to common ground, and to say to one another what should so much be said. And so we would plead with parents and with children to be more understanding with one another:

To you as parents, to remember when you were young; to remember why you wanted to do some things you wanted to do; to remember how eager you were for social acceptance —how sensitive you were to ill-timed criticism, and how easily your hearts could be hurt; and how some things, which now seem less important, once mattered very much. All this as parents we ask you to remember.

And now to you, our children, to you in your youth: Why should you suppose that the basic rules have really changed in the few short years since your parents were as young as you? The road seems new to you. It isn't new to them. They've been over it. They are still traveling it, and it is still essentially the same. We have more; we move faster; we have acquired some things and lost others—but it is still true that causes are always followed by consequences.

And as you ask your parents to remember this of you, will you also remember this of them: that they were young, not very long ago, as you are young today—that they once thought your thoughts; that they once felt they too had found new ways, and felt your longings for flight and freedom—and since have learned the wisdom of restraint.

Remember, too, that parents have hearts that can be hurt; that they, like you, are sensitive to ill-timed criticism, and to misunderstanding of their motives. Remember that there is nothing, in righteousness, they would not do for you. They are yours and you are theirs, and you and they together, have the privilege, the right, the duty, to sit down and share your thoughts and consider your decisions with one another, that both of you together may be listened to and respected— and work, and pray and plan together for the wholeness of your happiness—always and forever.

"... Not Responsible to Anybody?"

To repeat this self-evident sentence: "There is no such thing in human existence as being so high you're not responsible to anybody."[27] This applies to all people in all positions. It applies to the attitude (if we should ever be tempted to have it) that we don't need others, that we are self-made, self-sufficient, secure. But no man—no matter what his situation or circumstances—no man knows when he will need another—or when he will need Higher Help.

"There but for the Grace of God am I," is an oft-cited sentence. Any of us could find ourselves in urgent need. Any of us could find ourselves in greatly altered circumstances.

---

[27]Lawrence A. Appley, *Managers in Action*.

Furthermore, no one ever reaches the point where he doesn't owe much to many, or where he is accountable only to himself.

The employer and the employed are responsible to each other. Both are responsible to people who buy or use the product. People in the highest or lowest places are in difficulty if others are not working with them. Even in the least free countries and conditions, public opinion, the attitude of people, is important. Even the most absolute in authority cannot stand alone. Whoever he is, he is accountable both to other people and to a Higher Power—as all of us are.

We are indebted to those who work for us and with us; to those who risk their earnings to develop useful products; to those who make employment possible; to those who help make things go successfully, and help to keep society solvent. We are indebted to those who serve us, those who associate with us. We are indebted to those who risk their lives for the enforcement of law.

No matter what sense of sufficiency we may feel, we all have need of others, and we all have reason to give gratitude and recognition, with a sincerely humble sense of responsibility to each other, and to the Father of us all. "There is no such thing in human existence as being so high you're not responsible to anybody." This applies to all people.

"I Stood on the Shoulders of Giants . . . "

Perhaps this comment could be called Theme and Variation. The theme comes from an ancient Greek source. "A dwarf standing on the shoulders of a giant may see farther than a giant himself."[28] One variation is this: "I stood on the shoulders of giants."

The simple fact of life is that all of us stand on the shoulders of others—no man is self-made; no man is self-sufficient; no man of himself has brought into being all the

---

[28]Robert Burton, *Anatomy of Melancholy*: "Democritus to the Readers."

things that enrich his life. All of us inherit so much from the past that we have an obligation to serve the present, and to pass on an improved world to the future.

We all stand on the shoulders of parents, of teachers, of friends and benefactors, and of all who have contributed to all that is ours—for all things planted, for all things developed and improved; for all inventions, tools and medicines; for literature, for art; for education, for law, for cherished traditions, for freedom; for the heritage we have. And all this didn't just happen. It came from the toil and sweat and sacrifice, the study, the trial and error, the time and effort of others. No man stands alone. We all stand on the shoulders of others.

"The private and personal blessings we enjoy," said Jeremy Taylor, "the blessings of immunity, safeguard, liberty, and integrity, deserve the thanksgiving of a whole life."[29] And, as David Grayson said it: There is a "deep, deep connection of all these things with God." There is no place for selfishness and no such thing as a man self-made.

Thus all of us have reason for humility, for gratitude, for prayerful acknowledgement to the source of all truth, of all law, of all life, for the very purpose of life—reason for gratitude to God. And so we well would remember the hymn often sung, but not always deeply considered:

Count your blessings; Name them one by one.

Count your blessings; See what God hath done.[30]

Living into Loneliness

It isn't easy for those who are young to understand the loneliness that comes when life changes from a time of preparation and performance to a time of putting things away. In the eager and active years of youth it isn't easy to understand

---

[29]English bishop (1613-67).
[30]J. Oatman, Jr., Hymn: "Count Your Blessings."

how parents feel as their flock, one by one, leave the family fireside. To be so long the center of a home, so much sought after, and then, almost suddenly, to be on the sidelines watching the procession pass by — this is living into loneliness.

Of course we may think we are thoughtful of parents and of our other older folk. Don't we send them gifts and messages on special days and anniversaries? And don't we make an occasional quick call as a token of our attention? It is something to be remembered on special occasions, to be sure. But passing and perfunctory performances are not enough to keep loneliness in its place the whole year round. What they need in the loneliness of their olders years is, in part at least, what we needed in the uncertain years of our youth: a sense of belonging, an assurance of being wanted, and the kindly ministrations of loving hearts and hands; not merely dutiful formality, not merely a room in a building, but room in someone's heart and life.

We have to live a long time to learn how empty a room can be that is filled only with furniture. It takes someone on whom we have claims beyond mere hired service, beyond institutional care or professional duty, to thaw out the memories of the past and keep them warmly living in the present. And we who are younger should never become so blindly absorbed in our own pursuits as to forget that there are still with us those who will live in loneliness unless we let them share our lives as once they let us share theirs. When they were moving in the main stream of their own impelling affairs, we were a burden—or could have been if they had chosen to consider us as such. But now we are stronger, and they are less strong.

We cannot bring them back the morning hours of youth. But we can help them live in the warm glow of a sunset made more beautiful by our thoughtfulness, by our provision, and by our active and unfeigned love. Life in its fulness is a loving ministry of service from generation to generation. God grant that those who belong to us may never be left in loneliness.

"The Art of Living Long . . ."

If we are blessed with long years of life, this brings us to old age, and with old age there sometimes comes concern, not so much concern for growing old gracefully as for growing old usefully—"The Art of Living Long Without Growing Old"[31] as one respected person put it.

All reason and sense and inner awareness tell us that men are immortal. But we know what we have here, and we cling to it as long as we can, which always we should and must, seeking to make full use of all the life we live.

As to being well and happy in the later years of life: "A sense of purpose and the opportunity to contribute to others," said one physician, "—these are as vital to total health as are adequate nutrition and rest."[32]

"The happiest person," said William Lyon Phelps, "is the person who thinks the most interesting thoughts . . . As we advance in years we really grow happier, if we live intelligently. . . . To say that youth is happier than maturity is like saying that the view from the bottom of the tower is better than the view from the top. As we ascend, the range of our view widens immensely; the horizon is pushed farther away. Finally as we reach the summit it is as if we had the world at our feet."

Each part of life has its usefulness, its compensations; its challenges, its problems; its beauty, its service, its satisfactions. And as we live in honor, serving, as we can, as fully and in any way we can, keeping faith and peace within ourselves and with him who made us all, there is an ever added meaning to these lines from Karle Wilson Baker:

> Let me grow lovely growing old—
> So many fine things do;
> Laces, and ivory, and gold,
> And silks need not be new.

---

[31]Kenneth S. Beam.
[32]H. A. Holle, M.D., American Medical Association.

And there is healing in old trees,
Old streets a glamour hold;
Why may not I, as well as these,
Grow lovely, growing old?[33]

" . . . No Birds in Last Year's Nest"

These lines from Longfellow suggest some self-searching:

For Time will teach thee soon the truth,
There are no birds in last year's nest.[34]

Often we think of past decisions—of what we should or shouldn't have done. We dwell upon regret and brood about it. Or we think of what we should now be doing and are doing, of what we would like to learn, and it makes us uneasy.

We regret misunderstandings—words we wish we hadn't said—words we wish we *had* said—mistakes we have made, people we have offended, opportunities gone by—errors and carelessness that could have been avoided—places we might have gone, things we might have been.

The past has its place and is valuable for lessons learned. The present also has its place, and what we cannot change should not needlessly keep us from looking and moving forward. Nothing lost or left behind should keep us from now becoming what we can become, from learning what we now can learn.

There are new decisions every day, every hour, and reasons to improve and to repent. Whatever we are, wherever we've been, each day we have some opportunity to determine direction.

---

[33]Karle Wilson Baker, *Desk Drawer Anthology: Poems for the American People*.
[34]Longfellow, *It Is Not Always May*.

Each day we need to win, or keep—and certainly to deserve—the love of loved ones; each day to be more patient, more pleasant, more understanding. If there have been loved ones neglected, loved ones left, unreconciled differences, unspoken gratitude, unacknowledged debts, we ought to re-direct ourselves. If there has been within something that has soured us, we well would turn and look to the sweetening of ourselves, for we hurt ourselves as well as others when we live below the level that our possibilities permit.

Whatever the past or its meaning, or its length, or its losses, or its lessons learned or left unlearned, we go on from where we are—wherever it is—and become what we can become; with work, repentance, improvement; with faith in the future.

"For Time will teach thee soon the truth, / There are no birds in last year's nest!"

The "Get-out-from-under" Attitude . . .

There is sometimes evident an attitude of wanting to get out from under, not wanting to be accountable to anyone. Young people, for example, sometimes choose to move away from home and family and friends. Work, education, opportunities in other areas, are often good reasons.

But to leave just to cut loose, just to go it alone, just to be free from being accountable to anyone may well not be wise. And before we feel we want to get away, to get out from under, we ought honestly to make sure we don't want it for the wrong reasons.

No one is always safe. No one can know when he may become ill, or have an accident, or find himself in some serious situation. No one knows all the answers. No one can be sure he is self-sufficient.

Besides, others have much invested in us. Others have taught us, trained us, nursed and nourished us, loved us, and given us part of their lives—parents, teachers, doctors, friends, family have done this and much more—and they have a right to an interest in us, and we have an obligation to recognize that right.

There is also the fact that if we are alone and without the interest of others we could become indifferent and deteriorate. Much of our performance is for others and not for us. We do our best when others expect it of us. If life were simply a matter of satisfying our selfish selves, there wouldn't be much progress or improvement. The faith and interest of others leads us to be better—and surely we wouldn't, for the wrong reasons, want to separate ourselves from stabilizing factors and influences, and place ourselves in a position that would make it easier to lower standards or lose the most precious things a person can possess: virtue, honesty, honor, respect, excellence of purpose and performance.

Almost anything can happen to almost anyone, and the "cut-loose," "get-out-from-under," "leave-me-alone" attitude, in this sense, isn't sensible or safe. To cite a significant sentence: "There is no such thing in human existence as being so high you're not responsible to anybody."[35]

A Perspective on Being Busy

There are some startling contrasts and comparisons with the present and the past. In this prefabricated, prepackaged period, much of what makes up our material lives comes through machinery and assembly lines, so well organized and operated that we are hardly aware of the effort of anyone. Yet, with all this done for us by others, we seem to feel more crowded and hard-pressed than did people in the past.

[35]Appley, *Managers in Action.*

To put the picture in perspective, think a moment of the pioneer mother, father, family, wresting firsthand from nature the sheer sustenance and bare necessities of life. Think of being in the wilderness, nursing and caring for loved ones through injuries, illness, accidents, without professional help or facilities or much in the way of medicine. Think of breaking ground, of growing and grinding grain, of gathering food and storing it; of cutting logs, of building protection against the elements, insects, animals—in short, of living starkly next to nature without all the processing, packaging, provisioning, without the professional and personal services we have come to count on.

How did those who lived on far frontiers find time to do what they did—to fish, hunt, feed, and defend; to make a meal, or a shirt, or a shelter out of the simplest essentials?

The answer, of course, is work and faith—a great degree of self-reliance and a great dependence upon Divine Providence. But out of this there comes a question: What do we do—we who sometimes think ourselves busier than anyone has ever been before—what do we do with the time our forebears used in providing these absolute essentials? Our very busy-ness is a paradox, and we need to make repeated appraisal of what takes our lives, our time—what keeps us forever on the run. "Nothing is more unworthy of a wise man," said Plato, ". . . than to have allowed more time for trifling and useless things than they deserve."

Time is limited, and the things to be done with it are limitless. We are accountable for what we do with ourselves, our time and talents, our efforts and opportunities—with the hours and days that God has given us. "Spend your time," said Richard Baxter, "in nothing which you know must be repented of; in nothing on which you might not pray for the blessing of God; in nothing which you could not review with a quiet conscience on your dying bed; in nothing which you might not safely and properly be found doing if death should surprise you in the act."[36]

---

[36]English Divine, (1615-1691).

"Endure . . . for Days of Happiness"

There is a short sentence from Vergil that says: "Endure, and keep yourselves for days of happiness."[37]

There are times when we feel that we can't endure—that we can't face what's ahead of us; that we can't live with the disappointments, the problems; that we can't carry the heavy load. But these times come and go, as our strength and courage and circumstances run in cycles—from high to low to high—and in the low times we have to endure; we have to hold on until the shadows brighten, until the load lifts. "No one could endure adversity," said Seneca, "if, while it continued, it kept the same violence that its first blows had. . . ."[38]

People often issue ultimatums. They say they can't or won't stand this or that—not another minute. "I'm leaving it all. I want out." Such times could be likened to a circuit breaker or a fuse that blows when overloaded. We do wonder if we can take it at times—but there are built-in safety factors, and we find that the human soul—the spirit, the body, the mind of man—is resilient.

There is more built-in strength in all of us than we sometimes suppose. And what once we said we couldn't do or couldn't live with or couldn't carry, we find ourselves somehow doing and enduring, as time, reappraisal, readjustment, and sometimes sheer necessity, modify our sense of values and our attitudes, and we find strength and endurance and hidden resources within ourselves.

"Life is real! Life is earnest!"[39] as the poet put it, and facing facts, adjusting to life, isn't always easy. But before we give up, we should most seriously consider what we are giving up—and what we are going to. "The frying pan to the fire" is an old phrase that has much meaning.

---

[37]Vergil, *Aeneid,* bk. i.
[38]Seneca, *Moral Essays: On Tranquility of Mind.*
[39]Longfellow, *A Psalm of Life,* st. 2.

Well, thus endeth the lesson—to pause, to reappraise, to take time for hope, for faith, and for strength to return—remembering, as Solon said it: "If all men were to bring their miseries together in one place, most would be glad to take . . . home again . . . each his own."[40]

"Endure, and keep yourselves for days of happiness."

Loved Ones Waiting . . .

As we watched arriving passengers we saw an oft-repeated scene: a young mother with two young children, all dressed in their best, eagerly, anxiously looking. And then there was a light in their eyes as there came into view the one they were waiting for—the father, who completed the family circle: then running steps, and arms around each other, with everyone happily talking, as they walked to the waiting car. Father had come home. Mother and children were there. All were together again. If there is a picture in life sweeter than a sincerely loving family circle, we haven't seen it. Nor do we expect to see a happier scene this side of heaven. Just such scenes of wonderful reunion assuredly will be a most important part of heaven, with loved ones watching, waiting, as loved ones return, even as they do here from short periods of separation. God has not deceived us, nor placed in us a false expectancy concerning the reality of reunion with those who mean the most. And why should we doubt or quarrel with it? No matter how long we live there is always the certainty of separation—and we come to know that heaven would be no heaven without those we love—and so we seek assurances, which we find often and everywhere. We live in the midst of miracles—sunrise, spring; the awesome miracle of a newborn babe—living, learning, life, loved ones. And surely immortality is no more miracle than we now know. This doesn't

[40]Athenian lawgiver (638-558 B.C.).

make parting easy. Parting from loved ones isn't ever altogether easy. But he who has given us life here, has also given us life hereafter, as we move to more light, more living, to loved ones whose eyes will light at our coming, and we shall know that we are home again, as once we were. "I tell you they have not died; . . . They live, they know, they see: They shout with every breath: All is Eternal life! There is no death!"[41]

"To Be Born -- or to Rise Again . . ."

Here we are alive, on a planet suspended in space— a beautiful and wondrous one, with sunrise and sunset, and seedtime and harvest, and the changing seasons; and all that grows, and all that moves, with man and his searching mind, with the power to learn, and the love of loved ones, and all the evidence of the planning of Divine Providence. Is this natural or supernatural?

Perhaps some would suppose that the most natural thing is nothing. How did anything—or anyone—ever come to be in the first place? When was there a beginning of anything at all? "Who wound up the Universe?" is one of the classic questions. Who organized it—and who keeps it in its course?

You see, we live in the midst of miracles. We see them at our very side. The first flower of spring is a miracle, the first bud that breaks winter's death and dormancy.

Birth itself is a miracle—the awesome, sobering miracle of the newborn babe—with hands reaching, with eyes watching, with ears listening, and intelligence that responds to truth. The fact that we live, that we are, that we think and learn and love—all this is a miracle and a mystery.

---

[41]Song: "There Is No Death!" Lyrics by Gordon Johnstone.

Who gave instinct to animals? Who gave the body wisdom to heal itself? Who gave two cells the intelligence to join and divide, to become an eye, or a tooth, or the hair of the head? Natural or supernatural?

We recall the question of Pascal: "Which is the more difficult, to be born, or to rise again?"[42] Surely immortality is no more a miracle than mortality is. And the Lord God who gave us life here, can give us life everlastingly. To the believer there is the blessing of believing, even of knowing, beyond belief.

And to those who search and seek, to those who sorrow, to those who are fearful and frustrated, to those who wonder, and those who weary along the way, this is the certainty—this is the assurance of our Savior: that for us and for all men he did come forth from death to life; he did redeem us all from death. With Job we would witness with a certainty of assurance: ". . . I know that my redeemer liveth."[43]

To you who love life, and to you who have lost those you love, take this comfort, this assurance to your hearts, this day—and always.

Chance Could Not Have Done It . . .

As men move farther out from the magnificent earth that God gave us, and look back on its awesome beauty, its movement, its precision and proportion, upon the wondrous working, and magnificent majesty of it all, we come with souls subdued to the quiet conviction of these simple words: "In the beginning God created the heaven and the earth. . . ."[44] Chance could not have done it. "And God saw every thing that he had made, and behold, it was very good."[44]

Well, man, made in the image of God, has done much

---

[42]Blaise Pascal, *Pensees,* xxiv.
[43]Job 19:25.
[44]Genesis 1:1.

with his marvelous God-given mind, in the discovery and use of natural law. But much as man has done, he has scarcely touched the surface of all this majesty of meaning, and of infinite understanding.

Think a moment of the organizing and engineering and operation of it all—of keeping a world within a livable range of temperature; of air and water renewing themselves; of insect, animal and bacterial balance in infinite variety. And the creation is evidence of a Creator, design is evidence of the Designer, and law is evidence of its Maker and Administrator —evidence sufficient even for the most skeptical and unbelieving.

"When a load of bricks, dumped on a corner lot, can arrange themselves into a house," wrote Bruce Barton; "when a handful of springs and screws and wheels, emptied onto a desk, can gather themselves into a watch, then and not until then will it seem sensible, to some of us at least, to believe that all . . . [this] could have been created . . . without any directing intelligence at all."[45] Then and only then will I believe that this was done by chance—or without eternal plan and purpose.

"Behind everything stands God. . . ." said Phillips Brooks. "Do not avoid, but seek, the great, deep, simple things of faith."[46] "And God saw everything that he had made, and, behold, it was very good."

What Is It All Worth?

Many years ago Daniel Webster recalled a question: "How much is all this worth?"[47] As to liberty, or the lack of it, whatever the price, it is priceless, and the difference cannot be calculated.

---

[45]Bruce Barton, *If a Man Dies, Shall He Live Again?*
[46]Phillips Brooks, *The Light of the World and Other Sermons: The Seriousness of Life.*
[47]Daniel Webster, quoted by Joseph Roswell Hawley in an address titled *On the Flag and the Eagle,* 1874.

How much is it worth to live where one wishes? to work at what one wishes? to worship as one wishes? How much is it worth to have the right to live with loved ones? to listen to the laughter of children? to be unafraid of approaching footsteps? to walk home and find the welcome of loved faces unafraid?

How much is it worth to own personal property? to have personal privacy? How much is it worth to preserve human dignity? How much it is worth to choose leaders? to vote in an open and honest election? to have a voice in making and administering the laws of the land? How much is it worth to come and to go, to live and to choose, to think and to speak, to read and to search? to have an education offered everyone? How much is it worth freely to express an opinion, fearlessly to move from place to place, with an openness of life, a free ranging of the mind; and enjoyment of the great and goodly earth that God has given, with peace of mind and quiet conviction?

Despite all encroachments on freedom, and all unwise relinquishment of some rights, still blessed beyond belief, still precious beyond price, is the freedom our forebears paid for—the freedom which is God-given, which yet, paradoxically, has to be everlastingly earned and deserved over and over again, and can never safely be permitted to become commonplace.

How much is all this worth? All this must be worth the willingness to work, to defend, to give allegiance, to be a participating partner, to live with honor, justice, and respect for law, and the willingness to keep the commandments—for "No free government," wrote Andrew Jackson, "can stand without virtue in the people and a lofty spirit of patriotism: . . ."[48]

Thank God for liberty and for the privilege of preserving it at any price.

---

[48]Andrew Jackson, *Farewell Address.*

"He Teaches Well That Lives Well"

Somewhere in some rendering of *Don Quixote,* there seems to linger a line from Sancho Panza which says: "He teaches well that lives well. That's all the divinity I can understand."[49] It is profound, subtle, simple: "He teaches well that lives well."

This touches upon the question of our influence on others, what people see in us and feel from us, when the stage is formally set, and when informally it isn't. Teaching isn't just *saying* something. It isn't just the words we speak in the classroom, or the pulpit, or on finger-pointing occasions when we are laying down the law. It isn't something we can turn on and off at any given hour, because we are visible also at other hours. It is what we do, what we think, what we condone, what we condemn. It is both the subtle and obvious things that make up what we are.

"He teaches well that lives well." Sometimes we speak as if just *setting* an example were sufficient, but it isn't so much something we *set* as it is everything we are. Parents, teachers, everyone, and all of us *are* an example, no matter what we do—or don't do. Whether we are honest or dishonest, concerned or indifferent, fair or unfair, we *are* an example of some sort, every hour and every instant. The important point is, *what kind of example?* Where are young and impressionable people going if they go where we're going, if they do what we're doing, if they think what we're thinking—if they become what we are?

And there is really no way for anyone to separate himself into segments, to say "At this hour I will teach this, at another hour I will teach something else"—for a teacher teaches what he is himself as well as teaching his subject, and so does a parent; so do companions; so does a community.

---

[49]Cervantes, maxim quoted in *Don Quixote.*

And so we could say with Sancho: "He teaches well that lives well"—and might put it also in the opposite: He *doesn't* teach well who doesn't live well. It is a sobering lesson to learn.

We Are Not Alone in Life

As we see and talk to other people (and even sometimes as we look into our own hearts), it is apparent that there is much of loneliness in life—not only the loneliness that comes from lack of companionship with people—but also the loneliness that comes with lack of purpose, with lack of understanding of the reasons why we live.

No doubt some loneliness comes because we are always inseparably ourselves. Some thoughts, some experiences, some intuitions, some of the awareness we have within us we cannot fully share with anyone else. We come into the world alone. We leave it alone. We are always and eternally our own separate selves.

But loneliness is more than simply solitude. (A person can be very lonely in a crowded, busy place.) And there is a kind of loneliness that comes from a sense of not belonging, of not fitting in, of not knowing our part in the picture—of not knowing what we are, or who we are, or where we came from, or where we are going, or why we are here, or what life is basically all about.

The mortal years of life pass swiftly and soon. And except for some glorious, eternal certainties, there could well be a universal feeling of frustration. We labor long for things that sustain life and for things that afford a little passing pleasure—but there is nothing of these tangibles that we can

Address delivered on the CBS Radio "Church of the Air," October 1954.

take with us. These things we call our own are ours only for a short time. The farmer's fields not long ago belonged to someone else, and soon again will belong to someone else. The stocks, the bonds, the buildings, the houses we have, whatever we have title to, we all shall leave in yet a little while—and our going will make a mockery of all the titles of our earthly tenancy.

About all we can take with us after all, are the knowledge and character we have acquired, the intelligence we have developed or improved upon, the service we have given, the lessons we have learned, and the blessed assurance that we may have our life and loved ones, always and forever—as assured us by a wise and kindly Father whose children we all are. And knowing him, and what he is to us, (and what we are to one another), what his purpose is in sending us here from his presence, is one of the surest safeguards against loneliness and feelings of frustration.

Some few evenings ago, I sat at dinner by the side of a distinguished, successful industrialist, who told me simply and in a few sentences how he faced the heavy problems of his life, and met the decisions of each day.

"When I get up in the morning," he said, "I often feel that I can't face it, but as I get down on my knees and say simply, 'God help me to do what I have to do this day,' strength comes, and I feel that I am equal to it. And I think of him as my Father, and talk to him as simply and directly as I used to talk to my father when he was here."

And then he added: "Sometimes I do things I know I shouldn't do. But when I do, I don't lie to God about my motives. I know it's no use. I know he knows my heart, my thoughts. I know what I have done, and he knows what I have done. And I don't try to deceive him or myself."

I was mellowed and humbled by the direct and simple spirit of this friend with whom I sat the other evening. He was not of my faith, but in my own earnest belief, he could not have talked to God with so much satisfaction or assurance if he had thought of him merely as a force, or as an ineffable essence, the nature and purpose of which he knew nothing— or at least nothing that would bring to him the assured feeling that he was in fact talking to his Father.

It is urgently important in life to draw nearer to a knowledge of the nature of God, and of our relationship to him and to one another. And what better place to begin than with the first book of the Bible—what better place to turn than to literal scriptural language?

"In the beginning God created the heaven and the earth. . . . And God said, Let us make man in our own image, after our likeness: . . . So God created man in his own image, in the image of God created he him; . . . And God saw everything that he had made, and, behold, it was very good." (Genesis 1:1, 26, 27, 31.)

It was a good world; it is a good world—despite the foolishness and perversities of men. It is good because of its beauties and bounties, and because of the glorious purpose and limitless possibilities that a loving Father has given his children—a Father whom the scriptures testify is personal and approachable, even as Paul proclaimed in his epistle to the Hebrews that Jesus the Christ was in "the express image" of his Father's person. (Hebrews 1:3.)

Scripture records that many men have seen God, among them Moses and Aaron and the seventy elders of Israel (Exodus 24:9-11)—even as John recorded in Revelation that "his servants shall serve him: And they shall see his face." (Revelation 22:3, 4.)

And Stephen the Martyr, "being full of the Holy Ghost, looked up stedfastly into heaven, and saw . . . Jesus standing on the right hand of God." (Acts 7:55.)

And Jesus frequently addressed his Father. In Gethsemane: "O my Father, if it be possible, let this cup pass from me." (Matthew 26:39.)

On Calvary: "Father, forgive them; for they know not what they do." (Luke 23:34.)

And earlier with the Twelve: "These words spake Jesus, and lifted up his eyes to heaven, and said, Father, the hour is come. . . .

"And now, O Father, glorify thou me . . . with the glory which I had with thee before the world was. . . .

"Holy Father, keep through thine own name those whom thou hast given me, that they may be one, as we are. . . .

"And this is life eternal, that they might know thee the only true God, and Jesus Christ, whom thou hast sent. . . ." (John 17:1, 5, 11, 3.)

There is much more of scripture that affirms the oneness of purpose of the Father and of his Beloved Son—and that also affirms their separateness of person as a literal, physical fact. And as Jesus approached him, so also may we approach the Father, in all our needs. In every problem, in sorrow and success, in all the things we struggle with from day to day, we can reach out to him with the assurance that he is there. He lives. He speaks. His voice is not unto the ancients only, but even unto our own day there is witness of his personal presence. He is a God of continuous revelation, of continuous mindfulness for all of us, and he does not shut himself in the heavens if we will let him come into our lives.

He has sent us here, from where we were with him before birth, for a brief period of mortal experience, with our free agency, our right of choice, with principles and commandments, and with his Spirit to light us through life, and has assured us everlasting life with the glorious promise of limitless and eternal progress and possibilities, with all the sweetness of association of family and friends in the peace and protection of his presence—if we will. He has assured us that "men are that they might have joy" (2 Nephi 2:25), and has declared it to be his purpose "to bring to pass the immortality and eternal life of man." (Moses 1:39.)

Knowing our feelings for our own loved ones, for our own children, we can take confidence in the mercy and love and understanding and in the helpfulness of our Father in heaven, who will not leave the humblest child, or the most lonely among us, alone in life.

You who are sick, you who are wracked with pain, you who are confined with physical infirmity—you are not alone in life. There is faith, there is hope, there is mercy, there is help from him. "He that keepeth thee will not slumber." (Psalm 121:3.)

You who are discouraged, whose obligations are heavy, whose best efforts somehow seem to fall short of success; you who have been falsely dealt with; you who have met reverses and disappointments; you who have lost heart: There is a kind and just and merciful Father in heaven to whom you can turn, and who will see that you lose nothing that should have been yours. He can bring peace to your hearts, and restore faith and purpose. You are not alone.

And you who are tried and tempted by appetites, by evil in its subtle shapes; you who have been careless in your conduct, who have lived the kind of lives that fall short of what you know you should have lived—and are contending with conscience and are torn inside yourselves: You also are not alone in life, for the Lord God who gave you life has also given the glorious principle of repentance, which, upon sincere turning away from false ways, can restore again the blessed peace that comes with quiet conscience.

You who have been hurt—hurt in your hearts, hurt in spirit—you who have been offended and have withdrawn yourselves and become a little aloof—you need not be alone. The door is open.

You who have unanswered questions (which all of us have); you who are torn between the teachings of contending teachers, who are confused by conflicting theories—keep faith. Reserve judgment. Be patient. God lives. He is the source of all truth, and where there seem to be discrepancies it is simply because we do not know enough. The theories of men change swiftly, but "the glory of God is intelligence" (Doctrine and Covenants 93:36), and there is no truth in all the universe that the Father of us all would not wish you to seek and to accept—for man cannot be "saved in ignorance." (Doctrine and Covenants 131:6.) Keep an open mind and an open heart and a teachable spirit. "Seek learning, even by study and also by faith." (Doctrine and Covenants 88:118.)

And you who are young, who have ambitions for the future, but who face serious uncertainties: Go forward and live your lives with faith. Look far ahead; decide on some good goal. Study, work, and prepare yourselves. Make solid plans and pursue solid purposes and don't place undue emphasis on the passing, trivial pleasures. When the proper time comes, make your homes and have your families, and face your problems with faith. Your Father in heaven knows and understands you, and will help and lead you to happiness and usefulness here, and to your high destiny hereafter, if you will keep close to him and take him into your confidence.

And you who have lost your loved ones: You are not alone. God, who is the Father of the spirits of all men, has sent us here from his presence until he calls us to return. And our loved ones who have left us will always be themselves, and we may see and know and be with them again, always and forever—if we will but take the steps that lead to eternal family reunion. They are nearer to us than we know.

We are none of us alone in life. We belong to an eternal family. We belong also to one another—and God, who made us in his image, is the Father of us all. And there is justice and mercy and fair and adequate opportunity for all of us from him who is and has been mindful of us all, from birth and before—through death and beyond.

He is there and within our reach. He will guide and enlighten and lift. He is the source of truth, of comfort, of protection, and of the peace that passeth understanding, and the source of the sweet and satisfying assurance that life and truth are limitless and everlasting, and despite all problems and all perplexities we are not left alone in life.

We would testify to all who hear this day of the living reality of him who did make us in his own image—that he lives, that he has spoken, that he does speak; that he sent his

Son into the world, who is our Savior and of whose divinity this day we testify; and that the heavens have been opened in this day and dispensation.

We are none of us alone in life, but in the hands of him to whom his Son, our Savior and Redeemer, offered this sublime prayer:

"Our Father which art in heaven, Hallowed be thy name. Thy kingdom come. Thy will be done in earth as it is in heaven. Give us this day our daily bread. And forgive us our debts, as we forgive our debtors. And lead us not into temptation, but deliver us from evil: For thine is the kingdom, and the power, and the glory, for ever. Amen." (Matthew 6:9-13.)

THE MESSAGE

To The Church

Answering the Call

It seems that the usual radio technique is grossly inadequate for such a time as this. By the forewarning of a chance meeting with President Grant last Thursday evening, I thought that perhaps the shock of what has befallen me would have been somewhat alleviated yesterday morning, when it was announced here, and also this moment, but such seems not to be the case. I spent a sleepless night Thursday night, burning old bridges and building new ones. I think that perhaps this call would have come easier to me a little later in life, after I had had a better opportunity to make substance of more of my dreams, but perhaps this is not so. Perhaps I must just exchange old dreams for new dreams.

It is less than three weeks, during a nation-wide Tabernacle Choir broadcast, that I read from this pulpit as follows:

"There are two things that enter into the life of every man: Those things which we plan for ourselves, and those things which enter into our lives in spite of all our plans. Sometimes, happily, we fare better than we had honestly hoped, and sometimes, unhappily, we find we fall far short of achieving those things for which we have striven. But no matter how well we seem to control those elements which affect our lives, there are always to be considered things unlooked for. Surely it must be better that way. It would be difficult to imagine a more unsatisfactory existence than the life of a man into which nothing unexpected ever came.

"Furthermore, it is all part of a great plan. The Lord still chasteneth whom he loveth, and all those things which

Address given at General Conference, October 1938, immediately after being called to the First Council of the Seventy.

come into our lives in spite of our best-laid plans, are part of the education and enriching experience of every child of God who walks the earth. We may think what we would like for ourselves, and then, in the spirit of that resignation born of faith, we must reconcile ourselves at one time or another, to say as in the words of the hymn about to be sung, 'I'll go where you want me to go, dear Lord; I'll be what you want me to be.' "

I knew, when I sent out these words to a nation-wide radio audience, that they were true, but I did not know that they would return home so quickly. It is a conclusive thing for a man to stand convicted by his own words, and I now so stand before you.

My association with the General Authorities of the Church dates back to about eleven years ago, perhaps a little more, at which time I did not have a speaking acquaintance—with one exception, I think—with any of the General Authorities. At that time I found myself in the British Mission as a young man under twenty-one years of age and was aware of the penetrating eyes of Dr. James E. Talmage looking at me during my first meeting with him at a conference of the Norwich District, shortly after which I was called into the European Mission office at Liverpool and became associated with him in the editorship of the *Millennial Star*. Under his tutelage I found myself squirming at times, but nevertheless greatly benefited by his rigid scrutiny and exacting requirements. It was a good experience. And I love and honor the memory of the man who so painstakingly troubled himself to train me in ways of precision and exactitude, when ofttimes it would have been much less trouble for him to have done the task in hand himself.

That was followed by the coming of Dr. John A. Widtsoe, and I learned more from him. The rapidity with which he worked, the breadth of his knowledge and abilities, his powers to use other men and to help them realize themselves were a source of constant inspiration. Under him I later became secretary of the European Mission and visited countries from the Mediterranean up to beyond the Arctic Circle, and my heart is filled with thanks to him also for his belief in a young man.

Since that time it has been my privilege to become acquainted with all of the General Authorities of the Church, and their lives have been a testimony to me, because I know that they would not be doing the things they are doing, and would not have left the things they have left, to do the things they are now doing, except that they know of a surety that this is the work of the Lord, and must go forward.

I have been very grateful for the opportunity of engaging in the radio activity that it has fallen to my lot to be engaged in. One of the greatest satisfactions of my life is to read the letters that come in every day, week after week, from people who listen to the nation-wide program from the Tabernacle each Sunday morning, and who find their lives touched by the spirit of it, and find cause to inquire further.

I have known of some conversions that have come directly from this program, resulting in baptisms into the Church, which is an experience that I did not have the joy of observing in the mission field as a direct result of my own efforts.

I know from the character of the mail that comes in that tens of thousands more must be deeply touched by the things that go from here each Sunday morning on the Tabernacle Choir broadcast. The music of the choir and the organ prepares the hearts of those who listen for the reception of the spoken messages, and it is very encouraging to me to realize that a truth does not need to be shouted to be appreciated— that a truth quietly spoken has much greater effect than an untruth shouted from the housetops.

It has been a gratifying experience to me to be associated in the editorship of *The Improvement Era*. I struggled with myself for more than six months, from the time the Presidency first called me over and suggested that I take the editorship of this magazine until the time that it was actually undertaken. They did not make their request in the nature of a call. They left it entirely to my judgment, and it took me six months to reach the conclusion that they would not have called me over there if they had not wanted me to do it; but this realization finally settled upon my consciousness and I made the change— for what reason I did not know at the time. I am very grateful that the Presidency have left me some radio activity, because it has meant much to me and I feel that the results are gaining.

I spent a good part of the day yesterday trying to find sympathy from some of these my brethren, the General Authorities, who are sitting around me here. I found none, so I decided to like what has befallen me. President Clark told me yesterday morning that they had all been through it, and I might just as well cheer up. I reminded him that he had not been called into the work at my age, and President McKay, sitting by him, reminded me that he had; and President Grant reminded me also that no one who ever wanted one of these positions ever got one. So with all these unanswerable rebuttals, and finding no sympathy, I have sincerely decided to like my lot.

At an annual testimony meeting of the General Board of the Young Men's Mutual Improvement Association some months ago, I stated that the two paramount immediate ambitions I had were to assist in the editing of the best church magazine in the world, and to assist in the production of what I hoped to be the best church radio program in the world. So far as I am aware, my immediate ambitions have not changed. My remote ambitions will either have to be abandoned or await the direction of these my brethren, in whose keeping I find myself, and whose association I love, and whose judgment I trust.

I keep in my desk a comment by Abraham Lincoln to the effect that he who molds public sentiment does more than he who enacts laws or hands down decisions. I believe that to be true, and I believe that we in this Church must use every means that is available for molding public sentiment for truth, both within and without the Church. That is why I have been particularly happy with both my radio activity and editing experience, because I believe the press and the radio combined are the greatest and most effective means today of molding public sentiment, and we must use them to the utmost, because we must keep in mind that the same facilities that are being used to build public sentiment for truth are also being used to build public sentiment for untruth.

I have often pondered, in my own mind, the reasons why our missionary results have not been comparable to those of the early missionaries to Great Britain, into which history I delved at some length in the immediate past. When I learned of penniless missionaries converting whole communities and baptizing thousands of souls, I was worried and puzzled in some respects, wondering what was lacking in that we are not doing the same today. I have subsequently concluded that there are at least two partial explanations. One is that the Lord advised the Prophet in that day that the field was white and ready to harvest, and indeed it was. Another is that our advantages today are comparatively not as great, or not as much greater than theirs, as it would seem, because we must keep in mind that every means that is being used for the promulgation of the truth is also being used for the promulgation of untruth.

That is why we must not be found sleeping at any time. That is why we must be diligent with every means at our command, to use all modern facilities with greater intelligence, with greater foresight and with greater effectiveness. This we will do increasingly, I feel sure.

Those who were close to my feelings yesterday morning before the announcement of my appointment to the First Council of Seventy was made at this conference were aware that if there had been any way to turn back in honor I would have done so, but I do not know to what point I would have turned back, and I realize keenly that there was no turning back—that turning back would have been turning away.

If I had been of a mind to turn back I should have done it at my mother's knee. I should have done it before she taught me to pay out my first few pennies in tithing. I should have done it before her firm and gentle hand directed my steps into the ways of truth. I should have done it before I came up through the auxiliary organizations of this Church; before I went on a mission; before I went into the service of the Mutual Improvement Association and *The Improvement Era.* It was only necessary for me to think quietly for a few moments to see that there is no turning back for a Latter-day Saint, and he who thinks there is, finds himself not turning back but turning away. I think that lesson may well come into the lives of all of us.

I am grateful for the opportunity to serve. I have appreciated the kindness, the fatherliness of President Grant, President Clark, President McKay, Dr. Widtsoe, Brother Bowen, and all these brethren. They have all been kind, considerate and helpful to me. My own father died as the result of an accident when I was ten weeks old. My mother reared a family of nine children, all of whom at that time were under eighteen. With a meager and unreliable income, she immediately sent my eldest brother on a mission. Such faith as that in the home in which I was reared could only produce one result, and the result is that all of my brothers and sisters have come up through the program of the Church to be a credit to my mother and to all that this Church stands for.

I know, as well as I know any of the facts of life, that Jesus was the Son of God, the Redeemer of this world; that Joseph Smith was a Prophet of the Lord, as have been all his successors; and that this is the work of the Lord.

The young men of the Church are my friends. They belong to my generation. I know them. They have their difficulties, their problems, their struggles, economically and otherwise, but I have no fear for their integrity or their ability. I have no fear for their willingness to serve as the years roll along. I know that they say in chorus: "Our hearts are not turned back, neither have we departed from thy way," and that is my expression also, in their behalf.

I ask the blessings of the Lord upon all of us, and I do it in the name of Jesus Christ. Amen.

Facing War's Disruption

As always, I declare my dependence upon the Spirit that motivates all of these proceedings.

I was happy yesterday to hear President Grant and President Clark address part of their remarks to the young men of my generation who face a breaking up of the pattern of their lives by those events which we now face. We have lived to see the day when the best-laid plans of men have gone wrong, and these young men are facing the postponement or abandonment of many of their ambitions and most cherished dreams and plans for their own futures. And as the young men are affected, so are the young women. We sympathize with them greatly. I met with such a group a week ago today, a group of M Men, and I felt them reaching for a message on this subject. I should like to have the ability briefly to deliver that message to them.

I think it shouldn't be a time for too much pessimism and discouragement, in spite of all the uncertainties. I think we should remind ourselves of the fact that there has always been uncertainty. No one ever lived in a static society. No one has ever had fixed guarantees that his way of life would not be interrupted, and I am sure that it is not a time for disrupting our plans. The time for preparation in the lives of our young men is altogether too short, and I feel in my heart that they should go forward with whatever they have in mind, and let interruption overtake them when and how it will.

It certainly is not a time for living from hand to mouth. It is a time for laying broader foundations than ever before, because no matter what kind of world we find ourselves living in tomorrow, the best-qualified men will always be in demand, and whether we are living here or not, we shall be living somewhere, and those intangible things that we acquire we shall take with us wherever we go.

Some of our young men, and some of our mothers who are called upon to send them forth into service, wonder why

Address given at General Conference, April 1941.

they have to go. There have been some who have urged the Church and its members to declare themselves conscientious objectors. There may be some merits in this position. Perhaps we should reserve the right so to declare ourselves at some future time. I can think of possibilities and circumstances arising under which there could conceivably come some times and conditions for which we might want to reserve that right. But there are two sides to the question. Traditionally this has not been our position. In the century of our existence, no people of like numbers that I know of anywhere in the world have a better record for giving service when the call has come than this people.

No matter how ardently we may agree or disagree with those policies which have been and are being pursued in this regard, we are committed as a people to loyalty to constituted authority. That is true of our people in all the world, no matter what nation they may live in.

There may be another reason why our young men should respond to this call. Many people, and we are among them I am sure, bitterly regret the fact that when war comes it takes the cream of our manhood; it does not take the physically or the mentally unfit. It takes those who are best capable of rendering service, and we regret this fact most gravely.

But there is another side, and I would like to quote a paragraph from one of our nationally known commentators and columnists which appeared in the press a short time ago. Speaking of all our defense preparations and the creation of materials for defense, he stated that it also should be remembered that these things ". . . can be used against us by an *inside* enemy just as easily as we can use them against an outside foe. This means a character-building campaign should be a definite part of our defense program. Now, more than ever before in the history of warfare, it is vital that the people of the strongest character should furnish the men who are to be trained for this new and all-important branch of our national defense. Let religious and civic leaders who are serious in their prayers re-read this last sentence."

I am sure that you and I, since an army appears to be a necessary evil—it has always been so far as history tells us anything, in ancient Israel, in Book of Mormon times, and down to the present—under the conditions in which we live, I am sure that you and I would not care to have an army in our midst made up of the worst elements of our society. And I am sure that our young men who remember who they are and what they are can be a leaven and a wholesome influence in this service into which they go. This applies of course only to those who keep in mind their principles and their ideals and who always conduct themselves in accordance therewith.

I am reminded of the story of Jacob in the Old Testament, in Genesis, when he was traveling in a strange land. Up to that time he had had limited experience and had been held close to home ties. But in this strange place he awoke one night after a dream and said, "Surely the Lord is in this place; and I knew it not." (Genesis 28:16) I would like our young men to remember that wherever they are, God is in that place and they must take him into their confidence and conduct themselves in his ways.

We cannot departmentalize the eternal record of our lives. It is one continued story. As Latter-day Saints we don't behave one way in the army and one way in business and another in Church. That is, not if we give heed to our principles. We do not behave one way at home and another way away from home. Wherever we are, remember that God is in this place also, and when the final record is written and read, all that we have done and thought, at home and abroad, in all the occupations and in all the pursuits that we may be called upon to undertake, is all a part of the eternal record of all of us, and it stands unalterably for us or against us.

And to those young people who are inclined to be discouraged by the course of events, those who are oppressed with the spirit of "What's the use?" we say to them: There will always be a future. Again quoting from Genesis a passage that is a comforting assurance: "While the earth remaineth, seedtime and harvest, and cold and heat, and summer and winter, and day and night shall not cease." (Genesis 8:22.) And we must not cease in our preparations or in our living of life to the fullest that we are able to do it in accordance with the conditions and opportunities of our own generation. If we make the best of all the circumstances of our own generation and time, the Lord will ask no more of us.

Life is not very long, I think. In the normal course of events mine is now half over, and I feel that I have scarcely put my foot in the door. I am sure that it isn't long enough to gamble any of the values of eternity against the values of time. And this thought recalls one of the most impressive passages from the Doctrine and Covenants, in which the Lord spoke to the Prophet Joseph Smith in one of his hours of deepest despair:

"My son, peace be unto thy soul; thine adversity and thine afflictions shall be but a small moment; And then, if thou endure it well, God shall exalt thee on high; thou shalt triumph over all thy foes." (Doctrine and Covenants 121:7, 8.)

And so I say to these young men of my generation: Go forth and live your lives in all of the fulness that is possible for you, and remember who you are and what you are, whether you are at home or abroad, in the army or out of it, and the Lord will bless you and prosper you and comfort you and reward you, and bring good out of all the circumstances of your lives.

I leave you my testimony that I know that God lives; that Jesus is the Christ; that Joseph Smith and all of his successors have been prophets of God, and I do it in the name of Jesus Christ. Amen.

If Men Be Good . . .

I read not so long ago an article concerning the responsibility of those who speak and write in time of war, but I am convinced that the gravity of this responsibility is not limited to wartime. Those who speak or write, any time, for the influencing of others, have one of the greatest responsibilities, and surely one which we should not care to undertake in these gatherings without the sustaining help of our Father in heaven.

There has been running through my mind a statement by William Penn: "If men be good, government can not be bad." At first I was inclined to challenge it seriously, as we are inclined to challenge all statements of broad generalization. I challenged it because I thought of all the exceptions to the rule. I thought of all the peoples, historically and also in the present, who had become captive peoples and oppressed peoples quite beyond their choice or their power to resist. I thought of all the straight-thinking minorities who have resisted the popular fallacies in every generation and in every country. But I became convinced, as I thought further through William Penn's statement, that it had a broad and fundamental truth in it: "If men be good, government can not be bad"—in the long view of things, and admitting all the exceptions.

For convenience, historians have written history in a manner that gives emphasis to a comparatively few individuals— as though Alexander the Great conquered the world (we don't hear much about all of those who followed Alexander the Great and made this possible) or as though Hannibal did what he did, individually; or the Caesars, or the Pharaohs. Even though historians concentrate upon and would make history seem to be the doings of one man, or a few, in every generation, in every country, yet the great host of men and women who follow them carry their share of the responsibility, not discounting the importance of leadership, good or bad.

Address given at General Conference, April 1945.

We are inclined to repeat this fallacy of history in our own generation, if we are not careful. We have had the opportunity of observing at close range the leaders of the world in our generation perhaps more intimately than in any other for many centuries past, because of our facilities for rapid communication and travel in these days. Because we have heard the voices, read the thoughts, and have seen both in picture and in reality many of the leading figures of our own day, we are likely to think, if we are not careful, that all the acts of each nation head up in one man, or in a handful of men, that all of the troubles stem from them. We may think that the war is the cause rather than the result of our difficulties.

We are apt to oversimplify history both current and past, and to look for scapegoats and to fix responsibility too conveniently; but I am sure that if we will think a little more closely we will be impressed with the truth that a man isn't a leader unless he has followers, and that he couldn't accomplish those things which he does accomplish unless a very considerable number of people were willing that he should accomplish those things.

I am reminded of one of the statements of Heber C. Kimball, who in his characteristic and colorful way said, "I will tell you, the devil has his smart men."[1] Even Satan would be impotent unless he had a considerable following; and so I say, going back to William Penn, whenever and wherever there is deterioration in government, the people may look to themselves. Whenever and wherever there is corruption, the people may look to themselves. Whenever and wherever there is flagrant public waste, the people may look to themselves. Whenever and wherever there is loss of freedom, the people may look to themselves. I am sure that no man, great though he may be, or potentially great in the powers of leadership, could accomplish much of his purposes without a considerable following; and our responsibility for our allegiance as followers is likewise great.

---

[1]Heber C. Kimball, *Journal of Discourses,* Vol. VI, p. 35.

Of course we know that anyone who opposes a profitable evil or anyone who opposes a popular fallacy is certain to be deliberately misunderstood. Nevertheless, every generation and every people have produced those straight-thinking minorities who have seen what they have seen and who have felt an obligation to say what they have said; and any man who sees his own generation headed for a precipice at the bottom of which lie tragedy, destruction, sorrow, and misfortune, cannot honorably remain silent. He has an obligation to speak, even though he be misunderstood, and even though false charges be levied against him. This is true at all places in the world at all times.

We have a leadership in this Church, who have an obligation to instruct this people to do anything which the Lord inspires them to do, and I am sure that we must understand the Authorities in their fulfilling of this obligation. I am sure that the prophets of God throughout all the ages have not, in most cases, seen the end fully from the beginning, but it has been given unto them to know in what they must instruct their people, whether they could fully state the reasons or not. There are many things that we must still accept on faith.

I should like to read you a quotation from Brigham Young. He had his troubles, too; they are not all confined to our generation. It was at the time when the cornerstones of the Salt Lake Temple were being laid, April 6, 1853. Brother Brigham was the object of much criticism. The people had built their temples in the past, at Kirtland and Nauvoo, and had had to abandon them. They had many practical problems facing them—food, shelter, Indians, and many other stark realities were pressing them. No doubt many of the people thought it was folly at such a time to undertake so great a task. Said President Young:

"Some will inquire, 'Do you suppose we shall finish this temple, Brother Brigham?' I have had such questions put to me already. My answer is, I do not know, and I do not care. . . . I never have cared but for one thing, and that is, simply to know that I am now right before my Father in heaven. If I am this moment, this day, doing the things God requires of my hands, and I am precisely where my Father in heaven wants me to be, I care no more about tomorrow than though it never would come. I do not know where I shall be tomorrow, nor when this temple will be done—I know no more about it than you do. . . . This I do know—there should be a temple built here. I do know it is the duty of this people to commence to build a temple."[2]

I should like to leave this subject for just one moment, and close with another thought, and read a couplet which in a very few words states what I think our returning boys who have been serving their country expect. It is from a poem by Kenneth Parsons, just two lines:

> When we come home again, forget the band.
> Just have the things we fought for, understand?

I believe this is in the heart of every man who is away from home, in the armed forces. May God grant that they will return to find their homes as they would have them; their children reared in those paths in which they would have guided them; and find the free institutions and the free enterprise for which they have fought; and peace and happiness and the opportunity to live in peace with those they love.

God lives, and has given us life; he still speaks to us through his appointed servants; Jesus is the Christ—which is the testimony I leave with you, in his name. Amen.

The Blessing of Reconciliation

I am sure there is a well of tears in the hearts of each of us today. Our thoughts are with the parents of these children as though they were our own brothers and sisters, which

---

Remarks given at the funeral service of the three sons of Rulon and Emily Barnes and the daughter of Leland and Donna Preslar, March 1947.

[2]Brigham Young, *Journal of Discourses*, Vol. I, p. 132.

indeed they are. I can only pray that my Father in heaven will give me utterance and that through his spirit peace and satisfaction will come from this hour, for I know that I have no words of my own to say what needs to be said.

I bring first, by his express wish, the love and sympathy and the blessing, to Brother and Sister Preslar and Brother and Sister Barnes, of President George Albert Smith, who asked me to carry this message here today. I bring also to them a similar message from Dr. John A. Widtsoe, Brother Rulon's former mission president, who had hoped to be here on this occasion, but was unable to be.

These events bring us face to face with the uncertainties of our lives, but they also bring us face to face with some of the glorious certainties that rise above all uncertainties, of which I should like to speak somewhat today.

I came from a home of much happiness, but of sorrow and adversity, nevertheless. When I was not yet three months of age, my own father was killed in an accident, leaving my mother a widow with nine young children. Why should such a thing have happened? This was the question repeatedly asked by friends and family. It was never answered logically, so far as I know, but it was answered so far as the reconciliation of my mother was concerned, both in terms of her life here and in terms of the eternal future, and in the rearing of her family and in the conduct of her home she walked and talked with her Father in heaven in prayer, all the days of her life. And she received the satisfaction for which her soul yearned long before others who were less affected had found the answer.

I recall an accident that came into my own life as a young lad. I had been taught to pray and to have faith and I found myself praying and asking my Father in heaven to make it so that this accident had never happened. But it had happened and I came to realize that I was asking my Father in heaven too much. But I grew in faith that he could overrule it for good.

I have mentioned Dr. Widtsoe, Brother Rulon Barnes' former mission president in Great Britain, where I was also on a mission with Brother Rulon, and where I learned to love and trust him and to respect his fine qualities of character, and I think of him with deep affection in my heart. Dr. Widtsoe came to Great Britain just a few months after he had buried his last son, the only son who could have carried on the Widtsoe name. Dr. Widtsoe had had six children and had buried all but two of them, both daughters. He and his wife came over to Great Britain—sweet, trusting, full of faith and confidence in the future. Notwithstanding these tragedies in their lives, they had found answers that gave them satisfaction, though others had not. Even Dr. Widtsoe's only brother had died some few years before.

And so they came to Great Britain, bringing with them one of their two remaining daughters, at that time fifteen years of age. They had been there about a year when she was stricken with acute appendicitis, and was grievously ill with what later proved to be a ruptured appendix. With her life hanging in the balance, we found it necessary to commit her into the care of a surgeon and to carry her into a small private nursing home. Here we were with doctors of whom we had never heard before, in a strange land, among strange people. As she was being operated upon, I walked the halls of that small hospital with Dr. Widtsoe and was much disturbed and depressed, but I was also buoyed up by the calmness of his spirit and his unwavering faith. Although I was much farther removed from the outcome of what might happen than was he, I am sure that I showed much more agitation than he did. I commented to him concerning this and he gave me an answer which I have never forgotten. He said, "I have to trust the Lord for so many things that it isn't much to trust him in just this one more thing"—and thus he lived, and has always lived, with this philosophy of faith.

It happened that one other man with whom I have associated, whom I looked upon as a father and he upon me as a son, I am sure, buried his only two sons. It was President Heber J. Grant, and I should like to read to you just a word from him concerning the death of his last son and of some of his feelings toward that event:

"I have been blessed with only two sons. One of them died at five years of age and the other at seven. My last son died of a hip disease. I had built great hopes that he would live to spread the gospel at home and abroad, and be an honor to me. About an hour before he died I had a dream that a messenger came for him."

And he goes on to tell how he finally became reconciled not to hold onto his last son. He awoke, and within an hour his son died and he testifies that he saw him pass away without a tear, for he had become reconciled.

On the occasion of the death of President Grant's last son, President Joseph F. Smith delivered a funeral sermon in the home of President Grant, from which I should like to read a few sentences:

"If we have received the testimony of the spirit of truth in our souls, we know that all is well with our little children who pass away, that we could not, if we would, better their condition; . . . the gospel reveals to us the fact that they are redeemed, and Satan has no power over them. Neither has death any power over them. . . . They are absolutely beyond his reach. . . . To my mind this is a consolation and a glorious truth that my soul delights in. I am grateful to my Heavenly Father that he has revealed it unto me, for it affords a consolation that nothing else can give, and it brings a joy to my spirit that nothing can take away. . . .

"Under these circumstances, our beloved friends who are now deprived of their little one have great cause for joy and rejoicing, even in the midst of the deep sorrow that they feel. . . . They know he is all right; . . . Such children are in the bosom of the Father. They will inherit their glory and their exaltation, and they will not be deprived of the blessings that belong to them; for, in the economy of heaven, and in the wisdom of the Father, who doeth all things well, those who are cut down as little children. . . . all that could have been obtained and enjoyed by them if they had been permitted to live in the flesh will be provided for them hereafter. They will lose nothing by being taken away from us in this way. . . .

". . . . Joseph Smith, the prophet, was the promulgator under God of these principles. He was in touch with the heavens. God revealed himself unto him, and made known unto him the principles that lie before us, and which are comprised in the everlasting gospel. Joseph Smith declared that the mother who laid down her little child, being deprived of the privilege, the joy, and the satisfaction of bringing it up to manhood or womanhood in this world, would, after the resurrection, have all the joy, satisfaction and pleasure, and even more than it would have been possible to have had in mortality, in seeing her child grow to the full measure of the stature of its spirit. . . .

"It matters not whether these tabernacles mature in this world, or have to wait and mature in the world to come, according to the word of the Prophet Joseph Smith. The body will develop, either in time or in eternity, to the full stature of the spirit, and when the mother is deprived of the pleasure and joy of rearing her babe to manhood or to womanhood in this life, through the hand of death, that privilege will be renewed to her hereafter, and she will enjoy it to the fuller fruition than it would be possible for her to do here. When she does it there, it will be with the certain knowledge that the results will be without failure; whereas here, the results are unknown until after we have passed the test.

"With these thoughts in my mind, I take consolation in the fact that I shall meet my children who have passed behind the veil. I have lost a number, and I have felt all that a parent can feel, I think, in the loss of my children. . . . but I feel thankful to God for the knowledge of these principles, because now I have every confidence in his word and in his promise that I will possess in the future all that belongs to me, and my joy will be full. I will not be deprived of any privilege or any blessing that I am worthy of and that may be properly entrusted to me. But every gift, and every blessing that it is possible for me to become worthy of I shall possess, either in time or in eternity, and it will not matter, so that I acknowledge the hand of God in all these things, and say in my heart, 'The Lord giveth and the Lord taketh away, blessed be the name of the Lord.'

"This is the way we should feel with regard to our children, or our relatives, or friends, or whatever vicissitudes we may be called to pass through. . . .

". . . Let a man have the Spirit of God in his heart, that Spirit which reveals the things of God unto men, and makes them to know the truth as God himself knows it, he never can doubt those things which God has revealed. Therefore, I rejoice in these truths, for I know they are true."

It is as though Joseph F. Smith had been speaking to these beloved friends of ours on this occasion, although he was speaking, more than fifty years ago, to President Heber J. Grant and his wife, bereaved at that hour as we are at this.

I do not know, I cannot say, how reconciliation will come, but I know that come it will, in God's own time and way, and I should like to close with reading some paragraphs that I wrote a year or so ago for a memorial occasion on this theme:

"There are few of us but who have been touched somehow by death. Some may not have been touched closely by it nor yet have kept vigil with it, but somewhere along our lives, most of us are sorely bereft of someone near and deeply cherished—and all of us will some day meet it face to face. Perhaps most of us feel that we could accept death for ourselves and for those we love if it did not often seem to come with such untimeliness. But we rebel when it so little considers our wishes or our readiness. But we may well ask ourselves when we would be willing to part with or to part from those we love. And who is there among us whose judgment we would trust to measure out our lives? Such decisions would be terrible for mere men to make. But fortunately we are spared making them; fortunately they are made by wisdom higher than ours.

"And when death makes its visitations among us, inconsolable grief and rebellious bitterness should have no place. There must be no quarrel with irrevocable facts. Even when death comes by events which seem unnecessary and avoidable, we must learn to accept what we cannot help. Indeed, the greatest blessing that can follow the death of those we love is reconciliation. Without it there is no peace. But with it come quiet thoughts and quickened memories. And what else shall a man do except become reconciled? What purpose does he serve by fighting what he cannot touch or by brooding upon what he cannot change?

"We have to trust the Lord God for so many things, and it is but one thing more to trust him in the issues of life and of death, and to accept the fact that his plans and promises and purposes transcend the bounds of this world and of this life. With such faith the years are kind, and peace and reconciliation do come to those who have laid to rest their loved ones—who, even in death, are not far removed from us, and of whom our Father in heaven will be mindful until we meet again, even as we are mindful of our own children. Bitter grief without reconciliation serves no great purpose. Death comes to all of us, but so does life everlasting!"

And now, you who are bereaved: I am sure you will find the answer in your hearts long before some of us have found it, and while it may not be an answer of logic, it will be more satisfying than any logic that men could present before you. I do not know how your lives will be filled, nor how the pattern of the days ahead will be changed to satisfy you and give you purpose in the glorious future, but I do know that it can and will be done.

God be with you, and may his peace abide with you in all the days to come.

"God Is in This Place and I Knew It Not"

It would seem to be customary on such occasions to announce a text, which I should like to do. It is really a story rather than a text, a story from Genesis concerning Jacob, who, as a young man was traveling in a strange land. He had a dream one night in which he beheld the heavens opened, with angels ascending and descending a ladder set upon the earth: "And, behold, the Lord stood above it, and said, I am the Lord God of Abraham thy father, and the God of Isaac: . . . And, behold, I am with thee, and will keep thee in all places whither thou goest . . . And Jacob awaked out of his sleep, and he said, Surely the Lord is in this place; and I knew it not." (Genesis 28:13, 15, 16.)

Jacob was no more startled by this discovery than have been many men since his time. "Surely the Lord is in this place; and I knew it not." And now having announced a text, at this point I should like to depart.

You who graduate from Brigham Young University at this time of Centennial are gloriously fortunate and richly blessed. You begin your work in the world at a time that is unparalleled for interest and opportunity—and in a place which has been peculiarly blessed of the Lord God. When he said that a marvelous work was about to come forth, he meant just that. And then he said that this was a land choice above all other lands, he meant that also. And these are your heritage—both the marvelous work and the choice land.

And much as you may have cause to find fault with your own day and generation, much as you may be disturbed by some of the things that are happening, so peculiarly and abundantly blessed are you that it is extremely doubtful if you would choose to change places with anyone else at any other time of life or in any other place of living.

Baccalaureate Address given at Brigham Young University, June 1, 1947.

Of course there are some things about other times and other places that you might wish to have: But you wouldn't honestly want to go back to ancient empires with their slavery and superstition, with their hordes of captive peoples, and with their torn and toppled cities. It all has such a modern sound, but without the modern conveniences.

Perhaps you think you would like to have lived when knighthood was in flower. If your information comes from your romantic reading, perhaps you would. But if it comes from document and fact, likely you would not.

But maybe you would choose to have shared your lot with your Pilgrim or pioneer parents. Much of what we have we owe to them. But, honestly now, would you like to have faced the bearing and the rearing of children without possibility of medical assistance, whether you needed it or not? Would you like to be old in your thirties, or earlier, as pioneer parents often were? Would you like to make every shred of cloth and clothing and wrestle with the earth for every meal and morsel? They were days of courage and conviction. But would you like to have lived then?

Of course you would be willing to give up atom bombs and swindlers and slums, and gangsters and poison gas, and lewd literature and excessive taxes, and waste and want and warfare, and false friends and foul speech, and ignorance and unhappiness—but where on earth could you go back and not find these or their ancient equivalents?

A generation ago, two generations ago, ten generations ago, always you would have found human nature, sometimes at its best and sometimes at its worst; always you would have found war in the waging or in the making; always you would have found some men striving for better things, and some progress being made by some people, and the Spirit of the Lord God always striving with his children.

But never would you find back there more that could make more men happy than now you see before you— both of things material and things spiritual. Of course you hope, as all of us do, for a heaven on earth that will bring together all the good of all the ages, yet if you had to change all you now have for all you could have had at any time in the past, you wouldn't go back—unless we are much mistaken.

And so, be thankful for living now—and make the most of it.

And now that we have counted but a few of our many blessings, let us proceed with some further facts of appraisal as concerning our privileges and our obligations.

In addition to all the contributions of our own time, we have all that the past has given us—the experience of those who have preceded us is a great part of our great heritage. And the more we learn from it the less of life we waste. We can illustrate this by a very simple citation:

If every scientist, for example, insisted on going back to the beginning to perform all the experiments that all his predecessors had performed, there would be little or no progress in science. Life would be wasted in proving what had already been proved. If every explorer were to discard all maps and ignore all previous exploration, life would be wasted in finding what had already been found. We read with puzzled pity of the prodigal son who wantonly wasted inherited property. But deliberately throwing away experience from reliable sources is of the same cloth and color as deliberately throwing away tangibles. And if we were to disregard all that our parents have learned, all that our forebears have left us in experience, all that all men have proved about life, and all that God has given us in revealed and discovered truth, we would be guilty of committing a wanton waste.

But such is our heritage that we need not grope for truth that is already ours, and we must not spend our lives repeating past errors.

Now, another point. In appraising the past and in pursuing the present and the future, mere intellectual brilliance is not enough. Indeed, intellectual acumen without the proper mixture of humility, morality and spirituality is tearing the world apart. As an old phrase of unidentified origin says, "Talent without character is more to be dreaded than esteemed." So also is money without character, power without character, knowledge without character, science without character, men without character—all are more to be dreaded than esteemed. Even a club or a stone or even bare hands are a menace on a man without character.

Our fears are not of the forces that have been placed in our hands but of men who would misuse them. A sweet and lovely voice, for example, is a great gift of God. But the sirens of mythology used the sweetness of their voices to entice men to doom and destruction. The gift that enables a man to write an inspiring masterpiece may also enable him, if his thoughts are evil, to write debasing filth. The power of persuasion that moves men to good works may, in the possession of a false leader, move them to false ways.

Talent without character is indeed to be dreaded. Anything in the world without moral responsibility, sincerity, and humility is to be dreaded, and what this world needs is not more smart men, but more good men.

The devil not only has his smart men, but he himself was and is a brilliant personality, brilliant without humility—so stupidly brilliant that he has destroyed his own future and the future of all who have or do follow him. Ambition is an admirable attribute, but ambition that gives way to arrogance and opportunism is a soul-destroying ambition.

And anything in this world can be overdone. Any man can go overboard on any subject. And there are not many things that you of the Centennial class of 1947 could better remember than to live balanced lives. Any man who pursues his life, placing superlative importance upon mere intellectual brilliance, without the tempering, qualifying, saving factors of humility, sincerity, morality and spirituality, is on his way to disaster.

And remember as you make your many decisions, as you come to every crossroads, remember that there is only one question that should ever come first: "Is it right?" Many other questions may properly follow, but none should precede this. If the answer to this first question is "yes," then you may properly ask, "Is it profitable?" "Is it convenient?" "Do I want to do it?" But no question should ever be asked before this one: "Is it right?" If it isn't right, whatever else it is, it isn't worth it. And putting the wrong question first and giving it the wrong answer, may cost anyone his self-respect, his peace of mind, his happiness and his success, and may complicate and compromise life from that time forth. If it isn't right, leave it alone. If it is, then ask any other question you want to about it.

This next point is that there are no perfect people in the world. But don't let this weaken your confidence in principles. Regardless of what degree of perfection or imperfection you find in people, remember that it is always much more serious when we fail to distinguish between people and principles.

If a principle is right it doesn't matter who abuses it or who abandons it, it is still right. Because a man isn't honest it doesn't mean that honesty is discredited as a principle. Because someone else doesn't live his religion doesn't mean that we are justified in discounting the religious principles that would have made him a better man if he had lived them. This is not a world of perfection and we need not look for perfection in men, but principles should never be abandoned because of the imperfections of people.

Now may we suggest that you be ever cautious against becoming worshippers of words. Take for example one word that men sometimes falsely worship, the word *efficiency*. In making this point I have sometimes said that a juke box may be much more mechanically efficient than a boy practicing on the piano. It takes a lot of effort to get a little music out of a boy who would rather be playing ball, but it only takes a nickel to get much too much of what has sometimes been erroneously called music out of a juke box. But there are potential values in persisting with a boy which a juke box knows nothing about.

As a matter of mere mechanics it may be much more efficient to make all clothing in the same pattern, to build barracks instead of houses, to put men on a sort of human assembly line for all the services and attentions they need.

In the processes of propaganda we sometimes hear that dictatorships are more efficient than democracies, or that the safeguards and guarantees of the Constitution of the United States make for inefficient government. But when efficiency and higher human values come into seeming conflict, let us first face the question: Efficient for whom and for what purpose and to what end? Efficient for making men free or merely for moving masses? It is the avowed purpose of the Lord God, his work and his glory to bring to pass the immortality and the eternal life of man. And any efficiency that does not move toward this purpose, toward the freedom and happiness and salvation and exaltation of mankind is efficiency miscarried, and we want no part of it no matter what label it carries. We have already heard that a brilliant character named Lucifer had a very efficient scheme of his own whereby no man could have made a mistake nor could any man have been free.

Now some further facts on the question of becoming worshippers of words: Changing the name of a thing doesn't change its essential characteristics. Perhaps the most quoted phrase on this subject is from *Romeo and Juliet*: "The rose by any other name would smell as sweet." And, to paraphrase, evil by any other name would be as bad.

We hear of a great many names being misused. We hear of ancient evils renamed and presented as desirable modern discoveries. We hear of gangsters calling "extortion" by the term "protection." We sometimes hear of "licentiousness" being referred to as "broadmindedness." But it doesn't matter what we choose to call our vices and our virtues, they remain what they are and what they always have been, before men and in the sight of God. Evil is where you find it, and it is what it is no matter what you call it. And permitting it to hide behind polished fronts and chromium trimmings, and glamorous names is more dangerous. As long as evil appears in its true colors and as

long as it is known for what it is, the number who touch it will
be smaller. A barefaced evil issues its own warning. But whenever we let a thing of evil take on the appearance of respect-
ability we have advanced its cause immeasurably. But changing its name never changes its nature, and for this we must
ever be alert, even as we are alert by law to falsely labeled
commercial commodities.

In all the representations of life, if it is all wool, let's let
the label say so, but if it is false fabric, let's not be misled by
misused words.

And now another passing departure from our announced
text: You have been accredited for graduation because those
whose responsibility it is to do so have turned to your record
and have found there written that you are worthy of this recognition. This is just one of many times in your lives when you
will have reason to learn the importance of the record.

Many of you young men here tonight have come to learn
the meaning of the military record that goes with a soldier
wherever he goes, to explain his past and to qualify his future.
In civil life records are made of the least infractions of
the law that come under official cognizance. Records are
made of credit ratings, of the certainty and promptness with
which we discharge our obligations, and any future financial
help we may expect or hope for is qualified by the record.
Records, not official, usually not written, but nevertheless indel-
ible in memory are made by our friends and loved ones of our
daily conduct and consideration.

But beyond all these, the record of our lives is made
within us. Many years ago Edward M. Stanton wrote: "A man
of fifty is responsible for his face." Be that as it may, we are
the summation of all we have done, all we have seen, all we
have thought. And when the record becomes clouded, there
inevitably follows the heartbreak of wishing the record were
different.

Be straight, and open, and honest. Don't try to be all
things to all people. It isn't possible faithfully to serve two

masters who represent opposite objectives. This is no time for carrying water on both shoulders. This is no time for indifference about anything that is good or evil. This is a dress rehearsal for eternity, and you will play the part you have rehearsed. And when the final curtain rises you will see yourself as you know yourself to be—the maker of your own record and your own judge of the record.

Don't permit anything to get into your life's record that will not stand the searching scrutiny of the light of day. If you do, it will rise to plague you in the years to come, and your own thoughts will accuse you even when others do not, for we ourselves are the record of our eternal lives.

And now another subject which leads up to the final, or almost the final thing I should like to say. This is a day when books are multiplied almost without measure. There are books and books, and the books of men are no more infallible than are the men who write them. Books contradict each other even as people contradict each other. And an error is an error even in a book.

Indeed, if you want to see a prize collection of misinformation, turn to a textbook of a generation ago, choose your subject, almost any subject then taught, and you will be astounded at how much that has been proclaimed in print has since been accounted untenable and insupportable. And what reason have we to suppose that much of what is printed today will not likewise seem absurd to those who follow in fifty years—or in five—or even now. Our day will not be the exception.

Fortunately we are not obliged to believe everything we read anymore than we are obliged to believe everything we hear. Man-made theories come and go, and so-called "final conclusions" so often prove to be anything but final. Even the experts disagree. And even if all the experts of one generation were to agree (which isn't likely; it never has happened), the experts of the next generation may discredit them.

It is so seldom safe to attempt to force so-called "final conclusions" concerning clouded and controversial considerations, for the books of men and the theories of men are no more infallible than are men. What is written is written, but if what is written is not true, writing doesn't make it so.

One of the world's most eminent living scholars, Alfred North Whitehead of Cambridge University, England, of the University of London, and more recently of Harvard, has said this in his recently released book, *Essays in Science and Philosophy*: "Every single generalization respecting mathematical physics which I was taught [at Cambridge] has now been abandoned . . ." He further "deplores the educational anxiety to 'secure youth and its teachers from revelation.' " (*Time*, May 12, 1947.) Thus speaks Alfred North Whitehead, who looks back from the eminence of sixty-two years of teaching in the world's leading universities.

Men are still striving for greater knowledge and are finding a few fragments here and there, and revelation is continuous in science and religion and in all else, as Alfred North Whitehead suggests and, more important, as God has declared.

We can well afford to read and to think, to watch and to pray, and to wait, being ever grateful that we belong to a Church that will accept all truth that we or anyone else ever discovers, no matter where or when it is found or who finds it.

And now, we come back to the text with which we opened: "God is in this place and I knew it not." The spirit and influence of God is everywhere where there is revelation of truth: in the laboratory, in the rocks of the earth, in the depths of the sea, in the heavens above, and in the lives of man. He is the Creator and Administrator of the laws of the universe; and all there is of life and breath and being are subject to his infinite jurisdiction. He is our Father in heaven and we are his children.

Whoever we are, wherever we go, whatever we study, whatever we do, we shall never discover any truth that does not emanate from him. Nor shall we ever find anything that is worth while or conducive to happiness or to man's welfare, here or hereafter, which is not of God, whether we recognize it as such or not—not in the halls of learning, nor in the halls of government, nor in any avenue of activity.

Whatever any of us hope to accomplish in life, in any field, whether we be teachers or scientists, biologists or accountants, chemists or mothers, physicists or political philosophers, we shall find walking humbly with our God to be the greatest sustaining power of life.

God lives. Men were made in his image, and they become like him in accordance with his announced plans and purposes. And his purpose is to save and exalt us, his children, and not to condemn us, and this he will do if we give him a reasonable opportunity to do so.

I witness to you this night my conviction that God does live, that Jesus is the Christ, that the Father and the Son appeared unto Joseph Smith, as he testified, and that God continues to reveal his mind and will in the earth in this our day, through his servants the prophets, and in all the revelations of truth—in the laboratory, in the classroom, in our fields and factories, in our hearts and homes.

Life is waiting for you out there. Go out and live it. A confused and troubled generation needs such as you—men and women of faith and learning, of knowledge and conviction, of purpose and power, and of prayerful humility.

I congratulate you upon your accomplishment, and wish for you happiness and success and peace, this day—and always.

Faith in the Future

I have been impressed that the theme of this conference has been repentance. I remember a reassuring sentence from President's Smith's talk of two days ago to the effect that every blessing may be ours on condition of repentance and of keeping

Address given at General Conference, April 1950.

the commandments of God. I am very grateful for the privilege and the power of repentance, and I think there is evidence that we should all be lost without it.

I don't know what the Lord's eternal timetable is, but I am sure that he is happy to have it modified by the acts of men in the use of their free agency in bringing themselves to repentance. I feel sure that there is no dire prediction of any of his prophets that he would not be happy to have set aside by the repentance of his people.

You recall the experience of Jonah, that after trying to run from his responsibility he finally did what the Lord asked him to do and proclaimed that destruction should come upon Nineveh in forty days; and from the king to the lowest of his subjects there was repentance in that great city, and it was not destroyed. But Jonah, being human as well as a prophet, was somewhat disappointed that his prediction of destruction had not been fulfilled. He failed to understand, apparently, that the prediction was dependent upon obedience or disobedience, upon perversity or repentance, and that the Lord is happy to revise his timetable concerning the affairs of men on conditions of repentance.

Again I am grateful for the privilege and power of repentance and am convinced that there is nothing wrong with this world (much as there is to worry about) that couldn't be cured by repentance; and I find this hopeful fact, that regardless of what we may do with the opportunity, it is there. For a man to have a disease for which there is no known cure is quite a different matter from having a disease for which there is a known cure if he will only avail himself of it and pay the price. I am grateful that there is a known cure for the ills of this world. The picture would be one of darkest despair, much darker than any yet painted, if it weren't that there is a plan and a pattern for peace in the gospel of the Lord Jesus Christ, and that there is the power and privilege of repentance if men will only avail themselves of it.

I say again, I do not know the Lord's timetable, and I think there is ample evidence that it is not for us to know it;

"the day or the hour no man knoweth." (Matthew 25:13.)
We read in the first chapter of the Acts of the Apostles, before
the ascension of the Savior, this word to his apostles: "It is
not for you to know the times or the seasons, which the Father
has put in his own power." (Acts 1:7.)

There are many things that men are permitted by our
Father to change in the use of their free agency. In the use
of our free agency we have made a few and more than a few
mistakes. Some of them are costly, and we shouldn't repeat
them, and we should avoid making them in the first place,
if possible. But the contrary plan was the plan of Lucifer, the
plan whereby men would not have been permitted to have
freedom to make mistakes. Being able to repent is a great
privilege which our Father in heaven has given us.

I do not know what degree of repentance would be required of us to avert some of the things that might be imminent or at least remote possibilities. You recall Abraham's
bargaining concerning the destruction of Sodom, how he
pleaded that the city would be spared if there were fifty
righteous souls, then forty-five, and so on down to ten. I doubt
that we shall realize terms as favorable as Abraham was able
to secure for Sodom. Apparently he was an astute bargainer,
but the ten weren't found and Sodom wasn't saved. I don't
know that ten of a city would be enough to save us today,
but I am sure that the degree of our repentance will be taken
into consideration. I earnestly hope and pray that we may
give full repentance, and others with us, to the end that our
Father in heaven in his mercy and in his patience and in his
love for his children, which he has declared, and in whose
immortality and eternal life he has stated his earnest interest,
will revise his timetables, whatever they may be, according to
the degree of our repentance. If he would agree to save a city
for ten repentant souls, think what he would do for a whole
nation of people who repented!

I recall some five years ago one of the world's eminent
philosophers and historians—a British philosopher and his-
torian—making some dire predictions following shortly in the

wake of the war. He said, "It is the end," and then went on
to elaborate that statement. But it has been five years since
then, and I believe that this is a Church that has faith in the
future. The statement of President Smith here yesterday is
to me evidence of it—the statement that some two hundred or
more places of worship have been built by this Church since
the philosopher said, "It is the end." There must be many
more than this number in the building or in prospect, which
is another evidence of our faith in the future. It seems to me
that our building program alone, and all our other plans for
the future, are evidence of our faith in the future of this
Church.

We must have faith in the future regardless of the ultimate
eventualities. One of the greatest calamities in this world
would be the calamity of sitting down and waiting for calamities. We must not let the things we can't do keep us from
doing the things we can do. We must not let remote possibilities or even imminent probabilities keep us from moving
forward with all earnestness and all effort.

I should like to say to the young people of this generation
that they too must have faith in the future. In spite of all the
uncertainties, they must go forward and prepare themselves as
best they can for all the problems and opportunities of life.
Whatever may come, here or hereafter, the future will always
be better for those who are best prepared.

No generation has ever lived without facing uncertainty.
If those who faced the uncertainties of ten or twenty-five or
fifty years ago had sat by and waited for what seemed to them
to be imminent calamities, we should not have had the able
and ready and well-qualified men that we have today, and
that we need and shall need in the next generation.

So I say to these youth of ours: Go forth and live your
lives with humility, with gratitude, with repentance, keeping
the commandments of God and having faith in the future and
preparing yourselves for the future, as the Church itself continues its building. There is nothing to lose by having faith in

the future, but there is much to lose by not preparing for the future.

I recall a statement, attributed, as I remember it, to President Wilford Woodruff. Some of the brethren of his time are said to have approached him and to have inquired of him as to when he felt the end would be—when would be the coming of the Master. These, I think, are not his exact words, but they convey the spirit of his reported reply: "I would live as if it were to be tomorrow—but I am still planting cherry trees!" I think we may well take this as a page for our own book and live as if the end might be tomorrow—and still plant cherry trees! In worrying about things that are beyond our reach, we should not overlook our opportunities with our own families and friends; in worrying about possible eventualities we should not neglect the things that need to be done here and now, and that are within our reach; the things for which we are immediately responsible; we should not neglect our present opportunities and obligations.

I should like to close with a statement of William Allen White: "I am not afraid of tomorrow, for I have seen yesterday, and I love today."

I am grateful to my Father in heaven for the assurance in my soul that he lives and that he is mindful of his children. I am grateful for his assurance of everlasting life. It has sustained my family these past three months when two sudden deaths have fallen upon us, and we would not have been sustained except for this assurance. And I would leave with you the witness of my soul that God does live, that Jesus is the Christ, that these things to which we are committed here in this conference and in this Church are his work and are of divine origin, and that it is our responsibility to carry them forward.

May his peace be with each of us, and with our children in the perplexing problems that confront them, and give us guidance and give them guidance.

A Tribute

I think I need not speak to you of the acuteness of my feelings. There are times, as Tennyson expressed it, which are too full for sound or foam. I pray that I may be able to do what I have before me to do.

I can testify to you of my own intimate knowledge of a quarter of a century of sharing some of his love and counsel and encouragement and confidence—as one who has been given faith and strength by his understanding heart and helping hand—I can testify to you that not within my life have I known one better prepared to meet his Maker.

He served his Father in heaven and his fellow men in many fields. He had a great humanitarian heart with judgments that were not merely just but merciful. His days and energies and efforts were spent in encouraging others to live in health and happiness and to prepare themselves to lift themselves in life, here and hereafter.

It might sometimes be supposed that the life of John A. Widtsoe was free from the difficulties and discouragements that beset so many of us. To some it might have seemed that he walked through life serenely and successfully, with things easily unfolding for him. But lest it should seem so, let us look for a moment at a few of the facts:

He followed no well-worn road. He had no early advantage. He came to earth in an inconspicuous place, on a rocky island among fisher folk, on a winter night with the wind adding its cold and comfortless sounds to the breaking waves of the North Sea.

It was little expected that he should live. He was born with his hand attached to his head, and a crude operation had to be performed.

He was fatherless at six. His custody was in question not too long later, after his mother espoused an unpopular faith.

Remarks given at the funeral service of Elder John A. Widtsoe, December 1952.

At twelve he found himself in a frontier town, a foreigner and immigrant among people speaking a strange tongue, with the family livelihood at first dependent upon the seamstress hand of a widowed mother.

No one gave him his education. It was financed by mortgaging and borrowing, which he paid back, with interest added. But he went to the highest halls of learning to receive the highest degrees of the day, from the highest authorities in his chosen fields in this land and others, and with highest honors. Then he chose to return to serve his own adopted pioneering people, rather than accept offers elsewhere.

Repeatedly he was called upon to leave work that he most loved and to undertake difficult assignments in difficult situations. No man may now know the price he paid for the preferences he put behind him.

Nor was the personal side of his life without its sorrows. Of the seven sons and daughters who were born to him and his cherished wife, five were taken from them.

These two together came into my life a few months after they had lost their last son, a promising young man of twenty-four years, and the last of his line who could have carried on the Widtsoe surname. Deep disappointment and sorrow ensued, but no bitterness. Instead, they took unto themselves yet other sons, whom they counseled and encouraged and lifted on their way in life. I thank my Father in heaven that I was one of them, and a host of others would so testify if it were their privilege to do so here today.

No one may know the number he has helped. His heart, his home, were open to all, and when he was not at the office, those who sought him in solving personal problems beat a path to his home, even in his illness.

He has helped men redeem their lands and their lives, and has given as though the reservoir of his strength and his love were unbounded, which indeed they have almost seemed to be until these last few weeks.

He preached the doctrine of health and of happiness, of labor and of learning, and earnestly practiced and pursued what he preached, into the eighty-first year of his life. In the last public discourse that he gave here in Salt Lake City before the Sons of Utah Pioneers, he had this to say of himself: "I want to say to you frankly that I have nothing in my life to recommend me except one thing—and thousands of men can say the same thing—I have done an honest day's work all the days of my life; and if that can be spoken of me, I shall be quite satisfied."

Only a few days before he died he was working on a manuscript on a vitally important subject for young people. Some thirty books or so have come from his pen, plus perhaps another thirty or more courses of study, plus hundreds of scientific, religious, and educational pamphlets, tracts and treatises, all of which have been done simply as a sideline in the midst of all other work.

He had a profound regard for facts, and an insatiable appetite for the discovery of further facts. At his elbow, even almost unto the last, was a constantly replaced stack of significant books. His was an almost universal interest. He spoke the languages of many lands. He was at home, interested, at ease, wherever he went.

I shall not attempt further to elaborate the record. What is written is written. But I would speak another word or two of the faith that was within him.

When the call came to become an apostle, again there was no looking back. Years before he had in principle settled all such decisions. He had probed and weighed the things of earth and the things of heaven. The man of science was also the man of God who could see truth wherever it was as an eternal part of a great eternal plan and purpose and picture, and who humbly accepted his Father in heaven as the source of all light and learning. Decades before, as an earnest, searching student, he had faced and accepted the fact of the restoration of the gospel of Jesus Christ, in this our day and dispensation.

When he was a young man still in his twenties in Germany working for his doctor's degree, he sent home a manuscript written for the strengthening of faith. It appeared in the second volume of *The Improvement Era,* and could well have been called the first of his "Evidences and Reconciliations."

He was sensitive to the promptings of the Spirit, and was as convinced of his eternal continuance as most of us are certain of the dawn of this day. There are some men in whom faith in things not seen comes very close to certain knowledge; so close indeed that there is little or no line between the two; and in him there was such faith. He knew that his Redeemer lives, that God lives, that men are immortal, that life and truth are limitless, that time is only part of eternity, that we are children of God, our Father, in whose image we were made, and that his plans and purposes for us are limitless and everlasting, and that heaven could only be heaven with family and friends.

All this he knew with a sureness and certainty that in his own soul left no room for doubt.

He lived, according to his own testimony, in a sunlit land; not without its shadows. But he did not dwell in the shadows. He looked always toward the light.

All this he shared with the wonderful companion of his life. From their first days together, nearly sixty years ago, to these last difficult, but devoted days, I have never seen a sweeter association. Eternity is little enough for such completeness of companionship as theirs has been, and the ache in her heart, and in ours also, is softened by the assurance which the poet so well expressed:

> When sinks the soul, subdued by toil to slumber,
> Its closing eyes look up to thee in prayer,
> Sweet the repose beneath thy wings o'ershading
> But sweeter still to wake and find thee there.
> So shall it be at last in that bright morning
> When the soul waketh, and life's shadows flee,

O in that hour, fairer than daylight's dawning,
Shall rise the glorious thought, I am with thee—
Still, still with thee.

And that reunion, Sister Widtsoe, and you, his cherished children and grandchildren, will be as real as those you now hold in memory.

There can be no real regrets here. He has finished his life in the loving surroundings of his home. He was ill long enough to give warning and some preparation—but not long enough to extend suffering and sorrow. He passed mercifully, peacefully. The Lord has been good to John A. Widtsoe, and he has been deserving of God's goodness.

I cannot say how much we shall miss him. We shall miss his quick step. We shall miss the acute mind that quickly cut to the core of questions and problems presented. We shall miss stepping into his room, with his books and his tools of writing. We shall miss his kindly humor, his counsel, and his comfort and encouragement. We know not how much we shall miss him. But the years go quickly, and John A. Widtsoe is still himself, and should we ever come within reach of so high a place as where he is, we should like to take his outstretched hand and resume our talk where last we left it.

Almost to the last time he talked to us, he was earnestly anticipating other activities, and I doubt not that already he is engaged in them.

There are walls that will listen for sounds that are silenced. There are places and people that will be lonelier than they have been. But somewhere this past week there has been a glorious reunion, and the sweet sounds that have faded from our ears are somewhere heard in a heavenly setting.

For what he was, for what he has done, for what he has meant to many—and for what he is—God bless his memory; and may the peace that passeth understanding be with all of us, and especially with those who shall miss him most, I pray in the name of the Lord Jesus Christ. Amen.

A New Call

I have frequented these beloved walls for a period now approaching a quarter century in many situations and assignments. But this is the most difficult thing that I have here had to do. It seems that this chapter was not in the script which I had written for myself.

In the brief, but in some respects too long a time since first I became aware of this possibility, I have measured the full measure of my life many times over. There are those here who know much better than I the weight of this work. There is none here who knows better than I my own limitations, inadequacies, and imperfections, and the feeling of smallness which I have. But if you and my Father in heaven will accept me as I am, with your help and his, I shall earnestly endeavor to be better than I am or have ever been.

I should not want to pass without thanking God for a noble father whom I never knew; for a blessed mother who, in her widowhood, reared nine of us, and faced her problems on her knees in prayer and on her feet gloriously in courageous action; for brothers and sisters, who with their children, I have had no cause but to be proud of in their faith and their awareness of their responsibilities in life.

I thank him for the choice and lovely girl who has been by my side for twenty years and for the four sons that are ours. I pray for them, and for youth everywhere, for their guidance in the ways of truth and righteousness. I pray for their generation, that they may know of the promise of the future, that despite all uncertainties there are glorious certainties that transcend them all.

I would say to their generation: be prayerful, keep the faith, avoid cynicism, be not shaken by the waves of controversy and confusion which sweep over and are quickly spent, while the truth remains forever.

Address given at General Conference, October 1953, after being called to the Council of the Twelve.

This is a gospel, not of despondency and discouragement, not of ensnaring technicalities, not of quick condemnation, but it is a gospel of hope, of happiness and of helpfulness, of peace and of promise.

There is no act of man, nor any combination of men, despite what passing troubles they may bring upon this earth, who can thwart the purposes of our Father in heaven, nor stay him in his plans to bring to pass the immortality and eternal life of his children, and I thank God for it.

As to these, my brethren, they know of my affection for them. No one could be to any man more considerate or gracious or kindly than they have been to me.

I shall miss some of the intimate associations with my beloved brethren of the First Council with whom I have sat for fifteen years. God bless them.

May I leave with you the witness of my very soul that God lives; that Jesus the Christ is the Only Begotten of the Father in the flesh, our Savior and Redeemer; that the Father and the Son did appear in this dispensation to the Prophet Joseph Smith, and that he and all in line of succession, including our present President McKay, have held the keys and the powers of the priesthood, and do unto this day.

President McKay, I pledge my love and loyalty, and all that is good or useful in me, with gratitude to you for many kindnesses and considerations and for your confidence.

I beg of you, my brethren and sisters, your confidence and help.

May God bless each and all of us in the things we need most, in understanding and peace and joy in living, and in the realization of our highest possibilities here and hereafter.

The Spirit That Leads to Truth

I should like to speak first of the importance of participation—in life, in school, in every worthy endeavor. Sometimes we hear the phrase, in the vernacular of the day, "Shall we sit this one out?" It is all right, I suppose, "to sit one out" with your best girl at a campus dance. But let's not sit life out. The spirit of participation, of learning, of doing, of contributing, of understanding, of being a part of, is basically important. It is basic to the gospel of Jesus Christ itself. It is part of the fundamental difference between the plan that was accepted of the Father and the one that was proposed and rejected, whereby all of us would have been delivered back into his presence without any effort on our part, and without any growth either.

It doesn't matter what we know if we don't use it. It doesn't matter what we have if we don't deliver. It doesn't matter what we can do if we don't do it. I think it was Will James who said that "we should keep alive the spirit of self-effort, and do something each day constructively, even if for no reason than that we don't want to do it." This ties in somewhat with another greater statement by Herbert Spencer: "You are educated if you can do what you ought to do, whether you want to or not." It is a great and profound statement. I commend to you in life, the spirit of participation, of willingness, of work.

I used on the air a week or two ago, a great five-word sentence from Livingstone who spent some thirty years of his life in the dark continent of Africa, darker than it is now. These five words he spoke to some students in Scotland: "Fear God, and work hard."

Had he put *love* instead of *fear,* I should have liked it better, but fear in its proper interpretation, in this sense, is quite acceptable also. "Fear God, and work hard." I think that one of the greatest things that one could wish for you

Address given at Brigham Young University, December 1, 1953.

would be that you would close no day without a sense of accomplishment, without a sense of participation, without a sense of having filled the hours of that day with constructive and meaningful and worthwhile activity.

I see no evidence that the Lord God intended that any of us should live effortlessly. All the evidence is to the contrary, including his commandments. There is a striking illustration of what happens to men when things are too easy for them in the safety records of the New Jersey Turnpike, one of the best-engineered pieces of highway in the world, I suppose, where the going is about as smooth as the going could be. One would think that it would have a well-nigh perfect safety record. Quite to the contrary, there have been many major accidents, including fatal accidents. The explanation of some engineers is that it is too easy: that it is so easy to drive that it is almost effortless, and has a hypnotic effect. A driver loses his sense of responsibility in some degree.

I think it isn't too difficult to carry over the implications of this illustration in life. Some things could be too easy. Some of the difficulties of learning, of doing, of living, whether we like them or not at the moment, have their purpose and are for our good, and, indeed, we should not grow or develop without them. We should not want to drive through life in a hypnotic state. And more of the crashes and disappointments might well come to us (as they have been demonstrated to do in a physical sense) on a highway that is too easy to drive.

May I turn to another subject, a favorite theme of mine. I suspect that it always will be—the search for truth. I am grateful for membership in a Church that is committed to the acceptance of all truth—not all theories, not all suppositions, not all tentative conclusions, but all truth.

God who gave us life also gave it meaning, and made all else in the universe, or brought it together and organized it. He is not in confusion, even though men sometimes are. But truth and the universe are an integrated whole. They are not conflicting segments. And sometimes the things we don't know (of which there is infinitely much) become too large in our eyes; that is, we became too impatient. And sometimes this impatience (which may properly be a part of the desire to learn, of the urge to search, but which must be moderated) may lead us to jump to quick conclusions which seem appropriate at the moment, but which time may prove to be less than satisfying, less than true.

In one of the leading national magazines not long ago there was a summary of the views of some of the leading scientists of the world as to some of the questions that science cannot yet solve. They are very basic; they are very fundamental; they are very simple; they are very profound. There was a longer list, but I best remember three of them:

One is as to the nature of matter. Actually we don't yet know what matter is. (At least I don't know anyone who knows what matter is except that it is the very substance that we and all else, physically, are made of.) What holds it together—what is the binding force of the universe? You'd think that with all that has been discovered, someone could answer that. Many have speculated on it. What keeps creation in its course?

Another concerns the mystery of growth. By that I mean, what causes one cell to develop into one thing, and one into another; one cell to become a tree, another to become an elephant; one to become a toenail, another to become an eye? Do you know anyone who can answer it? I don't, and I don't know anyone who knows anyone who can answer it.

Then there is the mystery of memory. I talked about the mystery of memory on the air on Sunday, and quoted not a religionist, but an eminent scientist, Gustaf Stromberg, who said in one of his scholarly works a decade or so ago, in a book that had the commendation of Albert Einstein: "The memory of man is written indelibly in time and space." He said it in almost these words—that it endures for eternity (he used the word *eternity*), that it is a thing quite apart from the physical atoms of the brain, that the brain is periodically replaced, that we have a new brain from time to time in a physical sense. But this thing called memory is indestructible.

I am not quoting from scripture, or from LDS writers or thinkers. I am quoting in substance from a man named Gustaf Stromberg, an eminent Swedish-American scientist, a contemporary, and a well-respected one.

I am comforted by the fact, and I commend it to you, that with an insatiable appetite to know the answers we may also have the patience to wait for the right ones. Where there is controversy and doubt, remember there is time ahead and eternity also—and we can afford to wait. It is scripturally recorded that when the Savior comes he will reveal all things. Those words are used specifically.

Truth is a great thing. It is a thrill to search for it, a thrill to find it. Search insatiably, and have patience where there is doubt and controversy—for the Lord God is not in confusion, and one segment of truth is not in conflict with another. If it seems to be, it is simply because we do not know enough.

There are many things more we might say on this theme. Follow that Spirit that leads to all truth. Listen to the whisperings of that Spirit within you. You have a right to guidance. Live for that guidance. I know of nothing more wonderful than setting out to do something worth while with the feeling within you that it is right, that it is what you should be doing. There is no road that is too long or too difficult if it is the right road. And there is no journey that is satisfying, no matter how easy or short, or how long it may be if it is a journey on the wrong road. Consult the Spirit which our Father in heaven has placed within each of you for your guidance and direction if you will heed it. Cultivate it and listen to it. Don't try to tell the Spirit within what you think it ought to want you to do, but listen to it and let it tell you what you know you ought to do. "You are educated if you can do what you ought to do whether you want to or not."

Remember that the Lord God sent us here not to fail but to succeed. We are his children. He loves us. Much as we may love one another and our own loved ones, he loves us infinitely more. There is nothing that he could do for us that he would not do, if we will let him. He knows our hearts; he understands them. He knows our difficulties, our problems, our weaknesses, our strength. He will help us if we will take him into our confidence. If we trip he will help us to move with firm steps again, if we will keep close to him and take him into our confidence. If we trip he will help us to life if we will follow the Spirit that leads to all truth.

God bless you. There is a great future before you. Keep your lives balanced. Keep close to things of the Spirit as well as things of a temporal nature that you must deal with, in most cases, to win your livelihood. Search the scriptures. Don't become one-sided. There is a wholeness of man; there is a wholeness of truth; there is a wholeness of life. Partake of that wholeness as the Spirit of truth leads you to partake of it.

May I leave with you the witness of my soul that God lives; that Jesus is the Christ; that his gospel has been restored in this our day; that it is the way of life unto salvation, unto the highest happiness of which men are capable, of which God is able to give them. Follow it, and may God bless you.

Through Diligence and Obedience

It is interesting how, in reading scripture over and over again, one often, after many readings and a long time, quite unexpectedly finds some word or phrase that comes into his consciousness with a new and particular meaning. I have had, within the last few hours, just such an experience.

This scripture, so familiar to you, is no doubt one of the most quoted in the Church—one which I have read most often and heard most often, even unto thousands of times— that "Whatever principle of intelligence we attain unto in this life, it will rise with us in the resurrection. And if a person gains more knowledge and intelligence in this life" (and this is

Address given at General Conference, April 1956.

the phrase that struck me anew only yesterday) *"through his diligence and obedience* than another, he will have so much the advantage in the world to come." Not just a miscellaneous acquisition of knowledge, but knowledge and intelligence, through *diligence and obedience.* (See Doctrine and Covenants 130:18, 19.)

Those words are most meaningful—and I have no fear of learning, of the pursuit of knowledge, for any of our young people, if they will keep in mind *diligence* and *obedience*— obedience to the commandments of God, diligence in keeping close to the Church, in keeping active, keeping prayerful, keeping clean, keeping circumspect in their conduct. It isn't learning or the love of learning, or knowledge, or the pursuit of any subject that would take from a man his faith, but it is failure to keep the commandments, the failure of a man to feed all sides of himself.

Intelligence would not let a man lose his faith in finding truth. Learning does not lead to loss of faith. False learning might, but not true learning. Lack of learning may. Ignorance may. Failure to keep the commandments may lead to loss of faith. Loss of balance may lead to loss of faith. A man may pursue learning along too narrow lines and forget to feed all sides of himself; he may forget his spirit and starve it, but not learning itself leads to loss of faith, not the search for truth, for truth cannot come in conflict with truth. A man can have the pure love of learning and seek for it insatiably, and still keep a simple faith *if he will keep the commandments,* if he will feed his spirit, if he will be patient, and sweet in humility, and not commit himself to quick conclusions or tentative theories. If he will really seek for eternal truth, with *diligence and obedience,* he can keep and pursue an insatiable love of learning and still keep his faith, for "the glory of God is intelligence."

We are committed to continuous revelation, to an infinite search for truth, and there are some very significant lines accredited to Thomas Edison that I should like to share with you: "We don't know the millionth part of one percent about anything. We don't know what water is. We don't know what electricity is. We don't know what heat is. We have a lot of hypotheses about these things, but that is all; but we do not let our ignorance about these things deprive us of their use."

We don't altogether know what faith is, or prayer, and the ultimate meaning or power of them. We don't altogether understand all the commandments, but the limitations of our knowledge should not keep us from observing them and using them, as we pursue learning and the love of learning, keeping the commandments of God and keeping close to him and his truth, in a well-balanced life, in the gospel of Jesus Christ, and using it as our standard as the measure of all things.

I am not concerned about the unanswered questions. I should like to know all the answers, but those I don't know do not bother me. This I know, and leave it with you as the conviction of my soul—that God lives, that Jesus the Christ, his divine and very Son, lives and stands by his side in the Godhead; that these two did appear to a young man, more than a century ago; that we live; that God made us in his image; that he has unspeakably great eternal blessings in store for us as we will search and seek and keep faith and keep clean, and keep his commandments and live in obedience and keep our lives balanced, and keep close to him.

In the wonderful words of Emerson: "All I have seen teaches me to trust the Creator for all I have not seen."

God bless you, my brothers and sisters, in all things as you meet the daily decisions of life and move on to those great as yet unseen activities and opportunities of eternity, toward which the ways of all of us move.

A Reaffirmation:
"We Thank Thee O God for a Prophet"

I think to those of you who have heard what has preceded at this conference, it must be somewhat apparent that there has been a considerable and, I think, significant emphasis and reaffirmation of the principle of revelation, of continuous revelation.

There were some events associated with the dedication of the London Temple which I should like to relate, also. Our President went there, and we had arranged a press conference for him on the late afternoon following what was to have been the morning of his arrival, thinking that he would have time for rest and still time to face that arduous task. But his plane was three hours late, or more. He had been up all the night before with those who accompanied him, . . . and there was no time for rest; and he faced that battery of some thirty or forty newsmen representing the great London dailies and others of the British Empire and the wire services, and the BBC television camera.

They pressed many questions, difficult and sometimes tenacious and penetrating questions, as is the function of alert and seasoned newsmen. He met them forthrightly, with some declarations of affirmation as to things we would know and how we could be assured of knowing them. They were respectful, but one always wonders what will happen the morning after when what was said appears in print, with the reporter's personal color or understanding or misunderstanding on it. Some of us worried about it considerably. I saw the President in the lobby of the hotel that evening and expressed some of my concern, and he made a very significant statement. I do not know whether he remembers it or not, but I think I shall not forget it. He said, "When I have said what I know to be true, I do not worry about the consequences."

Address given at General Conference, October 1958.

This put me in mind of that great statement of the Prophet Micaiah as he declared to Ahab, the king, those things which the Lord God had given him to speak. The king had previously said that he hated the prophet because he never prophesied him good, and the prophet replied: "As the Lord liveth, what the Lord saith unto me, that will I speak." (1 Kings 22:14.)

It is the burden of the prophets always to speak what the Lord God saith, no matter who likes it or who does not, or what one would wish to be the truth. It takes a kind of courage beyond what most men have reason to reach down for.

We might just as well have slept, those of us who didn't sleep so well that night, because the newspapers the next morning were factual and respectful, and none of them that I knew of had reached for the sensational, or the old false representations that some of us had been accustomed to in times gone by.

Now, one thing these newsmen wanted to know, some of them, is, "How do you know? How can you know some of these things?"

Does it seem a thing strange that the Lord who admittedly had prophets in former days should have them in this day? Does it seem a thing strange that there should be living prophets as well as dead ones? Does it seem that this people in this time should need less, for these changing times and changing conditions, the interpretation of the everlasting principles and standards, and less need a living voice to help to find the way? Is there less of wilderness in our generation and in our world than ever there was? Or less need for living prophets?

Does it seem that the Lord would give prophets to one small people in one small place at one limited time, and leave all the rest of time without the living witness of his words, and the interpretation of them according to their own time and day? Just consistency and reason would seem to suggest living prophets and continuous revelation without any deep-seated affirmation of it within our souls.

As to answering the question of the newsmen, "How can

you know?" Of course, you can go back and read the record. We invited the attention of some of them to the fact that a prophet a century and a quarter ago had said that tobacco was not good for man, and that medical science was now affirming it. And they said, "Then in this respect your prophet was a century or so ahead of the findings of medical science." And we let them say it. We did not have to say it for them.

But beyond tangible and specific historical evidences, there are things a man can know inside his soul that are beyond the things he can touch and see and rest his feet upon, which are undeniable.

And as to those friends to whom President Richards spoke so earnestly yesterday morning, I would witness to them, also, with him, that this in which we are engaged is not merely a vocation or a profession, but the dedication of a life to a conviction that cannot be denied.

And as to how one can know: He who does not know cannot know that another man does know, and some things are so certain within the souls of men that they cannot be denied.

A few days ago President Clark spoke a sentence that I have not been able to forget. He said, "We are no better than we are." It is profound in its simplicity and it leads into many applications. Our positions do not make us better, or do not assure our being better than we are. I know of no generalizations that would save the souls of men. It is the specific performance of specific things that make men better —not theory, not merely the fact that there is a set of principles or that there are commandments, or that there is counsel, but the living of it.

I am thinking of the Danish sculptor of great fame, Thorvaldsen, who chose to be buried in the midst of his works— not in a cathedral or a cemetery, but in a museum among the monuments of his own making—in the midst of his statuary; and there what he made and what he did with his life surrounds him. He did not theorize upon sculpturing only, but with his hands and with his creative gift he fashioned those things and he lies there in the midst of his works, as we all shall do some day—and it will not be the theories or the discussions or the speculations or the set of principles or the set of commandments that shall save us.

We shall be no better than we are. We are no better than the tithing we pay, no better than the teaching we do, no better than the service we give, no better than the commandments we keep, no better than the lives we live, and we shall have a bright remembrance of these things and we shall, in a sense, lie down in the midst of what we have done when that times comes, and never in my life have I felt more fully to say with all the earnestness of my soul, "We thank thee, O God, for a prophet, to guide us in these latter days."

My beloved brethren and sisters, may we take counsel with each other. There is safety in counsel: counsel with our children, with the family, with our friends, with our Father in heaven, and not attempt to live life alone and to make the decisions alone, but to strengthen each other, and encourage each other, and go forward and do what there is to be done and follow the living leadership as the prophet interprets for us the great principles and commandments of all time.

I thank God for a prophet this day, for an assurance that I am not alone in life, and that you are not, that we none of us are, nor are left without inspired leadership. Thank God for it. And I leave this witness with you, in the name of him in whose name we do all things, and in whose name we are met, our Lord and Savior, Jesus Christ. Amen.

It All Adds Up

Some months ago, on a nation-wide radio network, we spoke on a subject which we called "It All Adds Up." We quoted from Emerson's remarkable essay on "Compensation" in which he said, "The world looks like a multiplication-table,

---

Radio "Fireside Talk" delivered in the Tabernacle, 1961.

or a mathematical equation, which turn it how you will, balances itself. . . . You cannot do wrong without suffering wrong. . . . A man cannot speak but he judges himself. . . . Every secret is told, every virtue is rewarded, every wrong redressed, in silence and certainty. . . . The thief steals from himself. The swindler swindles himself. . . . Men suffer all their life long under the foolish superstition that they can be cheated. But it is impossible for a man to be cheated by anyone but himself. . . . What will you have? quoth God; pay for it and take it . . . thou shalt be paid exactly for what thou hast done, no more, no less."

And in this same radio comment we further continued: "We have become increasingly aware lately of the so-called exact sciences, of mathematical formulas, for example, from which can be forecast the forces of the inner atom and the orbiting into outer areas. Order is evident in all of this— order and the mind of an Infinite Administrator. But he whose infinite orderliness is everywhere in evidence has not left his children without laws of life that lead to results as sure, as certain, as the laws pertaining to physical phenomena— laws of health, moral laws, counsel and commandments. There has been a tendency by some to say that this age-old counsel may have served a purpose in the past, but is no longer essential to human happiness. But it simply isn't so. There is no evidence that loose thinking or lax living or so-called emancipation from morals and manners has brought peace or happiness or progress to anyone, ever.

"And the Father of us all, in his love and wisdom pertaining to his children, hasn't said 'Thou shalt' and 'Thou shalt not' for no particular purpose. William James, the celebrated Harvard philosopher, said it in this way: 'Every smallest stroke of virtue or of vice leaves its never so little scar.' Every thought and act and utterance is being counted 'among the molecules and nerve cells and fibers. Nothing we ever do is in strict scientific literalness wiped out.' It all adds up.

"No amount of rationalizing can cancel out the fact that peace and quiet come with keeping clean, with keeping the commandments, and no amount of rationalizing can save us from the consequences of misconduct. We are the sum of the thoughts we think, of the habits we have, of all we do and have done. We are the sum of all our actions and attitudes and utterances, of all we have taken and retained in body and mind and memory. The laws given by a loving Father are always in force and always effective. His advice is worth taking; his commandments are worth keeping. It all adds up."

Sometimes people argue about the commandments, especially when they find them inconvenient to keep. And some would say that a loving Father wouldn't be technical with his children simply because of some small thing they had done or failed to do. But no matter how much our Father loves his children, he will not and does not ignore his own laws, which are the laws of life.

If I may use a personal example: I have had the privilege of serving as a member of the governing boards of two universities, but my sons still have to earn their degrees according to the requirements of the catalog. Perhaps many students at one time or another would like to quarrel with the catalog. They may wonder why it is necessary to take certain subjects. "Why do I have to take English," they ask, "if I am studying engineering? Why do I have to take social sciences and biological sciences? Why do I have to meet the requirement of the catalog?" But whenever we seek a privilege, or seek qualifying credentials of any kind, we have to do it according to the rules and the regulations. And if a son of mine should want a doctor's degree, no matter how much I loved him and no matter how much I would be willing to help him and to encourage him, he himself would have to learn the lessons, take the tests and meet the requirements.

It is so in seeking citizenship. A person who seeks citizenship must meet the requirements of the country, whether he understands the need for them or not. It is true of fraternities, of memberships, of licenses to do business or to practice a profession. In all orderly organizations and institutions there are requirements that must be met.

Many years ago the late Melvin J. Ballard of the Council of the Twelve Apostles delivered a remarkable sermon that was later published in a pamphlet. It was called "The Three Degrees of Glory." In it Brother Ballard told about the great objectives of life and the requirements for reaching those objectives and of how some people would quarrel with the requirements and how some people would wish to set them aside—how some would say, for example, that so long as you live a reasonably good life the rest doesn't matter very much. And then in a remarkable manner Brother Ballard went on, step by step, to enumerate the requirements and commandments of the kingdom, the purposes of the gospel, the importance of marriage for eternity, and the steps necessary to realize man's highest happiness. He indicated how every step is essential and how all requirements of the gospel pertain to the celestial kingdom. Strictly speaking, we don't even know how to get into the terrestrial kingdom or what the specific requirements of any lower kingdom are. Apparently the Lord God has only set out to teach us how to realize the greatest attainment, the highest happiness, the greatest opportunities and the greatest of the gifts. And we would be exceedingly foolish, exceedingly unwise, if we should set our sights for anything less than the best.

There are those who would remind us that all roads lead to London or that all roads lead to Rome. Yes, they do in a sense. I can go to Rome from where I am and you can go from where you are. But when we get to Rome we don't find everyone enjoying the same privileges or living the same kind of life. Some are rich and some are poor. Some are well and some are sick. Some are highly privileged and some are underprivileged, and some people in Rome live in jail. It is true that all roads lead into a hereafter, that all roads lead to some kind of continued existence. Our Savior assured us all of resurrection. But life hereafter is not the same for everyone any more than it is here. Our Savior said it very simply: "In my father's house are many mansions. If it were not so I would have told you." And we would be most unwise to decide to settle for something second-rate.

I've spent much of my life with nonmembers of the Church, among men of many professions and many occupations with whom I have had the privilege of associating, world-wide. I respect them and enjoy them and with many have found cherished friendships and affection, and I have never found any embarrassment, in any kind of company, in living according to our standards.

Many of these men who are not members of the Church employ our young men who are members—in many cases, young men who have been on missions. These employers may not themselves live according to our standards, but they would not trust one of us who didn't live according to our standards, because they would know that we were departing from our own principles. They would know that we didn't have the character to live our own religion. And while I respect other men and their beliefs, and while some things they do do not seem to them to be so serious, because they are not departing from their principles, yet for us such departure would be serious, because the Lord God has given us added knowledge concerning the purposes and laws of life.

And what we call commandments are really only counsel from a loving Father. Our Heavenly Father doesn't deal in unessentials. He hasn't set out simply to interfere with our fun, any more than our earthly parents have. But he knows us; he knows our nature; he knows what would be good for us, what would make us happy and what would make us unhappy. And he has given us some simple rules and some loving and wise counsel. That's all commandments are, and we shouldn't let ourselves think that they are arbitrary, or needlessly trying to interfere with our freedom.

There are those who would rationalize as to the Word of Wisdom. But wouldn't a loving Father—wouldn't any father, heavenly or earthly—be interested in everything that pertains to his children's health and happiness? And all the Word of Wisdom is, is counsel from a loving Father as to what is or isn't good for us. It all adds up.

When our Father says to us, "Thou shalt" or "Thou shalt not," I believe we should consider it much as if a wise and loving earthly father were to put his arm around us and simply say, "Son, I have lived a long life and have seen that some things make people unhappy and that some things make them happy, and I'd like to save you some sorrows, and I'd like to help you to success." If I had had a father to share his experience and his wisdom with me, I believe I would appreciate it; I believe I would take his counsel. This, largely, is what commandments are.

Cecil B. DeMille said something concerning these things in a remarkable commencement address at Brigham Young University not long before he left this life: "We are too inclined to think of laws as something merely restrictive, something hemming us in. We sometimes think of law as the opposite of liberty. But that is a false conception. That is not the way that God's inspired prophets and lawgivers looked upon law. Law has a twofold purpose. It is meant to govern. It is also meant to educate. . . . God does not contradict himself. He did not create man and then, as an afterthought, impose upon him a set of arbitrary, irritating, restrictive rules. He made man free and then gave him the Commandments to keep him free. We cannot break the Commandments. We can only break ourselves against them, or else, by keeping them, rise through them to the fullness of freedom under God. God means us to be free. With divine daring he gave us the power of choice."

This choice includes all things in life: habits, thoughts, actions, utterances, the places we go, the choosing of companions, the keeping of commandments. As to the places we go, many years ago President Heber J. Grant wrote this in a letter from Japan: "We have no right to go near temptation, or, in fact, to do or say a thing that we cannot honestly ask the blessing of the Lord upon, neither to visit any place where we would be ashamed to take our sister or sweetheart. The good Spirit will not go with us onto the devil's ground, and if we are standing alone upon the ground belonging to the adversary of men's souls, he may have the power to trip us up and destroy us. The only safe ground is so far from danger as it is possible to get. Virtue is more valuable than life. Never allow yourself to go out of curiosity to see any of the undercrust in this world. We can't handle dirty things and keep our hands clean."

Sometimes things happen all at once, but sometimes they happen a little at a time, a step at a time. I remember a comment from Brother Mark E. Petersen in one of his excellent sermons, in which he said, "It is possible to lose a little virtue." And if losing virtue itself is wrong, doing anything that might lead to the loss of virtue must be wrong. Even a half-step is unsafe if it is near the edge of a precipice. We should never tempt temptation or go near the edge of a precipice or see how far we can go without slipping. We don't really know our own strength. We don't really know at what point we will be swept farther than we intended to go, and the only safe practice is to keep a safe distance away from every questionable intent, from every unwise experience, from every situation that might lead us strongly into temptation.

Now as to companions, and especially as to the one life-long companion, it is most urgently important that that companion share our own principles and purposes. "Do you expect," said a Roman philosopher of many centuries ago, "that a mother will hand down to her children principles which differ from her own?" It is difficult enough to teach children when both parents are pulling in the same direction. It is unfairly confusing when each parent is pulling in a different direction. In this life which moves so swiftly and which reaches so far in its everlasting effects, those with whom we would want to live should lift our lives and bring out the best and help us to be better.

I would plead with you, beloved young friends, to live your lives with respect for yourselves, with respect for others, with respect for life, with respect for your Father in heaven and for keeping his commandments.

I would plead with you to respect the wonderful physical structure which God has given you by keeping it free from injurious substances, to respect the wonderful mind that God has given you by keeping it free from wrong and unworthy thoughts, from all evil intent. And if you've made mistakes, turn earnestly and soon to the principle of repentance, which means not simply being afraid of consequences but which means cleaning out your soul inside of you, starting a new way of life with sincerity and self-respect. Do the things that would entitle you to be with the kind of people you want to be with, always and everlastingly. The most rash and reckless kind of gambling is to gamble the values of eternity against the values of time.

I leave with you my witness of the divinity of the Lord Jesus Christ, of the reality of our relationship to God, the Father, and of his glorious plans and purposes for all of us, which is the whole reason for the gospel and the whole reason for its restoration in this day and dispensation. There are no short-cuts, but there is fairness, there is justice, and there is love. The Lord God does not expect the impossible of any of us, but he does expect a sincere and honest effort in the keeping of his commandments. I think it was Elbert Hubbard who said, "We are punished by our sins and not for them." It all adds up.

Live the good life, the clean life, the life that leads to self-respect, to health, to a sense of accomplishment, to a sense of cleanliness inside — the life that leads to peace and happiness. "It is impossible for a person to cheat anybody but himself." It all adds up.

I pray that for you it may all add up to happiness and peace and progress, to a life that leads to greater life, with limitless opportunities, always and forever.

This We Believe . . .

There is a salutation customary among us which includes all within sight and sound—"My brethren and sisters"—and I see no reason to modify it. I am grateful for the relation that all of us bear to all of us in the Fatherhood of God and the relationship we have to him.

Because of an unusual series of assignments, we have circled the world twice this past year—once flying east, and once moving westward. We have been in many countries, among many peoples, in many places. We have encompassed areas where hundreds of different dialects and languages were spoken. We have been in the midst of a diversity of men, and in the midst of many differing religions and philosophies of life.

We count among our friends, men of many races, many faiths, many backgrounds and beliefs, and these are not superficial friendships. They are part of our lives. We respect them and what they are and have an affection for them. We respect them and their beliefs, and we believe they respect us and ours.

As a consequence of this long journeying and these many friendships, we have been earnestly reading and seeking to understand the basic beliefs, the many philosophies of India and of Asia, and in doing so have consulted as closely as possible the people themselves and their authentic sources; and this we would ask our friends to do for us, as we would do it unto them also. When they want to know what we believe, we ask them to ask us, or consult our authentic sources instead of sources of intentional or unintentional distortion. No matter how many times an error is repeated, it is still an error. We believe that we ourselves are the best source of what we believe, as are other men of what they believe, and to those interested we should like to give the simple facts.

We have discovered, also, that mankind generally is sincerely searching—searching for the reasons, for the purpose of being, searching for the ultimate answers. "Man's success or failure, happiness or misery," President McKay has said,

Address given at General Conference, April 1962.

"depend upon what he seeks and chooses." What people believe is exceedingly important, because what they believe will determine how they live. A person prepares differently for a short journey than he does for a long one, and a person who believes that life here is the end of all would prepare much differently and live much differently from him who believes that life is everlasting.

Thomas á Kempis said, "Where my thoughts are, there am I," and might have added, Where my beliefs are, where my convictions are, there am I—or at least in that direction I am headed.

For these reasons and because we love our friends, and because many of them have asked us, and because even if they hadn't we would want to do it anyway, we would like to say some few things today basic to our beliefs:

First of all, in common with many millions of men, we are devoutly Christian. This is The Church of Jesus Christ of Latter-day Saints. Jesus the Christ, with the doctrines, the commandments, the revelation, the inspiration, the authority that come of him and through him, is the foundation of this Church. He is the chief cornerstone, and not any man.

We believe what Jesus taught, and in this we rely on scripture, including the Bible, which we believe as it came from the mouths of the prophets. We believe also other works, given to other peoples anciently and modernly, in addition to the word given to ancient Israel—works which are consistent with and complementary to the Bible.

In addition, we believe in the words of the living prophets. We believe in continuous revelation, for we feel that a loving Father still gives divine guidance, and would not leave his sincerely seeking children alone without counsel or direction, and him whose countenance you have seen this morning in conducting this conference—President David O. McKay—we accept and sustain as a prophet of God, as we accept Moses and Abraham, and Peter and Paul, and Isaiah and Elijah or any such others.

It does not seem a strange thing that God would speak to his children in the present as well as he would speak to them in the past. Certainly we do not need his guidance less today. What loving father would hold himself altogether aloof from his sincerely seeking children?

We believe in the literal language of scripture concerning the Fatherhood of God. We believe the language of Genesis which says that God made man in his own image. (Genesis 1:27.) We believe that God is an infinite intelligence with an infinite love for us, not indefinable, but a Father with a father's interest in us. This gives us a peace and purpose in life, a sense of belonging and of not being left alone.

We believe that the glory of God is intelligence; that no man can be saved in ignorance; that the search for truth is an obligation, as is education also; and that there must be freedom for the search.

We believe in the commandments of God; in causes and consequences; in the necessity for living within the law; and that there is real reason for every commandment and requirement.

We believe that the human body should be preserved in health; that it is unwise and ungrateful and unjustifiably foolish to partake of things that impair the fullest well-being of the body and effective physical functioning. What is not good for us simply should be left alone.

We believe literally in everlasting life, in the eternal perpetuation of personality; that whatever knowledge a man attains to in this life will rise with him in the resurrection; and we believe in a literal resurrection, remembering the words of Pascal, who asked, "Which is more difficult? To be born, or to rise again?"

Birth is a great miracle. Life is a great miracle, and he who gave us life here will give us life everlasting. This we believe.

We believe that all men will be resurrected; that all men in this sense will receive salvation, but that in the hereafter there are different degrees of glory (1 Corinthians 15:22-23,

40-42), entitlement to which will depend upon the life we have lived, and by the living of the law and the keeping of the commandments we shall be entitled to return to live with our Father and go back to him where once we were, to a place of peace and progress, where there will be everlasting life, with family and friends, in a relationship that is everlasting.

Thus we believe in marriage, not only for time but also for eternity, and that we have an inescapable obligation for the children God has given us to teach, to train, and to set before them a righteous example of the living of life.

We believe in the divinity of Jesus the Christ. We believe in the scripture which says that he was in the express image of his Father. (Hebrews 1:3.) We believe that he was born of a virgin, as the scripture says; that he lived, that he preached, that he ministered among men; that he was put to death, that he rose on the third day, that he ascended to his Father, that he will come again on earth to rule and reign.

This is a simple belief. It is a profound one also. It gives peace in life. It gives a sense of everlasting purpose. It gives the assurance that we are helping to shape our own future with our faith, with our works, with our learning, with our lives. It gives us the assurance that life is purposeful, meaningful, limitless, everlasting; that the gospel was given as a guide to help us realize our highest happiness; that all its ordinances are essential; that authority to administer them is also; and that this authority was again restored in the nineteenth century through Joseph Smith the Prophet, as the heavens were opened and the personality of God again revealed as the Father, pointing to his Beloved Son our Savior, said, "This is My Beloved Son. Hear him!"

In this brief time there is much omitted, but this in essence is the faith that gives us peace and purpose in life and freedom from many of its fears. We believe there are clear-cut answers to life's questions; that much of the groping of life can be eliminated.

In Calcutta, in India, we read in the notebook of a wonderful grandmother an inscription which, among others, she had cherished since she was a young girl—an inscription which India's great poet, Rabindranath Tagore, had written in there for her in his own handwriting: "Surrender your pride to truth."

These lines Tagore also wrote on freedom—freedom for the search and on the importance of such searching—(and we have altered a word or two by inserting "me" instead of "my country" in the last line) :

Where the mind is without fear and the head is held high;

Where knowledge is free;

Where the world has not been broken up into fragments by narrow domestic walls;

Where words come out from the depth of truth;

Where tireless striving stretches its arms towards perfection;

Where the clear stream of reason has not lost its way into the dreary desert sand of dead habit;

Where the mind is led forward by thee into ever-widening thought and action—

Into that heaven of freedom, my Father, let . . . [me] awake.

An eminent analyst has said: "I have learned in forecasting economic futures that what is going to happen is already happening." It is so in our lives. It is so everlastingly, and all of us ought to determine our ultimate objectives as early as possible and then faithfully pursue them. Life is not limitless here. Time soon passes. Every man takes himself and what he is with him wherever he goes, and he takes himself also into eternity.

What do we have to lose by indifference, by neglect? We have nothing to lose—except everything, and, conversely, we have nothing to gain—except everything.

In the words of Archibald Rutledge: "I am absolutely unshaken in my faith that God created us, loves us, and wants us not only to be good, but to be happy." No man can be indifferent to the issues of life and death. These are uppermost at one time or another in the minds of all of us.

With some awareness of the responsibility of doing so, with myself, my family, and to all men, I would bear witness of the truth of these things, of the everlasting importance of them, of the obligation that all of us have to seek and to search, of the interest that our loving Father who made us in his image has in us, and of the incalculable importance of the gospel he has given us.

How Much Is All This Worth?

As we have listened during these days, there is a question by Daniel Webster that has come to mind, "How much is all this worth?" It is a question that everyone might ask himself.

How much would it be worth to know the purpose of life?

What would it be worth to have an assurance of everlasting life?

What would it be worth to know that we may have life with our loved ones everlastingly?

How much would it be worth to have peace and quietness of conscience?

How much is it worth to be sustained in sorrow, in sickness, to know that the Lord God is aware of us, that he loves us, that we are his children, that he will not leave us alone?

How much is it worth to have a solid, sustaining faith in the future, despite the grievous problems and contentions that are prevalent among mankind?

Think what it would be worth to students, to young people who are torn between conflicting theories and teachings that change from time to time, with the many disagreements there are even among the experts, to be encouraged to search, to seek for truth, to know that the Lord God, whose infinite intelligence embraces the whole universe, is the source of all

Address given at General Conference, April 1965.

truth, and to know that there is no point or purpose in losing faith because of conflicting theories, because time and patience and research and revelation will sometime see them all resolved. After all, eternity is a long time, and there is infinitely much that men do not know. Why be disturbed about the little that we think we know? Many theories once thought to be true have since been set aside, and others will be.

What is it worth to be able to look at all things with patient faith, knowing that all the answers will sometime be in evidence?

What is it worth to have standards, commandments, moral laws, rules of life which are God-given, and by which to judge our choices, our conduct, so as not to be left to the perversions and sophistries of men for such decisions?

How much is it worth to those who are discouraged, to those who have been harshly dealt with, to those for whom life has been hard, to those who don't quite seem to have found their place; to those who have been misjudged, to those who have been deprived of opportunity, to know that God is our Father, that he is mindful of us, that all we cannot understand will sometime be understood; that all injustices will be corrected, that in the ultimate working out of our Father's ways, no one will receive anything he shouldn't, and no one will be deprived of anything he should receive?

As Emerson said in his essay on Compensation, "The world looks like . . . a mathematical equation, which, turn it how you will, balances itself." It is impossible for a person to cheat anyone but himself. It all adds up.

All this and much, much more is encompassed within the gospel of Jesus Christ. And certainly such peace and purpose, such assurance, would be worth the meeting of his requirements, and keeping of his commandments, and should give incentive for living clean and useful and honorable and dedicated lives.

All this should be worth young people's waiting for the proper time and season, waiting for life to unfold, with virtue, with prayerfulness, with respect for principles, with respect for parents, with the keeping of the commandments.

All this should be worth overcoming appetites, refraining from what the Lord has said is not good for man, heeding the simple counsel God has given, which will help us to have health and wisdom and knowledge and physical and spiritual blessings.

Often we rush. We sometimes aspire. We sometimes seek to acquire and accumulate. We live with many problems, with much unrest; we do much running around and take time for lesser things, looking elsewhere for answers, failing to find them.

And with all the many things that men are finding, it would seem that bedrock answers should not be so elusive. Indeed, they are not, but the answers go back to the commandments of God, to the principles given by our Savior, to what has been revealed through the prophets, to that which gives peace and high purpose, and the assurance of everlasting life. And it is worth much to know that there are answers, that to all of the problems and all of the contentions of the world, there are answers. The commandments have not been repealed. God has not changed his mind.

May I share with you one sentence from Carlyle. He said, "Over the times thou hast no power. . . . Solely over one man . . . thou hast a quite absolute . . . power.—Him redeem and make honest."

There are two pertinent lines from the closing of a beautiful song which the Tabernacle Choir sings, "America, the Beautiful": "Confirm thy soul in self-control, Thy liberty in law."

Sooner or later we learn that the commandments are self-enforcing. In all things there are causes and consequences. In all things there are standards, and all that we haven't yet reached or realized we must arrive at by repentance and improvement. There is no way except the Lord's way. As Dr. James W. Clarke expressed it many years ago in a radio sermon quoted by William H. Danforth:

"Christ is the greatest need of the world. Many of us profess to be Christians, yet we must confess that we do not take him seriously. Our surrender is but in part. We salute him, but we don't obey him. We respect him, but we don't follow him. We admire him, but we don't worship him. We quote his sayings, but we don't live by them. . . . There is only one way out for the world—the way of the Man of Galilee."

Jesus asked this of the Nephites, and then answered his own question: "Therefore, what manner of men ought ye to be? Verily I say unto you, even as I am." (3 Nephi 27:27.)

"And, if you keep my commandments," he said elsewhere, "and endure to the end you shall have eternal life, which gift is the greatest of all the gifts of God." (Doctrine and Covenants 14:7.)

How much is all this worth? It cannot be calculated.

"We have nothing to lose—except everything." And nothing to gain except everything—eternal life with our Father and his Son, and with our loved ones with us everlastingly, and peace and purpose and assurance here and now.

Leaving you my witness as to the truth of this work and as to how much all of this is worth, in closing there comes to mind these words from President McKay: "Go home and live your religion. . . . Radiate what you are and all who come under its influence will benefit from it."

May our Father's blessings be with you always.

The Test of Love

One of the most quoted New Testament texts is this from John: "For God so loved the world, that he gave his only begotten Son, that whosoever believeth in him should not perish, but have everlasting life." (John 3:16.)

Address given at General Conference, April 1966.

It is comfortingly familiar—the love of God simply stated —and what he did about his love is the evidence of it: He sent his Only Begotten Son that whoso believeth in him should have everlasting life.

Suppose God had loved the world in a passive way. Suppose he hadn't sent his Son. Suppose he hadn't given us his gospel. Suppose he hadn't set out to save mankind or redeem us from death. Suppose he had let his children drift without plan or purpose or counsel or commandments. Would that have been love? The point I hope to make, for a particular purpose, is the evidence, the proof, the test of love.

An editorial recently read in a medical magazine had an intriguing title: "Love Is a Verb." And from this the writer turned his attention to the importance of doing, of proving, of performing. The proof of any principle is what it does, and the proof of any person is what he does—how he acts, what he becomes—not simply what he says.

"Love Is a Verb."

We might paraphrase and say that service is a verb, that life is a verb; for it is in doing, in living, in learning, and not just in words that we perform our purpose. No one really proves himself or his principles in neutrality or indifference or inaction. No one proves himself by merely thinking or simply sitting.

The writer of the article referred to above said that in some primitive languages, with their fewness of words, the description of the movement of game, for example, is described simply by one word: *running*. Perhaps we could say much more with fewer words by simply indicating the action: *living, doing*. ". . . when a noun replaces a verb there is a disadvantage . . ." because a noun is static, and life is movement. Some people "assign an intrinsic value to 'things' like purity and gratitude. . . . They take credit for possessing nominal virtues. Or they punish themselves for having vices, . . . [but] we communicate with others in verbs. . . . Gratitude has not even been born until it has been actually conveyed in word or deed. . . ."

The same could be said for sanity, said this same physician. It "is not structural but functional. It is not something one has or is. It is a measure of what one does." (William B. McGrath, M.D., in *Medicine at Work,* February 1966.) If we do sane things, we are sane. If we don't do sane things, we are not sane. Actions do speak louder than words.

As to a young person who was speculating upon whether or not she loved someone, there is the reminder that love is not simply a noun and not simply a sentimental feeling. The proof of love is what one is willing to do for the loved one. The proof of love is how one behaves.

Dr. John A. Widtsoe turned his attention to this subject at times: "The full and essential nature of love we may not understand," he said, "but there are tests by which it may be recognized.

"Love is always founded in truth. . . . Lies and deceit, or any other violation of the moral law, are proofs of love's absence. Love perishes in the midst of untruth. . . . Thus, the lover who falsifies to his loved one, or offers her any act contrary to truth, does not really love her.

"Further, love does not offend or hurt or injure the loved one. By that test any human venture, past and present, may be measured for its real value. Cruelty is as absent from love . . . as truth is from untruth.

". . . love is a positive active force. It helps the loved one. If there is need, love tries to supply it. If there is weakness, love supplants it with strength. . . . Love that does not help is a faked or transient love.

"Good as these tests are, there is a greater one. True love sacrifices for the loved one. . . . That is the final test. Christ gave of himself, gave his life, for us, and thereby proclaimed the reality of his love for his mortal brethren and sisters. The mother gives of her own flesh and blood, and jeopardizes her very life, for her child. In family relationships, there must be mutual sacrifices among husband, wife, and children, else true love is not there." (John A. Widtsoe, *An Understandable Religion,* ch. 8.)

Thus, anyone who would induce someone to do that which it is unworthy to do, or to take advantage, or rob someone of virtue, or embarrass, or hurt, really doesn't love the person he professes to love. What he feels under such circumstances is something less than love. The proving is in the doing.

And so it is with all the virtues. Either we live pure lives or we don't. Either we think pure thoughts or we don't. Purity isn't simply a noun. It is a verb. It is the living of a certain kind of life. It is the thinking of certain kinds of thoughts. Its proof is in keeping the commandments.

Goodness is not theory, it is fact. We may think of tithing as a principle and discuss it and approve it, but if we are really convinced and converted, we will pay our tithing.

We may think well of the missionary system, but it works only because some leave home and sacrifice and serve sincerely — not merely because it is a good organization or idea.

We may think and talk of chastity as a virtue, but if we are converted and convinced, we will live chaste lives.

If we love our children we won't neglect them or let them run loose. If we love our children we won't leave them ignorant of the law, or of the commandments, or ignorant of how to behave, or unacquainted with sound habits of work, or ignorant of courtesy and acceptable conduct.

If we love our children we will urge them to prepare as fully as they can for life, persuade them to acquire all the training and education possible. If we love our children we will keep as close to them as possible and do our utmost to keep them free from sin and from anything that would clutter or scar their lives.

As parents there is no greater obligation that is ours—and neglect is not the evidence of love. Part of love is doing our duty in love and loyalty, "by persuasion, by long-suffering, by gentleness and meekness, and by love unfeigned; By kindness, and pure knowledge. . . ." (Doctrine and Covenants 121:41, 42.)

Jesus said: ". . . lovest thou me? . . . Feed my sheep." (John 21:16.) Elsewhere it is written: "If ye love me, keep my commandments." (John 14:15.)

Abstract qualities of character don't mean much in the abstract. It is how we live, how we serve, how we teach our children, what we do from day to day that both indicate what we are and determine what we are; and all the theory and all the speculation, all the quoting of scripture, all the searching of the mysteries, and all the splitting of hairs, and all the knowledge of the letter of the law don't in the final and saving sense amount to very much unless we live the gospel, unless we keep the commandments, unless we prove the principles, unless we live lives of effectiveness, sincerity, and service.

Sometimes we hear someone say, "My life is my own. I am going to do with it as I please." But no one's life is his own. Too much of others has gone into the making of all of us.

We cannot hurt ourselves without hurting others. A sorrow, an illness, a disgrace, an accident, trouble, or difficulty of any kind—any loss to loved ones is a loss to family and friends. We are too much a part of one another for this not to be so.

If we love our parents, wouldn't the evidence of it be to do something about it: to be grateful, to help to care for them in their need, to honor them by being honorable, to take them into our confidence—not to worry them? The best evidence of love for parents would be active evidence of kindness, consideration, appreciation, respect for their teachings and counsel.

The best evidence of love of country would be not what we say—or say we feel—but serving it, keeping the laws, preserving its principles.

The best evidence of love for our Father in heaven would be living lives of honor and reverence; not taking his name in vain; living useful, righteous lives; and keeping his commandments.

As to those who say they love the Church—the best evidence of that love would be serving, doing, giving of ourselves, living its standards, keeping the commandments. God help us to be members not of record only, but members who place doing and serving and living the requirements of the gospel above our comfort or convenience.

"Not every one that saith unto me, Lord, Lord, shall enter into the kingdom of heaven; but he that doeth the will of my Father which is in heaven." (Matthew 7:21.) It is important to believe; it is important to be; but it is also important to do. Even the devil believes. (See James 2:19.) "Conviction is worthless unless it is converted into conduct." (Thomas Carlyle.)

Thank God for the gospel, for the personal and literal reality of him who made us in his own image, for his Son our Savior, and for the blessed plan of everlasting life with our loved ones.

Thank God for his patience, for his understanding, for his comfort, for his commandments; for it would be a disillusioning life to be running loose without knowing what was expected of us—or why. Thank God that he sent his Only Begotten Son to show us the way, to redeem us from death, to lead us to everlasting life.

With you I offer gratitude and a pledge to do my best to demonstrate love for our Lord and Savior and his Father who gave us life by living the kind of lives that they would have us live, and leave my witness with you of the truth of that which gathers us here together, in the name of our Lord and Savior, Jesus Christ. Amen.

"If a Thing Is Right . . ."

We come back from having been on every continent and more than fifty countries, with gratitude for our fellowship with you and for the happiness of homecoming, which is one

Address given at General Conference, April 1967.

of the greatest blessings on earth. If the welcome in heaven is as happy as the welcome at home, it will be well worth all the doing and enduring, and well worth waiting for.

If we were to focus on this—a happy homecoming, here and hereafter—we wouldn't go far wrong in this world. May we live to be comfortable in the presence of our Father, with the assurance of a happy homecoming, and reunion with our loved ones everlasting.

We have met world-wide many wonderful people, many in positions of high public responsibility—heads of countries and communities, men of business and professional competence, men who make decisions and who do much to shape the future and much to run the world. Generally, we have felt their earnest sincerity as they carry a heavy complexity of problems. And often this thought has come: Without a source of guidance and inspiration and direction outside themselves, men of themselves, however earnest and able, are not equal to the problems and complexities of the day in which we live.

We have met no infallible men, no indestructible men— just men mostly honest and able, trying to do their best. And we have come to a deeper awareness than ever before of the need for divine guidance, for inspiration, for revelation, thanking God more fervently for a prophet to guide us in these latter days. We come with a greater awareness that without such guidance there are no adequate answers. Never in the past did we need revelation, inspiration, commandments, standards, principles, and a prophet more than in the present.

With the charge and admonition and appeal we have heard from President McKay, may we turn our hearts, young and old—indeed, all of us—to live and keep the counsels of God, to live and keep the commandments. In any other way of life there is frustration and sorrow and an empty rationalizing uneasiness within that never rests and never seems to satisfy. In answer to the question, "Shouldn't the commandments be rewritten?" someone thoughtfully replied, "No, they should be reread." This is true of things physical and temporal, as well as things spiritual and eternal. We need to look closely to the counsel and commandments God has given.

It isn't unusual—indeed, it is expected—that the maker of any machine should send a set of instructions on how best to use it, how best to care for it; and this our Father in heaven has done for us, mentally, morally, physically, spiritually. In the gospel are instructions from our Maker on how to care for and keep ourselves at our best for the purpose for which we were brought into being.

As to the physical side: More than a century ago, a prophet of God simply said that some things are not good for man. Now, knowledgeable and intelligent men of science and medicine also say so. But we had just as well have saved all the time and trouble, for the Maker knew it and said it to his servant. And what could be more important than a completeness of health and happiness—happiness and health of the spirit, the body, and the mind of man.

Some say there is no moral question on how we physically live our lives. But isn't it a moral question to abuse what God has given? And what a waste to abuse any useful creation of any kind. If someone were to give us a finely working watch, wouldn't it be foolish, indeed irrational, to put into it that which would corrode and defeat its purpose?

We have only one body. It is irreplaceable, indispensable, sacred. It has to last a mortal lifetime. With it, and the spirit within, we think, we plan, we work, we feel, we live our mortal lives. It is a miracle and most amazing: the housing for the spirit, the mind, the intelligence of man; the instrument through which we think and plan and pursue life's purpose.

Don't dissipate it; don't impair any part of it. Keep it clean and functioning. Don't quibble about words, about what is counsel and what is commandment. Don't rationalize. Don't clutter life with what is sure to distress and embarrass and lose peace and cause problems. Find what is good, and do it. Find what isn't good, and leave it alone.

If I may cite a phrase: "If a thing is right, it can be done. If wrong, it can be done without."

Don't let the temptations, the false advertising, the false appeals, the false endorsements, the glamorizing of evil, the cynicism and sophistry of those who would pull man down to the lower levels of life—don't let these impair health and peace and happiness and the everlasting possibilities of life. "If a thing is right, it can be done. If wrong, it can be done without." Basically, it is just this simple.

And don't expect life to be easy. It never was for anyone, and never was intended to be, so far as I know. On this point I quote from President McKay: "I am grateful for membership in a Church whose religion fits men for the struggle with the forces of the world," he said, "and which enables them to survive in this struggle."

Of course there are temptations, problems, things to overcome. Learning is a long and perennial process. The pursuit of excellence requires the best of all our effort. Life is for learning, and the lessons are clearly there to learn. The rules, the basic laws of life, have been given. The choice is ours. There is a law of cause and consequences. We realize the results of the lives we live. And we must live to respect ourselves and others also.

I would cite a sentence from Harold B. Lee: "Oh, God, help me to hold a high opinion of myself." That should be the prayer of every soul: not an abnormally developed self-esteem that becomes haughtiness, conceit, or arrogance, but a righteous self-respect, a belief in one's own worth, worth to God and worth to man.

Sometimes we may feel that it is easier for others than it is for us. But we all have our struggles. We all have our problems. We all have things to overcome, decisions to make, need for self-control.

Many years ago Phillips Brooks said: "But . . . some men live strongly and purely in this world, you say, and then go safely and serenely up to heaven . . . [men] who never know what struggle is. What shall we say of them? . . . you may search all the ages. . . . You may go through the crowded streets of heaven, asking each saint how he came there, and you will look in vain everywhere for a man morally and spiritually strong, whose strength did not come to him in struggle. Will you take the man who never had a disappointment, who never knew a want . . . ? Do you suppose that [any] man has never wrestled with his own success and happiness . . . ?" There are no such.

Blessedly, as we engage, each of us, in this struggle, we have the principles and the purposes. God help us to live by them, to live what we teach, for our own sake as well as for the sake of others.

There is no place, no people anywhere on earth, that would not be benefitted and blessed by the gospel of Jesus Christ. And ours is the opportunity and obligation of example, of sharing it with others. How can we be a light unto men if we don't live according to the light that God has given?

May I say, before concluding, how grateful I am for those who gave us this Tabernacle, with its organ, its traditions, and all that pertains to Temple Square, this year being the hundredth anniversary of this great building, at which thoughtful men the world over have marveled. It has been my privilege to spend much of my life here, for thirty-eight years, at every hour of the day and night, at every season, meeting visitors who have come from world-wide, and reaching out world-wide by radio and television through the facilities God has given.

We have performed in many of the great concert halls of Europe and America, and have talked in many auditoriums around the world, and find nothing to exceed this building in uniqueness of structure, in remarkable versatility, in its most pleasing and responsive acoustic qualities, in its simplicity and beauty and spirit. There have been some who would change it, some who have thought to "improve" it, so they say, even as to some of its basic essentials; but it satisfies my soul, and I thank God for the minds that conceived it, for the inspiration given them to do so, for the hands that fashioned it in their poverty and loving care and skill and devotion.

Many of the great artists and engineers and architects of the earth have commented on it. I give you one from Eugene Ormandy, director of the Philadelphia Orchestra. "We have, as you probably know," said Mr. Ormandy, "performed in almost every great hall in the world, but we have found no better hall anywhere than the Tabernacle. Its acoustics are superb, and I only hope that no human hands will alter them in trying to make improvements. It is as near perfect now as any hall can be, and it is a joy to perform in it for your wonderful audiences."

This is typical of many, many more, and I hope we may always preserve it in its simple and basic qualities and character.

With you I thank my Father in heaven for the heritage from our fathers, for the restoration of the gospel, for a prophet to guide us in these latter days, for devoted parents, for wholesome homes, for faithful young people, for our opportunities, for the beauty of the earth, for the commandment to subdue it. May we also subdue and control ourselves and realize the highest possibilities of life, physically, spiritually, mentally, and morally, in a completeness of the greatest possible attainments, now and always and forever.

God bless President McKay and these my brethren, and all of you, and your families, and our beloved friends, worldwide, that the spirit of truth may move upon us all and bring us closer together in a oneness of the gospel of Jesus Christ, and in the brotherhood of mankind.

And may we remember how many there are yearning in their hearts for what we have or could hold in our hands, and never turn away from our opportunities for education, for preparation, for improvement; never turn away from respecting life, respecting ourselves, our bodies, our minds, our spirits, our eternal opportunities—remembering that "if a thing is right, it can be done. If it is wrong, it can be done without."

I bear you my witness of the personal reality of God, our Father, of the divinity of his Son, our Savior, and the divine calling and authority and inspiration and prophetic office of

President McKay, and his predecessors. May the Lord bless our President and strengthen and sustain him, and each of us in our homes, in our counsels with our families, in our private and public performance; and lead us to know the truth, to live it; and help us in the struggle to become strong and improve and repent and refine ourselves so that we may face our Father and his Son, our Savior, straightforwardly when the summons comes to each of us as we must leave this life, so that we will be comfortable where they are.

God help us to live so as to have a happy homecoming always—here and hereafter.

Where Are You Really Going?

My beloved brethren and sisters—everywhere:

Some weeks ago some of us were considering what would attract the attention of people as they passed through a busy airport—moving to and from many places, intent on many purposes. The often-quoted questions came to mind: Where did we come from? Why are we here? Where are we going?— but a variation of one of these suggested itself: Where are you *really* going? And to this we might have added: What do you *really* want?

We use much of our time in rushing around, not thinking always what we ought to be, nor what it is that matters most. Sometimes we set our hearts on things we feel we have to have, and when we get them find they don't mean as much as once we thought they would.

And so the years move by—and even while yet young we become aware that we are older than we were.

Soberingly, more than one-fourth of this year already has passed partly in pursuit perhaps of things that don't matter

Address given at General Conference, April 1971.

very much—which reminds us of a dream that John Ruskin said he had:

"I dreamed," he said, "that I was at a child's . . . party, in which every means of entertainment had been provided . . . by a wise and kind host. . . . The children had been set free in the rooms and gardens, with no care whatever but how to pass the afternoon rejoicingly. . . . There was music . . . all manner of amusing books . . . a workshop . . . a table loaded with everything nice to eat . . . and whatever a child could fancy . . . but in the midst of all this it struck two or three of the more 'practical' children that they would like some of the brass-headed nails that studded the chairs, and so they set to work to pull them out. In a little while all the children, nearly, were spraining their fingers in pulling out brass-headed nails. With all that they could pull out they were not satisfied, and then everybody wanted some of somebody else's. And at last the really 'practical' and 'sensible' ones declared that nothing was of any real consequence that afternoon except to get plenty of brass-headed nails. . . . And at last they began to fight for nail heads, . . . *even though they knew they would not be allowed to carry so much as one brass knob away with them.* But no! it was 'Who has most nails? . . . I must have as many as you before I leave the house or I cannot possibly go home in peace.' At last they made so much noise that I awoke, and thought to myself, 'What a false dream that is of *children.* . . . Children never do such foolish things. Only men do.' "[3]

Well, I haven't dreamed a dream as Ruskin said he did, but countless times I have searched and prayed and thought this through.

Beloved young friends, beloved older friends, where are you *really* going? What do you *really* want?

Some months ago I spoke at the funeral service of a beloved old friend. He had, I would suppose, little of the *things* of this life, but I heard his grandson say, "Once a week Grandfather was with *all* his family—grandchildren and all.

---

[3]John Ruskin, "Little Brass Nails."

He taught the gospel to them. He was never negative. He always expressed faith and encouragement. There was no 'generation gap.' "

And I thought how blessed and satisfied I would feel if a grandson of mine could sincerely say this of me when this life runs out its short, uncertain length.

I thought of places where we've been, world-wide, where hundreds of millions have never had the privilege of learning to read and write. And then I thought of other places where young people drop out and ignore their opportunities. In a world that more and more demands training and competence and skill, where do they *really* think they are going?

My beloved young friends, *every* day is part of eternity. What happens here and now is forever important.

And I would plead with you, wherever you are, to prepare yourselves for opportunities that await you here and now, as well as for a future that is forever. "What is opportunity," asked George Eliot, "to the man who can't use it."[4]

The laws of nature, the laws of God, the laws of life, are one and the same and are always in full force. We live in a universe of law. Spring follows winter. This we can count on. The sun will show itself on time again tomorrow morning. This we can count on.

And the moral laws and spiritual laws are also in full force. This also we can count on. All of us will realize the results of how we live our lives. And don't let anyone say that mere men have the right or power to repeal God's commandments or ever set them aside—commandments that are so practical and essential, a part of life, dealing as they do with health and happiness and peace, with honesty and morality and cleanliness, and excellence, and all else that pertains to life.

If someone tells you, my beloved young friends, that you can set the commandments of God aside without realizing the results—if someone tells you *that*, then you may know that you

[4]Georgie Eliot, *Scenes from Clerical Life: Amos Barton.*

are listening to someone who doesn't know, or isn't telling you the truth.

These minds, these bodies God has given, with their wondrous physical functioning, must last a mortal lifetime— and to impair or dull the senses, or damage their physical functioning, or abuse or fail to care for them—to indulge in body-destroying, mind-dulling, spirit-blighting substances is a foolish, wicked *un*wisdom. Whatever is not good for man should not be used by man—or done by man.

But it isn't only physical punishment that comes from departing from the laws of life, but also mental and spiritual punishment, and the anguish of the soul inside. As Juvenal said: "The worst punishment of all is that in the court of his own conscience no guilty man is acquitted."[5]

Well, we ought to live as we ought to live, not only because it would please God, not only because it would please our parents, but as a favor for ourselves—for every commandment, every requirement God has given is for *our* happiness, for *our* health, and for *our* peace and progress. O my beloved young friends, even selfishly it is smart to keep the commandments God has given.

Now along with the physical side there must be concern also with pollution of the mind and soul—concern for the purveyors and exploiters of pornography, those who for profit or for other purposes would fill people's minds with vile, debasing pictures and impressions in print.

O surely we should use such means as are available to roll back such evil—an evil that will never put limits on itself, but will become ever more pervasive and sinister as long as we let it.

We have an obligation to safeguard children in their innocence and honesty. And besides the rising cry to clean up physical pollution, let there be like concern to clean up pollution of mind and manners and morals. Our concern for physical pollution is surely not more urgent than our concern for the pollution of the minds and souls of men.

---

[5] Juvenal, *Satires,* xiii.

Now, as we go along in life, two things should surely be considered: the power of prevention and the power of repentance.

Why run against the laws of life? Why run headlong into ill health and unhappiness? Why live contrary to conscience? Think of the heartbreak and waste and regret that could be prevented by living as we ought to live. No one can set aside consequences. As Cecil B. DeMille said: "We cannot break the . . . Commandments. We can only break ourselves against them."[6] O let us think and live and teach the power of prevention. "If it is not right," said Marcus Aurelius, "do *not* do it; if it is not true, do *not* say it."[7]

But wherein we may have failed in this (and heaven help us not to fail), then let us turn with all our hearts to the power of repentance.

The heavy weight of wrongdoing is too big a burden. I have heard President Lee say that the heaviest burden in all the world is the burden of sin. It isn't a happy sight to see those—young or old—in the anguish of carrying that weight around, wishing to heaven they had done differently.

But thanks be to God for the principle of repentance, for a Father who understands us and who has assured us he will accept our repentance so long as it is sincere. This he has said:

"By this ye may know if a man repenteth of his sins— behold, he will confess them *and forsake them.*"

". . . he who has repented of his sins, the same is forgiven, and I, the Lord remember them no more." (Doctrine and Covenants 58:43, 42. Italics added.)

This you can count on. O turn from those ways which will take you where no one really wants to go. Turn to that which will bring you peace and self-respect and cleanliness and a quiet conscience.

I don't presume to know the timetable of our Father's plans and purposes, but I do know that with each of us the

---

[6]Cecil B. DeMille, Brigham Young University Commencement Address, 1957.
[7]Marcus Aurelius, *Meditations,* Book xii, sec. 17, line 68.

time to turn and begin to go where we ought to go is not later than now.

Where are we *really* going? As we come again to the season that celebrates the coming forth of our living Lord and Savior, we would well remember the divine plan and purpose that in due tme would take us from this swift passing life to a real and personal everlastingness of life, with limitless eternal possibilities, and with our loved ones with us, always, and forever. This is our Father's plan and purpose. This is why it really matters where we're going and why we need his gospel to tell us how to get there.

Thank God for his revelations to his prophets, past and present, and for not leaving us alone. He has told us more than we have ever lived up to, and he will tell us more as we serve him and keep his commandments.

I leave you, my beloved friends everywhere, my witness that God does live, that same God and Father who made us in his own image; that he sent his divine Son, our Savior, to show us the way of life and redeem us from death; that the heavens have been opened and the fulness of the gospel brought again, to save and exalt us all, if we are willing, which is God's purpose: to bring our immortality and eternal life to pass.

I know that my Redeemer lives, and pray his peace and blessings upon all men everywhere, in the name of our Lord and Savior, Jesus the Christ. Amen.

THE MESSAGE

A Rotarian Speaks

If I Were Seventeen

If I were seventeen, or even if I had reached the ripe old age of eighteen or nineteen I would remember that in the matter of preparing for life, delays are seldom profitable. I would make a determined and unceasing effort to acquire whatever training I should need for my life's work without any delay of time and with all speed consistent with my means and opportunities.

Youth is the season for preparation. Maturity is the season for performance. And many of the unsuccessful and disappointed men of our day are men who have lived unseasonable lives. They have let spring pass by without using the season for its intended purpose, and then, realizing too late the error of neglect, they have tried to do spring's work in summer and summer's works in autumn, and winter has found them with no harvest. By youth may it be remembered that there are none so hopelessly handicapped as they who have let pass by this time for preparation and who go forth to live their lives out of season.

Soon we will realize that the world is no longer waiting for us to prepare for life. It is waiting for us to live it— to face its realities, to solve its problems, to improve its conditions, and to do for the next generation what has been done for us. To youth looking forward, life seems abundantly long, but to age looking back life seems all too short for the realization of things hoped for, for the accomplishment of things desired.

High school commencement address given at Weiser, Idaho, May 1939.

And that is why I say if I were seventeen I would get life's preparation behind me, whether I were destined to be a doctor, a farmer, a carpenter, or whatever occupation fell to my lot. There is no reason to suppose that the future by some stroke of magic will change essentially from the present, and there is no reason to suppose that while I am now free and unattached and relatively without responsibility that two years or five years from now—when the years have increased upon my head and the burdens have increased upon my back —I shall be better able to prepare for life than I now am.

So much for early preparation. And that brings me to another point, vital and fundamental. If I were seventeen I would not attempt to become something other than that for which I was best adapted. I would not strive to enter a profession in which I was sure to become a misfit. I would not grieve because of talents I did not possess and I would be grateful for those that I did possess and make the most of them. I would have the highest regard for physical labor and deep respect for the man who can do things as well as the man who can think things and plan things.

Our Father who is in heaven did not see fit to distribute the same talents to all men—fortunately for the world in which we live. Some can thrill millions with their voices; some can make the ground to yield abundantly the good things of earth; and some can fashion things of usefulness with the dexterity of their hands. And if I were seventeen I would look at myself honestly and attempt in all sincerity to find out that for which I was best suited. And I would value the skill of those who can create useful things with their hands as much as those who can speak lovely words with their tongues or think great thoughts with their minds. If I could fashion a house out of wood or stone I would attempt to build a better house. If I could move earth in the building of a road or in the making of a dam or in the landscaping of a park I would give the best thought and energy I had to that task.

If I were seventeen I would make up my mind to work

hard and unceasingly for everything that I expected life to give me, and I would not place my confidence in any system or organization or philosophy or individual that offered me something for nothing, because I would know that such is not the way of life and that anything I get for nothing now, either I or my children or my neighbors will have to pay for later. Since the Lord told Adam and Eve that they should eat their bread in the sweat of their brow, someone in the world has had to pay for everything that the world has gotten. And I am sure we want to do our share, for we have no appetite for the bread that other men have earned.

When the Lord said, "Six days shalt thou labor," he meant that men *should* labor. If I were seventeen I would remember that lesson well and I would never envy the idleness of anyone, whether it were in luxury or in poverty.

There is another commandment that the Lord gave that I would remember if I were seventeen—and from then on as long as life should last: "Thou shalt not covet." If my neighbor enjoys greater prosperity than I enjoy, if he seems to live a better life than I live, I may desire such things as he has and by my own energy seek to acquire a similar way of life, but I pray God none of us shall ever acquire the things our neighbor has by taking them from him. If each man in the world today, including individuals and nations, societies and groups, could remember what is mine and what is thine, most of the stresses we are undergoing would be relieved.

That there are social differences, we recognize. They make some of us unhappy at seventeen. They still make some of us unhappy at seventy. But they have always been and always shall be and there is no permanent leveling process. The elimination of social privileges was one thing that the Russian revolution attempted to do at the cost of millions of lives—but I read in a recent press dispatch from Russia that a new privileged class has arisen in the Soviet Union and in another generation or two the differences will probably be as great as they ever were. Men were created equal in their right to worship, equal in their rights before law—but men are different and always have been and always will be and no one will ever mold them into the same pattern.

If I were seventeen I would remember that all of the evils of the day have their root in disregard for law—disregard for the laws of men and of God—and if I should see someone gaining the material advantages of life by taking some unjustifiable short cut I would remember what the writer of the Psalms said many centuries ago, "The Lord knoweth the days of the upright: and their inheritance shall be forever. They shall not be ashamed in the evil times; and in the day of famine they shall be satisfied.

"I have seen the wicked in great power, and spreading himself like a green bay tree. Yet he passed away, and lo, he was not; yea, I sought him but he could not be found. Mark the perfect man, and behold the upright: for the end of that man is peace."

If I were seventeen I think I should try all the days of my life to remember that things—mere material things—are not nearly so important as they sometimes seem to be in our lives. Things are not as important as ideals, as principles, as character, as moral cleanliness, as faith, as happiness, as integrity. And in and of themselves, things are neither good nor bad. It is only men's use of them that makes them good or bad.

The airplane that keeps me in daily touch with my business associates in New York or Chicago is destroying life on other shores. The automobile which brings the doctor into my home quickly on a lifesaving mission, in the hands of a drunken or reckless driver may take a life. The water that helps me to mature my crops, when out of control becomes a ravaging flood. The money I accumulate for my own security and that of my family may teach them ways of indolence and may cause them to quarrel when I have passed beyond. The radio that brings me the world's finest entertainment and news may also bring into my home a message encouraging my children to bad habits or wrong thoughts by the use of those things that are not good for man. You see, material things are not nearly so important as they seem to be. It is only the use men make of them that makes them good or bad.

And in most cases it is only a comparison with what my neighbor has—the element of envy—that makes me want things that I cannot afford. I am content to drive a five-year-old car unless my neighbor has a new car this year. I am content to wear a four-year-old overcoat unless my neighbor has a new overcoat.

Fashion is a tyrant also. In some places it isn't enough to have good clothes. A person must have fashionable clothes or be a social outcast. That is one of the cruelest practices of society. If I were seventeen I would try not to let it make me unhappy because it isn't worth it.

If I were seventeen, I would remember that the kind of popularity that depends for its existence upon the sacrificing of ideals and principles never was and never will be worth the price that anyone ever paid for it. No one who sacrifices his own convictions for the superficial good opinions of others can ever hope to enjoy permanent respect or esteem.

I would not be afraid to be different if I were seventeen. I would remember that the most enviable grace, the most admirable poise, the most lovable ease of manner, and the most engaging attractiveness belong to those who, with sincere dignity and tolerant conviction, are true to their ideals on all occasions.

If I were seventeen I would try to remember that not everything that is written is truth merely because we see it in print. Not everything that is spoken is truth merely because we hear it said. Not everything that appears in books is truth simply because we find it between bound covers. Men write books, and men are not infallible. I would try to remember that the world is full of propaganda—of doctrines that are preached for selfish interest regardless of their truth or falsity. I would try to remember that one mark of an educated man—whether he is educated in school or out of school—is his ability to sit down calmly and think things through without being swayed by noisy oratory or subtle propaganda.

I would try to remember that not everything that is new is good merely because it is new. And I would try to remember that not everything that is old is outworn merely because it is old. I would try to remember that truth is truth, whether it is new or old, and I would try to cling fervently to all that is truth in the old and all that is truth in the new, and discard all else.

I would try to remember that the teachings of men change from year to year and that the teachings of our schools do also. I would try to remember that in most cases a textbook that is ten years old is outdated and has outlived its usefulness and that ten years from now my own textbooks will likewise be considered as belonging to another day. With this in mind I would try to determine what is constant in life and what is variable—and value them accordingly.

There is one other thing I would try to remember if I were seventeen—that the world has a place for me if I have something to give it. I would try to remember that there is as much work in the world to be done as there ever was; that there are as many unsatisfied wants—as many unfulfilled needs—and that which is as yet undiscovered is without limit. If there be those for whom gainful employment cannot be found, it is not because there is no work to be done—but because there is some breakdown somewhere along the line of human relationships. I would remember that there is dire need for men who will accept a trust and keep it; for men in whom are found intelligence and integrity; for men who will accept responsibility; for men who know how to serve with loyalty and remember what belongs to them and what belongs to others, and who are willing to give a day's work for a day's wage, and who know that the world owes them nothing except as they earn it.

I would remember if I were seventeen that there will never come a time when there are no more goals to reach, no more aims to achieve, and no more worlds to conquer—that there will never be a time here or hereafter when there is no more work to do.

If I were seventeen I would remember that youth, moving into the waiting future, must see the power within himself and create opportunities even as did his fathers. I would determine to be the maker of conditions and not the victim of them, and I would carve a place for myself in this world just as those who have lived in all the generations past have made their own opportunities, their own successes, and their own lives.

I would try to remember to be thankful for what I have and to strive for what I have not. I would try to know the zest for work without making gain my god; I would try to know the worthwhile contributions of the past without becoming enslaved to error, custom, and tradition; I would try to know the joy of companionship without fearing solitude; I would try to know the destiny of man and the purposes of God without becoming too self-righteous and too far removed from the world; I would try to have courage in the affairs of men, and humility before the things of God. I would never lose hope in myself, confidence in my country, or faith in the ultimate triumph of all good things.

These things I would do if I were seventeen, and I would continue to do them until I was called back to that eternal home from which I came—where all men shall one day go to answer for the manner of their living.

We have named a lot of things to remember for one who is seventeen. But it's not so difficult as it sounds. It simply means living each day as it comes with the best that we have in us, determining to make the right choices, determining to earn our own way, determining to be worthy of our parents, our opportunities and our Eternal Father.

We shall never be together again just as we are here tonight. We have spent happy years together. We have walked these halls and sat in these classrooms of our beloved school. We have formed friendships for our fellow students, and affections for teachers. We have gained many facts of knowledge. We have acquired ambitions. We have made plans. During the years that lie ahead life will end early for some of us, and others of us will go on to old age to see many things come to pass. Some of us will find the way difficult so far as the material things are concerned, and some of us will achieve financial success and professional eminence. It has always been thus and always will be. Some of us will make our homes and rear our children and some of us will not.

Some of us will render great service and some of us will accumulate much personal gain. But as life moves on toward its days of closing and as the ultimate destination of all men faces us, these things of a material nature will fade in their importance and the Judge of all of us will ask, "What did you do with what you had?"

A prophet going to his martyrdom said, "If my life is of no value to my friends it is of no value to me." No man who lives unto himself has lived. I think that is the final thought I would leave, and the thing I would try to remember if I were seventeen—if my life is of no value to my friends it is of no value to me.

May we go forth from here, from within these cherished walls, these pleasant associations, these happy days of our youth. May we go forth to live our lives in season—well and valiantly—and may God bless us every one.

Faith and Repentance

I should like to talk for a few moments about two basic principles: faith and repentance. We won't go past repentance tonight. We'll save the other principles for some later session. The fact that you are here is an evidence of your faith. We'll try not to make you repent too much because of your coming.

I am well aware that better men than I have been stoned and generally resented for crying repentance, or even speaking

Address given at Rotary District Conference, Salt Lake City, Utah, February 1953.

of it; but, as I am including myself as having need of it, and
if I reprove myself with you, perhaps you will be more indul-
gent with me.

Suppose we start with the Rotary phrase, *Service Above
Self,* which is certainly proper to introduce on this occasion.
It is a great statement with great implications. Sometimes it
is accepted too thoughtlessly. I think sometimes we mistake
the mechanics of what we do, and mere mechanical organization, for the real accomplishment. As Rotarians, as well as
citizens of this world, we must guard against assuming that
we have done something when we have simply set up the
machinery to do it. We form our organizations; we attend
our meetings; we pay our dues; we declare what needs to be
done—but beyond all this a man must put himself into actual
service in a very real way, or it is as "sounding brass." There
are some things we can't buy. There are some things in which
we can't simply give money as a substitute for personal service.
So I think perhaps we should repent of going through too
many mechanics, and assuming that we have done the job
when we have simply been through the motions—when we
have paid the dues, attended the meetings, set up committees,
and repeated the mottoes and the phrases. The gift without
the giver is a very empty and hollow thing. Service must be
an experience in the giving of oneself as well as of material
things. It is a sharing experience, or it misses much of what
it might hold for all of us, and much of the result that is
hoped for it.

I think we should repent also of judging and misjudging
men too freely. I am very grateful that the ultimate job of
judging man is preserved to a wisdom and intelligence—a
power which is beyond ours. Knowing how quick I am to
judge and misjudge; knowing how embarrassingly wrong
I have proved myself to be on so many occasions and with
so many people, I think the quick judgment and the imputing
of motives to men—assuming that we know what is in their
hearts and what moves them to do what they do, and presuming to pass judgment upon them—is one of the errors

that most of us often commit and have great need to repent of. I say most sincerely: the longer I live, the less I want to judge men, the less I feel disposed to judge them, and the more thankful I am that I don't have to judge, ultimately or now.

There is so much that we have in common, there is so much that we can find in the hearts and souls of all other men that is good, and I submit to you that the only way to lead a man is to lead him from where he is. We have to find some common ground with him first. And we can't do that by presuming a superior attitude or presuming to prejudge him. Furthermore, we can't lead where we aren't going. We can't take anyone with us where we aren't going. Again, our motives, our declared intentions as Rotarians, must be demonstrated as an evidence of our sincerity, and by an example that will become contagious.

We know so much better than we do. And the reason we get into trouble, most of us, is not because we don't know, but because we don't live as well as we know. Our knowledge in this world is far beyond what our conduct gives evidence of. I quote Eugene O'Neill, but I have to edit him a bit before I quote him, and any of you who know the quote in the original will recognize the editing. He uses some expletives which I shall not attempt.

"If the human race is so . . . stupid that in two thousand years . . . it hasn't had brains enough to appreciate the secret of happiness contained in one simple sentence that you'd think any grammar school kid could understand—then it's time we . . . moved over and let the ants have a chance. That sentence is the Golden Rule."

We *know* much better than we *do*. We have the laws, the commandments, the rules of life. We often ignore them, but it is wonderful that we go along as well as we do, and enjoy one another as we do, and serve one another as we do.

We should repent from letting doubts dominate our thinking—not wholesome doubts (doubt is an invitation to learning)—but doubts that make us fear to attempt. As Shakespeare said: "Our doubts are traitors and make us lose the good we oft might win, by fearing to attempt." We often take more time to explain to ourselves why we can't do some things than it would take to do them. In fifteen minutes a day we can do a great number of things in a year's time— while we're waiting for some other things, while we're arguing with ourselves about some things. I don't have the figures before me, but I went through some calculations at one time, and I think that I arrived at the conclusion that you could read all the plays of Shakespeare through once in a year in fifteen minutes a day, the Bible twice through or maybe more in fifteen minutes a day.

There are many basic college courses that require less than the total number of hours which fifteen minutes a day add up to in a year's time. I suggest to all of us that we repent of thinking we don't have time to do some of the things we ought to be doing.

As another commonplace thing, I suggest that we repent of losing our tempers—for our own sakes, as well as for the sake of those around us. There was a well-known physician who knew what he was talking about when he said, "My life is in the hands of any darn fool who makes me lose my temper." He later died of a stroke, brought on by a "darn fool" who made him lose his temper. He *knew* better than he *did!*

I think we should repent of assuming that collectively we know much more than we know. When we think we know too much, it takes from us the spirit of humility—sincere humility—sincere humility before God, and before the great vast infinite unknown. Sometimes when we discover something, we act as if we were the creators of it. We discover a new star, or a new galaxy of stars through a telescope that man has made, or discover a little something about how the universe moves in its majesty, and we sometimes act as if we were on a par with the Creator, or at least one of his first assistants.

There is quite a difference between being the discoverers of truth (laws, scientific facts, or other facts), and in controlling them or presuming that we are the creators of them. We have learned how to split an atom, but we haven't learned how to create a single living cell or a single blade of grass. We have learned how to see stars a billion light years away, but we haven't learned yet what makes a muscle move. Actually, I don't know anyone, medically or otherwise, who can tell how what a man eats can instantaneously (with scarcely a thought, a thought so quick that we are ourselves often unaware of it) become controlled motion. And until we learn how to make a blade of grass, or a single living cell, or what makes a muscle move, I think we have need to walk humbly with our God.

Now may I suggest that we do a bit of self-searching, and read a series of self-searching questions, which some of you have heard, and some of you may not have heard. I wrote them some time ago for another occasion:

"If you were choosing someone to trust, could you trust yourself?

"Would you like to meet yourself when you are in trouble?

"Would you like to be at your own mercy?

"If other men didn't put locks on their homes, and on their barns and on their banks, would you ever walk in where you knew you had no right to walk?

"If there were no accounts, no bonding companies, no courts, no jails, no disgrace, none of the usual fears except your own soul inside of you, would you ever take what you knew you had no right to take?

"Would you serve a man without influence as fairly as you would a man with influence?

"Would you pay a person as fair a price for something he was forced to sell as for something he didn't have to sell?

"Would you honor an unwritten agreement as honestly as if it were written?

"If you found a lost article that no one could possibly know you had found, would you try to return it, or would you put it in your own pocket?

"Would you stay with your principles no matter what price you were proffered for forsaking them?

"Would you compromise on a question of right or wrong?

"Do you talk as well of your friends when they aren't around as when they are?

"If you made a mistake, would you admit it, or would you pretend to be right even when you knew you were wrong?

"Could you be trusted as well away from home as you could where people know you?

"Do you make an earnest effort to improve your performance, or have you been hoping for an undeserved improvement in the pay of your position?

"Do you try to get the job done, or have you been loafing along for fear you were doing too much?

"Would you hire yourself?

"Would you like to work for yourself?

"If you were your own partner, would you trust yourself?

"If your partner were to die, would you treat his family as fairly as if he were alive?

"If he lost his health, would you still deal with him not only justly, but also generously?

"Let's look again—inside out. Would you like to work for yourself? Would you like to live with yourself?

"This is admittedly a severe scorecard, but sometimes it's a good thing to turn ourselves inside out, and look at ourselves as honestly as if we were someone else."

I see in this audience men whom I have learned to love and respect — men of widely different beliefs from mine, of widely different backgrounds and manner of life. I am grateful for what Rotary has done to bring me to an understanding of some of you—and, beyond understanding, to appreciation and affection and sincere respect. It is a glorious association that cuts across the lines of many interests, of many activities, of many convictions. I am grateful for it.

It is a glorious and interesting world we live in, despite all the uncertainties, despite all the discouragements. I am even grateful for uncertainty. It may seem to be a peculiar thing to be grateful for, but I shouldn't want to carry a foreknowledge of the events to come. It would be too ominous a thing to carry on one's shoulders; and I am sure that the plan of the Creator is the wise plan, which lets us live from day to day, enjoying the goodness that comes and meeting the difficulties as they are imposed upon us. I enjoy the fine things that life has to offer, and I have great faith in the future—faith in the final purpose of an Eternal Father who sent us here not to fail, but to succeed, and who will help us to succeed in life and to enjoy all its glorious opportunities and privileges and experiences, if we will give him only half a chance. There are many things we don't know. There are many puzzling things, many unanswered questions. The realm of the unknown is infinite, but we do know enough to live gloriously happy and wonderful lives together in cherished association.

I commend to you that we all cultivate the power to appreciate the present. I know that we all become depressed at times. I suspect you do; I know that I do, and I rather think it is a universal experience. But beyond these periods of discouragement and depression, there are glorious certainties, glorious things to enjoy in this world.

May you go forth from here and into all the days ahead with sweet, satisfying experiences and associations, with wisdom and strength to meet all the problems, all the opportunities, all the disappointments—and may God be with you, this day—and always.

Meaningful Service

All of us know that we have had a most unusual morning and that there has been a meaning in this meeting here, far beyond the mere mechanics and formalities of any such occasion. Yesterday coming in the train from Bombay we had the delightful experience of a visit with Mr. A. D. Shroff, and I can tell you that I go away with a brighter and a deeper understanding of India than I had ever anticipated. In the course of one's lifetime a few people take on a particular and personal meaning, as your District Governor Ebrahim and his wife Shireen have with us. You have in Ebrahim a man of heart and deep inner substance. We all have known the external abilities and talents that he has always displayed, but this deep inner substance of his head and heart has become obvious to us today.

Alice and I have come from a far-off place. We wanted to come to you not as tourists, not as superficial observers, but as individual friends. We have covered India from North to South and from East to West. We have been guests in palaces; we have been guests in mud huts. We have had poor people who could not even afford it offer us their milk and cocoanuts. We go away stirred and moved.

If a man lives seventy years, he has about twenty-five thousand days from the time he is born till he dies. He cannot do everything with them—he has to choose what he does. He can go through life using mere mechanics or he can live his life in meaningful service and contribute to the needs of his generation. He cannot be everything; he cannot join everything; he cannot do everything.

Now you here have chosen to join Rotary. You have chosen to be here today because it means something to you, and the evidence of what it means is what happens—whether we live our lives as worthy and responsible citizens, as dedicated Rotarians—when we go back from here. Now, yesterday

---

Address given at the Rotary District 315 Conference, Poona, India, February 1962.

Alice and I stood in front of the subway exit near the hotel in which we were housed in Bombay on the great circle of streets there, and watched wave after wave of white-clothed humanity emerging from the subway entrance. We felt almost as if the waves of the ocean were moving on us, a small part of the 440 millions of which Mr. Shroff has been speaking, each one to be clothed, fed, taught, cared for, and housed; each one to realize his highest potentialities in life, the mission that all men of goodwill have.

Sometimes men feel that they are trapped in life, and they wonder about the meaning and purpose of it all. I should like to witness to you here today that there is a purpose in it, that it is not just an accident, that there is an intelligent creation and a Creator, that life has a meaning and a purpose for each man, that the great enemies that we all face, besides many others, are those of ignorance and fear, and that our first job is to do what we can to help eradicate these. We need to know more, we need to do more, and we need courage and conviction.

I come from a people and a faith little known to you here, not known at all to many of you. We have a scripture that says, "The glory of God is intelligence," and another says, "It is impossible for a man to be saved in ignorance." Jesus said, "Know the truth and the truth will make you free." Tagore said, "Surrender your pride to truth."

We all go through life making mistakes. We have to be tolerant and considerate and understanding of each other, because we all make our share of mistakes and because life is a search for all of us. We all ought to have humility, because none of us knows all the answers, or indeed in detail any of the ultimate answers, and we have to have a great, deep-seated sincerity. And the evidence of that sincerity is the service that we give. There was a great Rotarian who died some years ago, a French Canadian. He said: "Whenever I am asked to do something by anyone, I ask two questions— If not by me, by whom? [If I do not do it, who is going to? Somebody has to do everything.] If not now, when?"

There is a certain timeliness in life. There is an old Greek proverb which says: "He gives twice who gives quickly." The time to feed a man is when he is hungry; the time to clothe him is when he is naked; the time to nurse him is when he is sick; the time to teach a child is when he is with us and can be taught. If not now, when? Almost anybody will agree to do amost anything, if you do not put a time limit on it. We have four sons. They never refuse to do anything when we ask them, if we do not say when. The minute you say when, you have a problem. Then begins the argument. If not by me, by whom? If I do not do it, who is going to? Somebody has to do it. If not now, when? Life is perishable, and so are all its opportunities.

I should suggest to you one more thing besides the importance of belief and patience, humility, sincerity and service, and that is the importance of hope, and another tied to it— the danger of complacency. People are patient if there is hope; they have not much reason to be patient if they have no hope. As long as they can see a hope for the future, they will endure much. I suggest to you that we renew our dedication this day, our commitment to hold to our hope to the best of our ability, to do something about something even if it be so small and so little.

I will remind you about an old proverb: "A journey of a thousand miles begins with but a single step." Sometimes we give way to slogans and phrases and generalities. I am thinking of the man who said, "I love humanity but I cannot stand people personally." This is sometimes the result of generalizing and not particularizing. It is not enough to love humanity. We have to do something for people personally, as Mr. Shroff has so well said this morning. We must seek to achieve peace in a free world, and we must seek constantly to improve the living standard of all peoples everywhere. As Hendrik Willem van Loon said: "We are all passengers on the same planet and the safety of any of us is the safety of all of us." It is so.

At one of the universities in Dharwar, we talked to some graduate students the other day. One of the professors of

economics there said by way of emphasizing this interdependence of people, "When America sneezes, the rest of the world
gets pneumonia, economically speaking." Though it is an
extreme statement—not literally quite true, there is a basis
of truth in it and it applies not only to nation and nation, but
also to person and person. We have influence—each of us
has more influence than we suppose. We shall be accountable
for what we do with it, and I think we shall also be accountable for what we don't do with it. I appeal to you this morning therefore to exercise your influence judiciously and towards
proper action. Nothing can stay the progress of an ideal, and
though we be few in number, with courage, conviction, and
service, mixing the ideal with the practical, we can do much
more than we sometimes suppose.

Now I should like to share with you just a few quotations
which seem to summarize the things that all of us here since
the beginning of this most meaningful conference have been
trying to say. This comes from Kipling:

> . . . The best thing, I suppose,
> That one can do for his land
> Is a thing that lies under his nose,
> With the tools that lie under his hand.

A contemporary American said, "The history of our time
will be written by what happens in the everyday life of men
and women as we see them on the street, in the factories and
on the farms." I give you a sentence from George Bernard
Shaw. A keen, incisive, challenging mind, whether you agree
with him or not (and great even to quarrel with). He said
that the worst sin against our fellow creatures is not to hate
them, but to be indifferent to them. I will give you one more
from Edward Everett Hale. You have heard it many times,
but I recall it here for its particular pertinence: "I am only
one, but I am one. I cannot do everything but I can do something. And what I can do, I ought to do, and what I ought
to do, by the grace of God I will do."

Now Ebrahim, I am proud of you as a pupil this morning. I hope I have not disgraced you as a teacher. We are glad that you made it possible for us to come to your conference. We are here because many wonderful friends wished us here. You made us feel at home and welcomed us wonderfully. I think it is best expressed in the lines of Tagore:

Thou hast made me known to friends who I knew not.
Thou hast given me shelter in homes not my own.
Thou hast brought the distant near,
And made a brother of the stranger.

Alice and I feel that nearness to you. We are grateful for it, and I would like to close by sharing with you this sentence of hope and faith: "I am absolutely unshaken in my faith that God created us, loves us and wants us not only to be good but to be happy." I have a conviction that Rotary has a mission here in India as well as world-wide, and I am proud to be associated with you as part of it, and to challenge you and ourselves this morning to rededicate ourselves and commit ourselves to do something about something in Rotary.

We Need Each Other

Will you permit me this morning a rather relaxed informality? I have a manuscript with me, and would rather not read it. I would rather talk to you out of my heart, and consider this something of a family gathering. Let us all relax into a very comfortable informality, if you will.

I am always especially grateful for the presence of the ladies, and for those occasions in which they are included. You add so much with your graciousness. You do so much for us: you lift us when we are down, and you level us off

Address given to Rotary International in Great Britain and Ireland Convention, April 1967.

when we are too high up. I have heard, in time past, of the typical helpfulness of the wife who was approached by her somewhat hopeful husband who said, "Darling, how many truly great men do you think there are in the world?" She replied, "I don't know, sweetheart, but I am sure there is one less than you think there are." For this and for other things we thank you.

We are impressed with your presence, and one would wonder what to say to a group seasoned in Rotary as you are. There would be nothing to say that you do not already know. I make no apology for repetition, for the process of learning is a process of repetition—an everlasting one, and we go about it day after day, and all of us need reminding, I think, more than we need being taught. I recall the occasion of a young six-year-old boy coming back from his first day at school, and his very fond mother, in typical fond-motherly fashion, said, "What did my son learn today?" And with typical six-year-old cynicism the boy said, "Not enough. I've got to go back tomorrow." Well, all of us are doing it—going back tomorrow and tomorrow, and I hope we shall do so everlastingly. It would be very dull if everything had been learned and if we were without challenges and without reminders.

As we have indicated to you before, Alice and I come to you with a genuine feeling of oneness with you—a genuine sense of somehow belonging here. I don't know what rights we have, but we have history and tradition and kinship and some common ancestry that we are proud of. We have a little different mixture between us. Two or three days ago we were out at Haverfordwest, which is where my Evans forebears came from centuries ago. Somehow a little English and Scottish blood got mixed in with the Welsh. I don't know whether it enriched the mixture or diluted it, but it's there. And Alice is English and Scottish with some Irish and I don't know what that does to her. So we belong to you, and we feel that you belong to us. We come to you with a sense of closeness, and of so much in common.

I think first of all we owe you some report of the trust that you have given to us, which we have all but completed. Some two and a half months are left of a year of responsibility, and we would share with you some impressions of Rotary world-wide. In the pursuit of this trust that you have placed upon us, we have visited every continent and perhaps more than fifty countries officially. It has required, in less than a year's time, a very rigorous schedule. We have moved early and late; we have found that there were more Rotarians than there were of us; and that anyone can wear anyone down in relays. We have found ourselves mingling with friends very late at night and moving on very early in the morning.

We come from a long line of pioneer forebears—some of those who settled the valley of the Great Salt Lake—and we remember of them that in their ruggedness they did not think anything of getting up at four or five in the morning. (We don't think much of it either!) We have been on trips where we have had to accommodate ourselves in one way or another to as many as ten different languages—one such beginning in Iceland and ending down in Morocco. It has been a wonderful experience—and we promise never to do it again! At times we had thought that we had come to look like our passport pictures, and anyone knows that anyone who looks like his passport picture isn't well enough to travel.

We are grateful that we can bring to you a report that in something more than 50 of Rotary's 134 countries we find that Rotary is solid and forward moving. We have found many of your friends world-wide, and we have found many clubs that your fellow countrymen have established as you of this great country have moved over the earth. We have seen your traces in many places.

Paul Harris, the founder of Rotary, said this:

"My hope for the future is that Rotarians will continue to be ambassadors of goodwill to all races, to persons of all religious faiths—that Rotarians will continue to be purveyors of tolerance, helpfulness, kindliness and friendliness—and that through our world-wide fellowship we shall ultimately achieve our goal of international understanding, goodwill, and peace."

I don't come to you with any conviction that Rotary has all the answers, or that it can solve all the problems. It is not a religion, nor a substitute for one; it is not a panacea for any purpose; but I have found it to be the most effective organization I know for bringing together men who would not normally come and sit down with one another; for bringing men to cross chasms that sometimes separate them, to cross borders and prejudices and interests, to cross the lines of professions and social circles, that they would not normally move out of or into. I suggest to you that the fact that Rotary has gathered you here is most significant—you who come from all over this beloved land of yours and sit down together in confidence and understanding. I suggest that if it had done nothing more significant than that, it would have more than justified itself.

You may ask us, and we ask ourselves, why we take time for this. There is only so much time in life. Benjamin Franklin said, "Time is the very stuff that life is made of," and there isn't much that we can do about it. Time moves at its own pace, and it moves one way only. Sometimes we would like to freeze life, we would like to hold it as it is; there are times when we have our families with us, when we have health and the good things of life, and we would like to hold on to them; but it moves on.

I shocked myself some years ago by making a simple multiplication and discovering that in some seventy years of time, there were only about twenty-five thousand days. And I multiplied once more, and discovered that there are only about six hundred thousand hours in seventy years of time. It shocked and startled me. I was then at an age when I began to think how many of those six hundred thousand hours I had already used. And then I began to think how many I might have left if the good Lord were that generous with me. And I began to be very discriminating as to what I did with every hour, and with every day of life.

And so the question comes, Why Rotary? Why take time for it? And I can only say to you that in my conviction and experience I have found it good for people. I think this is the measure of goodness. I have found that it contributes to understanding and communication and goodwill and peace and service and the relieving of human want and suffering among men. I can only say to you that Alice and I would not take a year of our lives, nor any part of it, for Rotary if we didn't have a conviction pertaining to its purpose and its future and its effectiveness. And this we bring to you as our witness from these wanderings around the world, as well as nearly thirty years of association with it at closer range.

On one of our official calls we had the very sorrowful experience that some of you are aware of. Down in Singapore there lived the 3rd Vice-President of Rotary International and many of you would know him: Doctor Arthur Thevathasan. Born in Ceylon, he had lived most of his life in Singapore. A medical doctor, his father was a Methodist minister. He was a man of great stature, of great service, beloved and respected in Rotary world-wide. We were there at an inter-city meeting at Singapore. The President of the Republic was with us and a very distinguished company gathered there. I had spoken, and Arthur had spoken, and we had together cut a Rotary birthday cake. Arthur was sitting between Alice and his wife Gnana, and we were in the midst of a ten-course Chinese dinner, and Arthur's head just slowly drooped to his chest, and he was gone—at fifty-three years of age, seemingly of great promise. Four doctors were there present, and did all they could, and there must be great frustration at times among the men of medicine when all of their skill, and all of their knowledge, and all of their facilities don't change the outcome. Well this deeply sobered us, of course. We went on up to Malaysia and filled some assignments that Arthur had asked us to fill and made them in the nature of memorial services for him, and then returned to Singapore and spoke at his funeral service. And there was a great outpouring in that city for this lost and beloved man.

I think we should face ourselves soberly with this inevitable exit from mortality for all of us. This dramatized it for us, and we shall never forget it. And the summons that sometime will come to each of us, I think will be of this nature. The Maker of us all and the Father of us all will in some sense say, "Come now, and come just as you are." There won't be time to correct the past, to do much about the undone things, to change much the nature of us within our hearts and inside ourselves. The readiness is the important lesson of this occurrence. "Come just as you are, and come now."

I think that whatever we ought to be, we ought to be becoming; and whatever we ought to be doing, we ought to be doing. We ought to be about our business. I feel in Rotary that we may well rededicate ourselves to a deeper—not only conviction—but a proof of that conviction. Carlyle, I believe it was, who said, "Conviction is worthless unless it is converted into conduct." I would plead with Rotarians everywhere, and you associated with them, for a rededication to "service above self."

In our visits we have called upon the leaders of many nations. We have been privileged to represent you in these official calls on the heads of countries and states and cities. I think a comment on this for a moment may be not out of order. Generally we found these men sincere and earnestly trying to solve the problems of this complex time of life in which we live. But we elect men and sometimes expect them to be more than they are. We often expect too much of our leaders and too little of ourselves. We have seen some very sincere and able and dedicated men, but we have seen no supermen, no indestructible men, no infallible men. I think that we must face the fact that to solve the problems of this world is going to require the best effort of each and all of us and our sharing of the problems. I like a sentence from Albert Camus, Nobel Prize author, now deceased, freely translated something like this: "Since I cannot separate myself from the time in which I am living, I have decided to become a part of it." One of the greatest determinations we could make is to become part of our own time and each assume our share of responsibilities and obligations. There is no country that can carry the whole world around with it. There is no man who can carry around a whole community. We shall solve the problems of the world as we assume our share of them and begin to do something about something, whatever it may be that is within our reach and according to our talents.

Sometimes, romantically I think, we suppose that we would have liked to have lived in the past. We read of times when knighthood was in flower and of the golden age of one era or another. But I have never read in history of any time in the past that didn't have its problems. I think this is mere romanticizing. I don't think there is any time back there when we would rather have lived, in reality, if we faced all the facts. There is so much missing back there that we have.

Sometimes we think that we would like to live at some time in the future, in some Utopia when all the problems have been solved—and what we're really talking about, I suppose, is heaven, and I have a literal belief in such a time. I come to you with a conviction in the personal and eternal continuance of each one of us, and I think that if we don't solve some of the problems here, we may well have to face them hereafter. I think that we will find the heaven that we so much seek. But the present reality is that this is our time of life, so far as the here and now are concerned. This is the planet on which the Lord God has placed us, these are the people he has given us to live with, these are the problems, and the sooner we face up to the facts of our own time the better. It doesn't matter how we got the problems, whether we inherited them or whether we created them, this is our time, our day, our generation, our opportunity. Life slips away swiftly. I think that to face up to becoming part of our own time and helping to solve these problems is the most forthright, wise and rewarding thing that we can do.

I have a great conviction about the world-oneness of Rotary—this internationality that crosses borders and brings us together on common ground that is so much needed. Not long ago I was restlessly reading in a hotel room the famous lines of John Donne, the words of which you would so well know: "No man is an island entire of itself." And then he went on to say in his own poetic language that if a clod is washed away from the shore the continent is the less. "Any man's death diminishes me," he said, "because I am involved in mankind." And then he added, "Therefore never send to know for whom the bell tolls, it tolls for thee."

All of us need each other. In a sense, what happens to any of us, happens to all of us. Countries need each other. Our great countries have needed each other in the past and we never know when we shall again, and we continue to do so. There is no such thing as self-sufficiency. I have never met in a true sense a self-made man. There is a great interdependence. John Muir, the great naturalist of the Sierra Mountains, wrote about a century ago that "whenever you pluck up anything from nature you find that it is attached to the whole universe." All of us are attached to each other, and to the whole. I am grateful for this world-oneness of Rotary and for your part in that world-oneness. "There are no distant places in the world anymore." We all have an interdependence.

Just a few weeks ago Alice and I were in the Ndola area in Zambia where Dag Hammerskjold met his death in the great copper belt. And I have carried around with me a sheaf of things he said—a man whose tragic death was a great loss to the world. One of the sentences was this. "Thanks to your success you now have something to lose." All of us here have received much and have much to lose. He also said, "You have not done enough, you have never done enough as long as there is something more that you can contribute." And then he added, "We act in faith and miracles occur." We come to you with great faith in the future, with faith in people and in the basic things of life, and in the everlasting things of life. What happens to people is exceedingly important. All of us need each other.

Now we pay our respects, as we leave you, to the leadership which you have contributed to Rotary International and the great part you have played in its traditions and its strength and its world-wide spread and oneness; to your present leadership—to Roland Richardson and his predecessors and his successors—thanking you for your graciousness, for your hospitality, your warm welcome to us, your making us feel that we were indeed back home.

Saying goodbye is difficult always. We shall not leave you the same as we came, but we shall take part of you with us and shall not forget this occasion that has brought us here. We are grateful to have this fellowship with you, and these few moments with you in an informal sharing of our hearts, our thoughts, and our feelings about the great organization that has brought us together.

May you have every blessing that you need in life: health and happiness, a deep enjoyment of each other, a fulfillment of all that you are capable of doing or becoming. Thank you, God bless you, and may peace be with you, this day—and always.

Looking Back, Looking Ahead

We come to you today on the Côte d'Azur deeply impressed with your presence, with an awareness that it is thirty years since we gathered here together as members of Rotary International. Not all of us; indeed, not many of us, but some of you were here thirty years ago, and what has happened since is such as to marvel, to frighten, and yet to reassure with faith.

Will R. Manier, Jr., of Nashville, Tennessee, was presiding here thirty years ago, and a young man named Maurice Duperrey of Paris was here elected to become president of

Address given at May 1967 Rotary International Convention, Nice, France.

Rotary International for 1937-38. He is still a young man—eighty-nine years young—and we shall hear from him tomorrow morning.

There were some 6,000 registered here at the convention in 1937. As of eight o'clock this morning there were 18,579 paid registrations at this convention. There were 180,000 Rotarians world-wide in 1937 and about 615,000 today. There were more than 4,000 Rotary clubs in 1937 and almost 13,000 today; 82 countries in 1937, 134 countries today. In several ways we have increased virtually three times or more what we were.

Nineteen thirty-seven was a world between two wars —a world of change and tensions. An unbelievable succession of events has occurred since then and a momentous cast of characters—for good and ill—have walked across the world's stage to play their various large and little parts, and then to leave, and thus life moves men through its swiftly moving scenes with the imponderable and eternal things remaining always and forever.

In all history, so far as we are aware, events have never been so momentous nor changed the lives of more men than in these thirty years since Rotary last gathered on the Côte d'Azur. An amazing, startling, discouraging, puzzling, productive, frightening, fabulous thirty years. Most of the people of the world have been born since then; most of the scientists of all time have lived since then—indeed are living today. Most of the nations of the world have in a sense been brought into being or have modified their borders since 1937. Communication, travel, tools, techniques were not then known as now we know them. Most of the currently used medicines were not then known. A social, political, economic, scientific revolution has occurred since 1937.

Indeed, so much has happened, so much has been discovered, so much has been made and modified, that one might presumptuously pose the question: What was there prior to 1937?

But to keep ourselves in focus and to balance the preeminent importance that each generation presumes, we could well look back to what had been brought into being before.

To begin the list modestly, Rotary was already thirty-two years old by 1937. In that same year Walt Disney released his first full length cartoon, "Snow White," which some of you will well remember.

Shakespeare had written his plays; Michelangelo had produced his matchless art; Pasteur had made his momentous discoveries; Wagner had written his music; Confucius, Buddha, Mohammed had made their contributions to moral and ethical life; Aristotle and Plato had left their imprint among men; the Pyramids had been built; the Vikings had sailed the seas; Columbus had "discovered" America (and found people already there, so it was apparent someone else had done it before!).

The Ptolemies, Copernicus, and Galileo and others already had some fairly solid ideas about the nature of the universe. The Crusaders had come and gone, printing and gunpowder had long since been discovered; Lindbergh had flown the ocean ten years before—ten years I believe, this very month (3,800 miles in 33½ hours at about 113 miles per hour). Marconi had long before sent words without wires.

Moses had received the Ten Commandments; Jesus had lived and left his message of the meaning and the everlastingness of life. The world had been brought into being—and it was good and beautiful and there was life, and loved ones, and human nature and people and problems. And all the basic laws were all then and long before in evidence—and in this sense we should have to go along with him who said: "There is nothing new under the sun."

And where does all this bring us? It brings us to the present, which is a very important place. It is interesting and often pleasant to dwell upon the past. But we are here, now, in Nice, in 1967, with all the complexities and problems and opportunities of the present. And if I had a theme today, or a selection of several, one would surely be this, as expressed in some lines from Longfellow:

> And let time teach thee soon the truth:
> There are no birds in last year's nest.

Sometimes, romantically, we think we would like to have lived in the past. But I know of no time that did not have its problems.

Now since it is Rotary that gathered us here, we must have the forthrightness to examine and appraise Rotary and the part it has or does or can play in all the relationships of life—for no organization has a right to take men's time unless it lifts men's lives.

And so there must be compelling reasons for Rotary.

I am not unmindful of the Rotarian who recently said, in substance: "Why are so many Rotarians gathered in Nice . . . is it merely for festivities . . . for relaxation . . . for spring-time on the Riviera?" Rotarians will not content themselves with statements on rules of membership. No call is made to so many important men for mere mechanics . . . and even if only part of them say so, all of them are asking themselves questions concerning the future of Rotary—concerning forceful actions in the international field.

I think Rotary can and must face such honest inquiry. To cite a provocative sentence: "There is no point at which we may arrive, and having arrived, remain." We must move on. We must be responsive to present problems. To justify the time and travel represented by your presence here, Rotary must have a very important purpose. With this in mind, I have reviewed the Object of Rotary and would encourage your re-reading. And I sample just a few phrases: "To encourage and foster the ideal of service . . . The development of acquaintance . . . High ethical standards in business and professions . . . dignifying his occupation as an opportunity to serve society . . . The advancement of international understanding, goodwill, and peace through a world fellowship of business and professional men . . ."

Rotary is first a fellowship from which flows confidence, communication, understanding and service world-wide. It is *not* an organization of political action. It *is* an organization of self-initiated service wherever there are human needs, however they may be served.

We have seen for ourselves Rotarians communicating and serving together between countries that are not so successfully communicating. We have seen Rotary bring men to cross chasms that might not otherwise be crossed—the chasms of prejudice, of ignorance, indifference, of differing backgrounds and beliefs.

We offer no grandiose answer, no easy prescription for the problems. We still live in a world of trouble and tension as we did in 1937. And often we overlook the simple answers, the law of cause and consequence, the basic laws of human relationships. But Rotary has done what it has done for more than sixty-two years with increasing success and acceptance, world-wide. And the fact that it brought you here together from eighty-eight countries is exceedingly significant, but it can and must do much more.

As we said at Denver last year: "The needs of the world are insatiable—and while we can't do everything for everyone, we can do something, for someone, somewhere."

If I may quote Winston Churchill, he said: "It is no use saying 'We are doing our best.' You have got to succeed in doing what is necessary."

Now since this is the President's report, we must mention a few specific matters pertaining to the trust that you a year ago at Denver entrusted to us, to represent you and Rotary International world-wide. Since then, in addition to administrative duties, Alice and I have traveled most earnestly and widely over the world.

We have seen many impressive Rotary projects. With our own eyes we have seen magnificent service and evidences of effective international fellowship. We have seen a single, small Rotary club with members holding passports from more than twenty different nations. We have seen busy, competent, professional men take their precious time to bless the lives of impaired children and others in remote areas of the world.

We come back with an awareness that Rotary not only has a past, but a present, and a future mission far beyond what its founders could have foreseen in this its sixty-third year—it being also the fiftieth year of The Rotary Foundation. We have seen what we sincerely feel is a resurgence of Rotary.

And so the year has gone—and so again we are gathered together in this beautiful and favored place. But the questions are ever present—people—their problems, life—its purpose, the why of things—and how we use our lives, and what we take our time for—our precious irreplaceable time.

What's life all about? It goes so swiftly. It means so much. The question is with us always—and so each man searches.

One of the answers is that people are everlastingly important—and that life is for learning, and one of life's lessons is learning how to get along with others—and this is one reason for Rotary.

Sometimes we oversimplify the problems—or overcomplicate them. Sometimes we blame almost everything on some currently emphasized problem, such as population explosion. But underpopulated places have problems as well as overpopulated places. As I remember reading, Adam and Eve had problems, and it wasn't the problem of overpopulation.

The problem is human nature—people—and the opportunity is people—the most important thing on earth is people—and the greatest resource on earth is man's resourcefulness—and we come to you with the conviction that there is virtually no physical problem on earth that men of intelligence and goodwill cannot solve, if unselfishly and earnestly they will turn themselves to such solution with patience and understanding and work and faith before the Father of us all, before him who keeps creation in its course.

And along with our world-wide activities and interests, and wide-ranging fellowships and service, we need to look inward as well as out and to put the home, the family back where it belongs.

Sometimes it seems we approach problems from the wrong end. We create agencies and institutions to do what the home should do—but the world will never be stronger than the strength of our homes. No nation will ever be stronger than family love and loyalty. No one has more responsibility to shape the character of our own children than we have. If we cannot set their character, who can? We cannot escape first responsibility for our families. We cannot abdicate the relationship that God has given. And if we do not begin with sound relationships at home, how can we hope to be convincing anywhere else in the world? How can we hope to solve other peoples' problems if we can't solve our own? How can we be convincing world-wide if our own houses are not in order?

"No other success can compensate for failure in the home" (David O. McKay), to use a quoted sentence. We need to keep our families close to us—and teach them. How can we expect others to do for us what we fail to do ourselves? And wouldn't it be tragic if we reached out for others world-wide and failed to save our own families—or failed to save ourselves? We need to look at where we live as well as where we work. Any Rotarian who is too busy to be on the best of terms with his family is too busy. He's overbalanced.

Home and family—no other interest should supersede it. And this isn't only personal. This is service to society. For the solid, wholesome home and family is the strength and salvation of society. Let no Rotarian forget it. If we are not successful at home, we're really not successful.

Keep close, draw near to one another in the home with your whole hearts—and for this purpose take whatever time it takes, for if we are not convincing at home, we are not convincing anywhere in the world. "No other success can compensate for failure in the home."

Some years ago, President Dwight Eisenhower said approximately this: "I would not move my little finger to defend the Western world if I thought that man were just a machine, with no spark of divinity in him." In this materialistic age there is sometimes a tendency to think of man merely as a machine, as an assemblage of atoms. And if he were merely a machine, what happens to him wouldn't matter very much.

But I come to you with the conviction that the most meaningful things are everlasting, including life and truth and intelligence and personality and family and friends, always and forever—and how we live is important, how we serve is important, what happens to every person is important.

The problems are perennial—but people are important, and despite the complexity of problems, I come to you with a conviction that the Creator is still in command, that there are eternal purposes that prevail, and that as we do the best we can from day to day and move forward with faith we shall find the answers we so much seek and shall look back and see that there was a pattern, a plan, and a purpose—an eternal purpose. And in the working out of this purpose we are all dependent upon one other. All of us have need of each other. There is no man, no nation that is self-sufficient. There is no man, no nation, that can afford to live in isolation. We have needed each other in the past; we need each other in the future. In a sense, what happens to any of us happens to all of us.

And so, with you, I reaffirm my faith in the function Rotary has to perform—but Rotary and all of us should and must be doing much, much more. In the words of Robert Louis Stevenson: "To be what we are, and to become what we are capable of becoming, is the only end of life."

Heaven help us to get back to simple faith and trust and honest respect and courage, doing our best to do what needs to be done, humbly and with patience, with understanding.

As we enjoy this conviction, as we enjoy each other, as we search ourselves, as we rededicate ourselves to "Service

Above Self," may we remind ourselves of the words of Albert Camus: "We have nothing to lose—except everything!"

May God help us to move into the future with faith and peace and hope, enriching each other's lives, and the lives of all men, everywhere—and may peace be with you, this day—and always.

THE MESSAGE

From "The Pen Of A Ready Writer"

Quest for Contentment

When we cannot find contentment in ourselves it is useless to seek it elsewhere.

—La Rouchefoucauld

Perhaps you have never heard of Jabinbar. Perhaps no one has. But it doesn't really matter. We will say that he was a man who lived in a far country, and that he was happy, almost, and contented, almost. Did he not have a water buffalo and a wife, and did they not both work well? Why should he not be happy? That is, why should he not, until one day across the field there was his neighbor plowing with two water buffaloes. Now Jabinbar is not contented, almost; nor will he be until he, Jabinbar, also plows with two water buffaloes.

And that is the story of Jabinbar, for whom perhaps we smile a bit indulgently—inwardly if not outwardly. But are we so different?

Contentment is a relative and comparative term, as is wealth, as is comfort—as are many other things in the minds and in the lives of men. We are rich, or we think we are, by comparison with what our neighbors have, rather than by any absolute standard of our own.

For example, good fortune has been ours, some of us have been soundly sure, in driving a car with perhaps only half a dozen years or so behind it. But one day (remember Jabinbar), three doors down and across the street there came a car made this year! Shades of discontent tinged with envy! Our car hasn't changed appreciably these past few days, but the one across the street has changed everything.

As long as happiness and contentment are thus more subject to what other people have and do than to what we have and do, most of us perhaps are going to be relatively unhappy and relatively discontented—until we learn to carry our contentment within us, and not turn the color of green inside or out when our neighbor's wife appears wearing a newer hat, or when our neighbor mortgages his future for something we don't have and can ill afford. Usually no more can he afford it.

This elusive contentment isn't a question of being poor or of being rich. There are both contented and restless people in all financial and social brackets. It isn't what men have. It is what they permit themselves to think, whether they have it or not. There are many things all of us cannot have. There are none of us who have everything we want. Perhaps there are none of us who ever will have them.

Furthermore, there are many things we could have that we shouldn't have—things that would contribute to our discontent if we had them. And parents who deny their children nothing, deny them a chance for real happiness. Any child who gets everything he wants, whether it is good for him or not (or any adult either, for that matter), is having piled up inside him one of the worst cases of chronic discontent that anyone was ever afflicted with—as surely as though it had already happened.

But having said this much about contentment, may we guard against confusing it with indolence, idleness, or indifference. To be contented does not mean that we shall not have ambitions, or that we shall not set our hearts upon worthwhile things and work toward them. No man who doesn't want something is going to do much that amounts to much for himself or anyone else. We should always have urgent objectives and always be in pursuit of them. Even if all our material wants were satisfied, we should be ever earnestly seeking more knowledge, greater understanding, better ways of doing things. A wholesome unrest is the moving power of progress.

The answer then—or part of it at least—honest effort (let's even dare to call it *work* if the word is not too much in disrepute!) for anything we want that would be good for us if we got it. But in all conscience, may we never let the things we can't have or don't have or shouldn't have spoil our enjoyment of the things we do have and can have. If we value our happiness let us not forget it, for one of the greatest lessons in life is learning to be happy without the things we cannot or should not have.

He who has learned this can go his way with a quiet contentment that neither the discontented rich nor the discontented poor nor the discontented world (nor perhaps we ourselves—nor even Jabinbar) can easily understand.

Which Road?

Common are the stories, in literature and in life, of those who have searched long and distantly for things which finally were found very close to where their search began. And perhaps neither in literature nor in life is anything so constantly pursued or so frequently missed as happiness.

Some thoughtful thinking went into the making of the now immortal phrase, "Life, liberty, and the *pursuit* of happiness." There are shrewd distinctions in these seven words: Life—an inalienable right, an eternal fact. Liberty—a right, also, but less certain than life. But with happiness—only the right to *pursue* it!

You can give a man his liberty. He may not use it well or keep it long, but you *can* give it to him. But not so his happiness. You can help him on his way, but you cannot "give" it to him. Ultimately he works it out himself, or he does not find it at all.

But this one thing all men have in common—we are all looking for it. And if there were no reasonable chance of finding it, we had just as well ring down the curtain on time and eternity, for happiness is properly the chief business and the ultimate end of life.

And yet some of us get some very queer notions about this most sought-after thing in life—and many of us pass it by without seeing it. Some of us are so hotly in pursuit of some counterfeit kind that the real thing wouldn't have a chance of being recognized. But when we miss it, it is often easy to look back and see where we might have found it.

And yet, in making the many decisions of life, in living the pace we live, in hearing the confusing opinions we hear, it isn't difficult to understand how so many of us miss finding what we are most pursuing. But our bitterness and disappointment may well be tempered by knowing that our failures are not planned.

We don't deliberately set out to make a mess of our lives—not any of us. Some people do make such a mess of their lives that it would seem they couldn't possibly have gotten into that much trouble without deliberately working at it. But no man wants to be unhappy, no man tries to be unhappy. Unhappiness, of the kind which men bring on themselves, is the result of error, or a succession of errors, which mislead us into looking for the right thing in the wrong way.

Among the many common misconceptions concerning happiness are these:

1—That money makes happiness. False. With no money it may be difficult to find. Some money helps. Moderate living is often an antidote to neurotic discontent. But, in any case, much money is not the answer. Paradoxically, some men may have sold their happiness, but no one was ever able to buy it.

2—That pleasure is synonymous with happiness. False. You can wear yourself ragged in pursuit of pleasure in all the so-called bright spots of the earth—and still wake up in dull despair.

3—That fame brings happiness. False again. Fame of the right kind can be a satisfaction, but not a guarantee of happiness. At the height of his fame, Alexander Pope is thus quoted: "I am so tired of being the 'great Mr. Pope.' I want only the common joys of life." Mark the marital muddles in America's "movie" manors—and then mark off fame as a factor of happiness.

4—That happiness is found by restless running up and down the world. False. We carry it with us—or we don't have it. And sometimes after we've pursued it on a far journey, we find that we have left our happiness at home. But why couldn't we see it before we left?

The things that make men happy have been written in the experience of the ages as far back as the record goes. A few among them are these: A quiet conscience; useful work; love and respect; an awareness of being needed and wanted; the ability to meet our obligations and to live within our means; conformity with the spirit and the letter of the laws of men, the laws of decency, the laws of God.

Others could be added—but if we want happiness, we had better look for it where it is—and not where we think it ought to be or wish it were. We are all looking for it—but it is available on its own terms, not on ours. Our only "inalienable right" where happiness is concerned is the right to pursue it, and there is no point in pursuing it where it never was and never will be found. No one ever overtook anything—including happiness—by pursuing it on the wrong road.

The Forgotten Freedom

Be not made a beggar by banqueting upon borrowing.
—Ecclesiasticus 18:33

Wilkins Micawber is speaking: "To leave this metropolis . . . without acquitting myself of this obligation . . . would

weigh upon my mind to an insupportable extent. I have therefore prepared . . . a document which accomplishes the desired
object . . . I beg to hand to my friend, Mr. Thomas Traddles,
my IOU . . . and I am happy to recover my moral dignity,
and to know that I can once more walk erect before my fellow
man."

Thus Wilkins Micawber walks through the pages of
Dickens' *David Copperfield,* dodging dunners, decrying creditors, and discharging debts with IOUs—always with the
avowed expectancy that "something will turn up," but what
"turned up" usually were more badgering bills.

But Wilkins Micawber assuredly was not the last man
to delude himself into thinking that an IOU or a promissory
note discharged a debt. And while the old debtor's prison
which Dickens so fondly portrayed, and which Micawber so
frequently favored, is not now with us, yet many a man has
lost his freedom behind walls of debt as unyielding, and bars
as unbending, as those of stone and steel. But, with hearing
much about many freedoms, perchance we have heard too
little lately, and perchance have heeded too little what we
have heard, about the forgotten freedom—freedom from debt.

There are many reasons for going into debt—some
good, some bad. There is legitimate borrowing, of course.
There are some necessary things most of us could never acquire
except by incurring an obligation. And there are some great
ventures that would never be born without borrowing. But
there is also debt induced by extravagance; debt that comes
by appeasing appetites; and debts fostered by false philosophies. And the burden and the bondage of an unbalanced
budget are such as to suggest some reminders of this forgotten
freedom:

One—It is difficult to preach this philosophy, but more
people have been made unhappy by what they bought too
hastily than by what they lost by "thinking it over."

Two—Salesmanship is a desirable and necessary art. But
so, at times, is sales resistance. It may be the other fellow's
business to be persuasive, but it is our business to be realistic—

even if he is "our friend"; even if he is letting us in on "the chance of a lifetime"; even if it is "going, going, gone." Saying "no" at the right time may be embarrassing, but never as embarrassing as saying "yes" at the wrong time.

Three—Universally, and almost invariably, things cost more than first seemed likely. Nearly always we underestimate the extras, and miscalculate the emergencies and the misfortunes. Because of the unforeseen and the unpredictable, it is unsafe to live to the last margin of our means.

Four—A wise and seasoned traveller once said—and he had been over the road, both down and up financially— "You get so little when you go up, and you give up so much when you come down." How heartbreakingly true. The pleasure of acquiring things we don't need is not to be compared with the pain of giving up things we have become attached to.

Five—There is a further phase of this question, exceedingly important to anyone who has a mind for his future: How can anyone who can't keep his own affairs straight expect others to trust him with their affairs? If our own lives are habitually in a financial muddle, how can we expect employer, friends, or anyone, to impose confidence or give us important responsibility?

Many have started out with the false feeling that the ability to incur debt gives the right to live beyond our means, and have ended up with the badgering embarrassment of dodging dunners, and cringing from creditors, while trying to answer the unanswerable: How do we spend more than we make, and still come out even?

The most important business in the world is the business of your life. Keep it solvent—for much of happiness, of content or discontent, of comfort or discomfort, is involved in this financial factor. Overhead is the burden of business—often the cause of its failure; and it is often also the burden of our private lives, the weight of which has crushed many a man who manacled himself with more than he could manage.

There comes to mind a conversation between Paul the Apostle and the captain of the Romans: "And the chief captain answered, With a great sum obtained I this freedom. And Paul said, But I was free born." (Acts 22:28.) But no man is free if he is born with a debt; if his world is in debt. No man is born free if preceding generations have not paid their obligations. No man is free who has debts of his own— for "the borrower is a servant to the lender." (Proverbs 22:7.)

Let Wilkins Micawber speak again: "Annual income twenty pounds, annual expenditure nineteen (pounds), nineteen (shillings), six (pence): result—happiness. Annual income twenty pounds, annual expenditure twenty pounds, ought and six (pence): result—misery."

May we not forget the forgotten freedom—freedom from debt.

Forgiving and Forgetting

"I can forgive, but I cannot forget," is only another way of saying, "I cannot forgive."

—Henry Ward Beecher

Quoting Kin Hubbard: "Nobuddy ever fergits where he buried a hatchet." (Abe Martin's Broadcast, p. 52.) And an unidentified author has observed that "a woman may consent to forget and forgive, but she will never drop the habit of referring to the matter now and then."

So comes the question: How much is "forgetting" a part of "forgiving?" Can an old grudge be fully forgiven if it's not forgotten?

There is no one who does not sometimes need to be forgiven, and there is no one who does not sometimes hope his errors will be forgotten. But a verbally proffered forgiveness comes much easier than an actually accomplished forgetfulness.

Suppose we look in on two people:

Years ago, months ago, weeks ago, one of them made a mistake which affected and offended the other. Anger and accusation, resentment and recrimination prevailed for awhile, but seemingly burned themselves out, and were followed by reconciliation. Forgiveness was asked and given.

But still come the questions: Will there be recurring reminders? Will there be rankling resentment? Or will forgiving be followed by forgetting?

If every time we are miffed we remind a man of all his mistakes, we haven't fully forgiven. If we are constantly throwing up the past it is exceedingly doubtful if we have given forgiveness.

People can't move forward on a new footing if the old false footing is always there to stumble over. People cannot live together in happiness until differences are settled between them. And differences are not settled as long as they are bitterly remembered. To remember a grudge is to hold a grudge, and to hold a grudge is to be unforgiving.

Of course, we may say that we can make ourselves forgive, but we cannot make ourselves forget what is firmly fastened in memory. But we do have some control over forgetfulness as well as over remembrance. We can crowd out thoughts with other thoughts. We can refuse to dwell upon one thing by dwelling upon another. We cannot will our minds to be a blank. But, with patience and perseverance, we can select the thoughts we think, in some measure, at least.

But of course, the offender has some obligation. If sincere forgiveness is expected, sincere repentance should be offered. And sincere repentance is more than saying we're sorry. "Forgiving the unrepentant is like drawing pictures on water."— Japanese proverb. And we have it on good authority that he who expects forgiveness must be forgiving: "For if ye forgive men their trespasses, your heavenly Father will also forgive you: But if ye forgive not men their trespasses, neither will your Father forgive your trespasses." (Matthew 6:14, 15.)

There is good reason for concluding that forgetting is essential to sincere forgiveness: "I, even I, am he that blotteth out thy transgressions for mine own sake, and will not remember thy sins." (Isaiah 43:25.) If we see ever before us the picture of former offenses, then every present prospect will be marred with old marks. If we let the snarled past continually tangle up the present, there isn't much chance for unfettering the future.

There is little hope of walking in new ways as long as stumbling blocks from the paths of the past are constantly strewn before us. If there are those who have past grievances and who want to walk together again, they will literally have to learn to forget as well as to say that they forgive. Otherwise they will likely find ever-increasing friction as past accounts accumulate. If they would find a new footing of faith, understanding, confidence, and love, they must learn to leave unwelcome pictures in the past.

It isn't often easy to forgive, and it is still more difficult to forget, but no one has done either completely unless he had earnestly tried to do both. Resentments remembered and nurtured through the years offer evidence that forgiveness has not been fully given.

Forgiving is more than merely saying so. Forgetting is much of forgiving.

Tomorrow May Be Better

Tell me, . . . when does that tomorrow of yours come?
—Marcus Martial

This week we are worried. This week we are crowded. This week we are frantically trying to do some of the things we have left too long. But next week—next week is going to be different. Next week things will ease up. Next week we shall have time to take care of those long-neglected loose ends. Next week we shall be "over the hump"—and then—then—

Tomorrow — always tomorrow. Tomorrow we shall breathe easier. Tomorrow our work will be in better order. Tomorrow we shall relax. Tomorrow we shall live! But "tell me," said Marcus Martial some nineteen centuries ago, "tell me . . . when does that tomorrow of yours come?" Tomorrow —next week, next month, next year!—always we live for the relief that is not now—always we live for the time when we shall live more in the manner we would like to live.

But next week isn't likely to be much different—unless we do something to make it different from its predecessors. This is true for several reasons—because many of our muddles are of our own making. We often say "yes" when we know we ought to say "no." We often say we will do things that seem easy a few days off—but which are difficult to do when the day comes for doing them. We incur debts, and promise to pay next week—next month. Right now it looks like it wouldn't be too difficult. But the future comes fast when a debt is due.

People frequently apologize for their failure to visit a sick friend—because they have been "so busy." And yet those same people (and its *us* we're looking at) have found time to idle away an evening, or to do many other things they wanted to do.

Often when we say we don't have time, it would be more accurate to say that we don't take time. Or, to put it another way: We give our time more to the things we like more, and less to the things we like less. We usually find time to do what we really want to do.

Sometimes when we see someone playing the piano, we wish we could play the piano. But we don't wish it to the point where we are willing to take the time to practice— because, with most of us, there are other things we want to do more.

Of course, making a living, and other "unavoidable" activities, often press us into patterns that are not of our choosing. But even those of us who are most pressed do some things we want to do. Even those of us who have the least choice have some choice. And the fact that we choose to do some things and don't choose to do other things, is an indication of what we want to do.

If we really want to play the piano—or if we really want to see a sick friend—we'll likely take time to do it. And there isn't much reason to suppose that there will be any more time next week, or tomorrow, or next year. The difference, if there is any, will be a difference in what we do with our time.

As Ed Wynn used to say to Graham McNamee each week on the air: "The show is going to be different this week, Graham!" But each week, as we well remember, the show was essentially the same!

Next week may be better. But it will have a better chance of being better if we do something to make it better.

Can I Count on You?

Have you ever put your foot on something that wasn't there—on a step that you had counted on, or the rung of a ladder that gave way at the wrong time, or on a brake that didn't hold when you urgently needed it?

One more question: If you were crossing the desert and were desperate for want of water, would you rather have the promise of a full gallon, or one pint that you knew you could count on now? If you have ever been in want of water, you'll know the answer. A pint may save a life, but a promise without performance won't save anyone.

It is important to remind young people of the importance of dependability, because they may not yet have found out how far it will take them if they have it, or how far the lack of it will leave them behind.

Of all the important qualities of character, none that we know of is much more important than dependability. And many men just miss being what they might have been by lacking this one great ingredient. A person may be brilliant, talented, generous, witty, kind, considerate, and many other things, and still not go very far without dependability.

It isn't a question only of what he is able to do; it is a question also of what he does do. It isn't a question only of what he will do; it is a question also of when he will do it. It isn't a question only of can he pay or can't he; it is a question also of will he pay or won't he?

Actually we may often be much better off with a person who has half as much ability but twice as much dependability —with a person who is half as "smart" and always there, rather than twice as "smart" but unpredictable. No matter how much anyone has to offer, if he doesn't deliver it when and where it is needed, it isn't worth much.

Wars that could have been won have been lost by the failure of reserves to arrive at the appointed time and place. A safety device that is dependable only part of the time, isn't safe to rely on any of the time. A fire alarm that sometimes works and sometimes doesn't may be worse than no alarm at all.

Men need to know what they can count on. A youngster jumping into outstretched arms must know that he is going to be caught, or he loses all confidence. Investors need to know that their security is safe. A bank depositor must know that his money is there when he wants it.

People can't live on promises. They can't pay on promises. If a person is honest one day and dishonest the next, perhaps we can only conclude that he is dishonest, because we can't safely conclude anything else.

If a person is loyal one day and disloyal the next, perhaps we can only conclude that he is disloyal, because we can't safely conclude anything else. With an undependable person we don't know when to relax and when to worry—and so we have to worry all the time.

Suppose that spring came some years and that some years it didn't come? *We need to know.*

It would be difficult to name any activity in life in which undependability is not heavily penalized. It would be difficult to name any activity in life in which a dependable performance is not held at a premium. There is a great reward for consistency. And the man who does what he says he will do when he says he will do it can more than hold his own in competition with people who are more brilliant but less dependable.

Indeed, being where we ought to be when we ought to be there, and doing what we ought to do when it ought to be done, are among the greatest factors of success and safety. Beyond all brilliance, beyond all talent, beyond all ability, beyond spectacular performance and pleasing personality, there is a premium on dependability that no other quality of character can ever replace.

If you find a man you can count on, you had better hold onto him. The "little man who isn't there" isn't worth much to anyone.

"What's Wrong with Work?"

Somewhere recently I read this intriguing title. I don't know who wrote it and I don't know whether the author was "fer" it or "agin' " it—but I'd like to take his title and talk to it. Work can become terribly tiresome—but so can anything else. Let's look at golf, for instance.

Suppose someone were to make men walk around an eighty-acre field and knock little white balls into little holes, with long sticks! Actually, they would want money for it, with shorter hours and more pay and time and a half for overtime. And it's more than likely that they would form a golfer's union to see that they weren't imposed upon. And many of them would quit the job because it was too boring, too tiring, too difficult. But now we do it for recreation, and pay plenty for the privilege!

Some men enjoy chopping wood—in preference to playing golf. But people who chop wood when we want it chopped call it work. Youngsters often play football and baseball in preference to coming in and eating. But when a person plays football or baseball for a living, it comes under the category of "work."

The Tom Sawyer episode is an apt illustration. His friends competed for the privilege of whitewashing a fence. But if some adult had told them to do it, they would have disappeared like dew before the summer sun.

Many men work harder physically at fishing than at the office, but call it recreation. Many men work harder on their vacations than they ever do at their vocations. Many men think harder at chess or checkers during the evenings than they usually do during the working day—but they call it relaxation!

People dance into the early hours and are pleased to pay for the privilege. And some people sing until we wish they were silent. But if they do the same thing on schedule, or at the instance of someone else, they quickly call it work. Actually a man may willingly work his muscles or his mind to absolute exhaustion—and call it play, because he has his heart in it.

In other words, work is often only a matter of attitude and interest. And what is work at some times is recreation at other times. What is work to some people is recreation to other people. It is the set of the mind, as well as the set of time and circumstances, that makes one thing work to one person and the same thing pleasure to another person.

But men become bored with their pleasures and pastimes. They become discontented in their leisure. We need no more evidence than all of us see every day of the restless discontent of our own generation. And it is a discontent that is difficult to explain in face of the fact that we have more hours free from work and more comforts and conveniences than any other people ever had.

No ancient king or caliph of fact or of fable could, with all the power and wealth of his sovereignty and subjects, see what even the least of us can see, or hear what even the least of us can hear, or be served as even the least of us is served—and yet, there is much discontent among us, and no mistake about it. Could one cause of our discontent be that too many of us are working too hard at trying to avoid work?

"Happiness," wrote David Grayson in his *Adventures in Contentment*, "is nearly always a rebound from hard work. . . . Happiness . . . loves sweat, weariness, self-sacrifice. She will be found lurking in corn fields and factories and hovering over littered desks; she crowns the unconscious head of the busy child. If you look up suddenly from hard work you will see her, but if you look too long she fades sorrowfully away."

One thing we often forget is that the fourth commandment not only says that we shall observe the Sabbath, but it also says, "Six days shalt thou labour, and do all thy work."

We may live on the labors of others, but we cannot take from anyone else the surpassing satisfaction of work well done. And if the whole idea of work were ever to become too tiresome to us, we should surely be lost. Work is essential to human happiness and survival.

Everyone should enjoy the thrill of doing his best work willingly. And when anyone withholds his best work, there is corrosion of mind and muscle—and of spirit.

What's wrong with work? One thing wrong with it is that too many people have the wrong idea about it. Another thing wrong with it is that it's too unpopular with too many people in too many places.

The Great Gift of Gratitude

Give a grateful man more than he asks.
—*Portuguese Proverb*

Until this morning, I felt that I had been very much imposed upon. At a cost of considerable effort and inconvenience, some days ago I performed a difficult service for a friend—at his urgent insistence. So far as I knew he hadn't made any effort to see me since then. There was no word of thanks—no evidence of any appreciation—no suggestion that my services had been satisfactory—just silence.

Silence—that is, until this morning, when a sincere and satisfying note of appreciation came from him. And in the moment or two it took to read it, it warmed my heart and altered my outlook on the whole episode. Writing it had cost him only a very little time, but it had rewarded me richly.

There is hardly anything within reason that seems too much trouble for a sincerely appreciative person. But almost anyone might begrudge almost anything to an ungrateful person. Almost any relationship is unsatisfacory when it is all one way among strangers or friends, between parents and children, or between man and his Maker.

I also well remember some months ago being asked to do something for a rather remote acquaintance. (It took almost a day—and at the rate life moves, a day is something to consider!) While he was on the "asking end" he was so sweetly solicitous, so complimentary, so ingratiating! But from the moment I undertook to do what he wanted, I have seen no evidence of any gratitude.

No doubt we have all had such experiences. We can all recall occasions when we have done something for someone who seemed to be so sincerely grateful that we have felt embarrassed because we didn't do more. And, in contrast, perhaps we have all had occasion to feel deeply disappointed in those who have accepted services in cold and uncommunicative silence.

No one who hasn't had it happen will ever know how much it means to a speaker to have someone come up after and express appreciation. On the other hand, it is terrible to see one's listeners fade away without any word of thanks, and to feel that one's efforts have fallen flat.

When someone asks us out to dinner or invites us into his home for an evening, even if we aren't too pleased with the prospect, the least we can do is to offer sincere appreciation—for it takes time and effort and expense to entertain others.

It is disappointing when a child accepts gifts and services and simply says, "What else have you got for me?" But when this fault is found in adults, it is magnified many times.

Of course, some people sometimes perform services purely for their own pleasure. Some people find their pleasure in making a display of their gratuities and good works. And, as it says in the Sermon on the Mount, ". . . they have their reward." (Matthew 6:2.)

On the other hand, there are those who hope to pay their way with a counterfeit kind of gratitude. They hope to cancel obligations with superficial thanks. They know that talk is cheap, and they would rather pay by expressing profuse appreciation than pay in more substantial ways. But all debts cannot be discharged simply by saying "thanks." Some debts call for a return of service and consideration.

But gratitude offers an extra premium in all personal relationships. It is the added interest that makes every favor, every service, every consideration mean more.

For a parent, there is nothing within reason that is too much trouble for a grateful child. But there is little satisfaction for parents who labor the best of their lives for children who accept their service and sacrifices as a matter of course, and who offer little evidence of gratitude or of anything else in return.

There may be times later in life when we shall need much more from our children than a "big bear hug" or an enthusiastic "Gee, Dad, thanks! . . ." And the ultimate evidence of our children's gratitude will be what they do for us when we need them in material and substantial ways, as they once needed us. But until that time comes—as in so many cases it does come—a sincere expression of thanks goes a long way in adding to the sweetness of service.

"Gratitude," says an old French proverb, "is the heart's memory." It is a social grace and an essential quality of character. And beyond our gratitude to men, there must always be the earnest gratitude of man to his Maker—for life, for food, for freedom, for friends, for family—and for many things unmentioned.

The sin of ingratitude is grievous.

"Whence Cometh My Help"

As four of the foremost enemies of mankind, one philosopher has listed: worry, hate, doubt, fear. There are many other enemies also, including illness and accident, greed and guilt, war and want, disease and death—and an endlessly long list. But they all somehow seem to tie themselves to these four: worry, hate, doubt, fear—and they all ride roughshod over our personal peace.

It would be terrible to meet any of them without the sustaining power of prayer. It would be terrible to face any serious situation without the privilege of approaching him in whose image men were made, and who is mindful of the men he made.

It would be terrible to feel alone in the world, beyond the help of human hands.

Dr. Alexis Carrel, Nobel Prize winner, once wrote: "As a physician, I have seen men, after all other therapy had

failed, lifted out of disease and melancholy by the serene effort
of prayer. It is the only power in the world that seems to
overcome the so-called 'laws of nature'; the occasions on
which prayer has dramatically done this have been termed
'miracles.' But a constant, quieter miracle takes place hourly
in the hearts of men and women who have discovered that
prayer supplies them with a steady flow of sustaining power
in their daily lives . . . When we pray we link ourselves with
the inexhaustible motive power that spins the universe . . .
Even in asking, our human deficiencies are filled and we arise
strengthened and repaired . . . Whenever we address God in
fervent prayer, we change both soul and body for the better.
It could not happen that any man or woman could pray for a
single moment without some good result."

In every problem of every passing day, in the classroom,
in the sickroom, in the shop, in the factory, in the field, in the
office, in halls of government and in humble homes, the
power of prayer is (or can be and should be) an inexhaustible
source of strength, a comforting, sustaining force.

But the fact that there is power in prayer doesn't mean
that everything we pray for will immediately be ours, or that
everything we pray against will immediately be wiped away.
We well remember the observation of the small girl who said
in Sunday School: "Just because we don't always get what
we pray for doesn't mean that our prayers aren't answered.
It may mean that the answer is 'no!' "

Fathers don't always give children all they ask for—
not even if they can afford it. Wise fathers know that children
must do many things by their own effort. And a mere petition,
a mere request, may not immediately bring all the things
a child thinks he wants.

A wise Father may show us other ways to get what we
think we want; or he may show us the wisdom of waiting—
or he may show us the wisdom of changing our wants.

Obviously all men cannot (and should not) have everything they pray for. This is true because people often pray

against one another, as in war when two opposing sides both pray for victory; as in a race when two contestants both want to win; as in a lawsuit when two parties both want to possess the same piece of property, or as with the weather, when one man wants rain for his crops and another wants clear skies for a picnic or an outdoor performance.

If we are disappointed in prayer it is often, perhaps, because we don't quite understand the purpose of prayer (or perhaps because we don't quite understand the purpose of life).

Most of us might be disposed to pray for unbroken good fortune, for uninterrupted happiness, for perpetual prosperity, for victory, for assured success, for affluence and ease. But life isn't an uninterrupted holiday; nor, obviously, was it intended to be. Rather it is a time of training, and often of trial, of education, and of self-effort, as evidenced by the Lord God when he expelled Adam and Eve from Eden and said that they should eat bread by the sweat of their brow.

It is not the usual purpose of prayer to serve us like Aladdin's lamp, to bring us ease without effort. Prayer is not a matter of asking only. It should not be always as the beggar's upturned hand. Often the purpose of prayer is to give us strength to do what needs to be done, wisdom to see the way to solve our own problems, and ability to do our best in our tasks.

We need to pray not only for freedom from difficulty but for strength to endure, for faith and fortitude to face what sometimes must be faced. ("Nevertheless not my will, but thine, be done.") Prayer is also partly appreciation, and partly a petition for others and for all the world, as well as for "me and mine."

Prayer is communication between man and his Maker, between child and Father. The power of prayer is from him who gave us life, and whose power is apparent in all Nature, in all its wonder and variety and endlessly evolving purpose.

Prayer is an unfailing source of strength and understanding and endurance. It is the source "whence cometh my help." (Psalm 121:1.) "More things are wrought by prayer than this world dreams of."—Alfred Tennyson, *Morte d'Arthur*.

How Close Can You Come?

The pitcher that goes too often to the well is broken at last.
—Old English Proverb

There is an old tale told about Ben Holladay, the colorful nineteenth-century character who operated the Overland Stage Line. It is reported that he once asked three prospective employees how safely they could drive a stagecoach around a certain precipitous curve.

The first applicant replied that he could drive within a foot of the outer edge with absolute safety and assurance.

"Very good," agreed Mr. Holladay.

The second man was even more brash in his boasting: "A foot!" he exclaimed. "Why, I can drive with the rim of the wheel half over the edge. I know where every horse is going to step and I have every horse in hand!"

"Very good. Very good," conceded Mr. Holladay.

He then turned to the third driver, who somewhat hesitantly said: "I don't know how close I kin come to the edge—but I'll keep as far away from it as I kin."

It is reported that the third man was hired.

Courage is a great quality of character. (So is confidence —if it isn't overdone.) But courage should never be confused with carelessness or overconfidence. Doing something dangerous that needs to be done may indicate great courage. But taking useless chances and deliberately and needlessly doing something dangerous is evidence of lack of judgment, lack of maturity, lack of simple common sense.

Not long ago, over one of our nation-wide highways an airplane pilot, who apparently had a flair for showing off, swooped down on a moving car, misjudged the distance, and crashed the top of the car with the plane's undergear—for no apparent reason except to frighten the driver and "see how close he could come."

Only a few days ago three bystanders lost their lives when a plane "buzzed" a small town a time or two, and then cracked up in front of a confectionery store. In this case the pilot was killed, so no one definitely knows why he did what he did—but to observers it seemed that he, too, was seeing how close he could come.

Youngsters who drive cars sometimes see how close they can come. They hug the center line and force others over. They "peel" their tires in screeching starts; and they rush up to the stop signs and pedestrian lanes and squeal to a standstill, with only a hair to spare—"just for fun." But lost lives and crippling crashes are never "for fun," and the driver who deliberately sees "how close he can come" should be ruled off the road.

As the old and unconfirmed legend has it, William Tell was forced to shoot an apple from his son's head. (Fortunately he had the skill—but even so, the result might have been otherwise.) But the character of William Tell would have come down to us with quite a different color if legend had said that he had shot an apple from his son's head "just to see how close he could come."

Sharpshooting or knife-throwing with live targets may be all right in a circus or a sideshow—but no action that needlessly jeopardizes the life or health or happiness or the peace or property of people is ever sane or sensible.

But it isn't only in physical feats that people see how close they can come. Often they dabble with other practices that endanger them. They come too close to the limits of the law. They come too close to forming harmful habits. They come too close to compromising situations. And often after they have found how close they can come, they find that they have come too close to pull back in time to save themselves.

In one of his lectures on "Representative Men," Emerson tells of the inscription on the gates of Busyrane—" 'Be bold'; and on the second gate—'Be bold, be bold, and evermore be bold'; and then again . . . at the third gate—'Be not too bold.' "

Simple common sense suggests keeping away from the outer edge.

Tell Him Now!

You know, it is strange what we can see when we want to. It is strange what we can see under some circumstances that we can't see under other circumstances. Take a man who has died, for example. His neighbors who may have criticized him caustically but a day or two before quietly come to call, and are sorry for some of the things they have said, and begin to think of the finer things about him that they hadn't thought about before.

It is a well-known fact that when people pass away, the living mostly remember and mostly speak of the better things about them, and their faults do somehow seem to fade. There are exceptions to be sure, but we can recall comparatively few occasions when the kindliest possible comments were not made about the person who had passed.

The woman whose husband has been abusive nevertheless thinks of his virtues (whatever they were), and of how much she will miss him. The father who has been much less than he might have been is nevertheless mourned and missed, and his commendable qualities are clearly recalled. And the friend with whom we have had some friction may, in memory, again become our fond and faithful friend. When death comes, censure seems to soften even for those who have strayed far from being what they should have been.

In short, when people pass we seem less certain of our own judgments, and we seem more willing to leave judgment in the hands of him whose final right it is to judge the hearts and minds of men. And I wonder if "over there" it will not be somewhat the same. I wonder if the worthwhile things people have done won't weigh rather heavily on the right side of the scales and their superficial faults a little lighter.

I wouldn't want to be misunderstood; I believe that every man will have to face his every act. I believe that neglect and indifference will have to be accounted for, as well as deliberate misdoing. I believe that consequences follow when causes are set in motion. I believe that people will have to pay the penalties for their failings and their faults. But I am also well aware that there aren't any perfect people, and that all men are a mixture of some things they should be and of some things they shouldn't be.

I am aware that it is easy to find fault with anyone— or anything—if we are looking for faults. I am also aware that we can and do overlook much that we don't like in other people, when we want to. (We do it with our own children. Others often emphasize their faults while we emphasize their virtues.)

If we were to look upon those who are present a little more like we look upon those who have passed, we would all be much more kindly and comfortable. Many misunderstandings would be mended if we would mellow before people have departed as we do after they have departed. Many burdens would be lighter if we would lift them when we could, instead of waiting until we wish we could. Much bitterness would be avoided if we would only go halfway when there are still two parties to appreciate it, instead of waiting until one of the parties has passed.

And there would be much more human happiness if some of the eulogies we offer after others are gone were uttered before they go. And there are many things we would be grateful we had done, if we wouldn't wait until we wish we hadn't waited.

The person who has passed away still has in his record the faults and flaws he had before—and also all the virtues. It isn't his record that has changed; it is our attitude that has changed. And he might have been better (and we might have been better) if our attitude had altered while he was here.

So don't save all those sweet songs and charitable thoughts and kindly words for funerals. Put a bit more of the "funereal philosophy" into the living of life while there are still ears to hear and eyes to see and hearts to understand. Let failings be forgiven and virtues be appreciated in the present—instead of waiting for some future funeral.

The Loneliest People

Considering the fact that there are several billion people in the world, there is an amazing amount of loneliness. And another ever-startling fact is that the loneliest people aren't always found in the loneliest places. Some of the worst loneliness in the world is found where people mingle with other people, but where there is no meeting of minds, no understanding, no warmth of welcome.

Some people are lonely with their own families. Some are lonely with those they work with. Some parents are lonely with their own children; and children likewise are sometimes lonely for lack of sympathetic association. Loneliness has little to do with population per square mile. It is more a matter of people "per heart."

Some evenings ago I saw a distinguished man sitting "alone" among many acquaintances. He was what people would call a self-sufficient person—prominent and influential in public affairs, successful in private affairs. He didn't need money. He didn't need influence. To look at him casually, he didn't need anything. But one understanding person looked more than casually, and went over and sat with him and talked easily and understandingly. Tears came to his eyes. "Thank you," he said, "for what you have done tonight. No one knows how lonely it is sometimes."

Loneliness can come to anyone, on every level of life— to prominent people as well as to little-known people, to young people as well as to old people, to people who live with other people as well as to those who literally live alone. Young people sometimes suffer the loneliness of those who haven't found "their place" with others of their own age.

Older people are sometimes lonely because they seem to have outlived their lives. At least, they have outlived those who knew and loved them in their younger years. They may be cared for kindly, but the swift sweep of family affairs may rush around them at a pace at which they cannot fully participate—sometimes because they aren't able, sometimes because they aren't willing, and sometimes because they aren't welcome. In any case, they cannot enter into everything as once they did when their generation was riding the full tide of affairs.

The loneliness that comes when life has been lived long is a tired and tragic kind of loneliness that any of us may some day see—and that all of us should seek to alleviate for others.

We might sometimes suppose that loneliness is most common among inconspicuous people. But some people who meet the most people are the loneliest people. Celebrities, so-called, are often subject to severe loneliness. They have plenty of "company," and precious little privacy. But often they are isolated from their former friends, and often they are forced to leave behind those who best understand them.

They may be constantly called upon to meet many people who envy and admire them, who seek their favors, who compliment them and sincerely wish them well. They may be constantly before the public and the press, and be known in every crossroads community, and still be acutely lonely for want of simple understanding and association.

The star, the prima donna, or the president, or the man of money has his personal problems, his personal sorrows, his personal side. He also has his fears, and may even have an unsuspected shyness inside.

The man in the front office is as likely to be lonely as anyone who works for him. He is as likely to have a sick youngster at home, or trouble with the plumbing, or a headache. And despite the "front" that his position imposes upon him, he may want as much as anyone else to talk about the ball game, or about his troubles, or about the best time to plant petunias.

Everyone on every level of life is subject to the aches and ailments and fears and hopes that the rest of us humans have, and everyone is sometimes subject to loneliness. Some are lonely because they are separated from their own kind for some cause. Some have made mistakes. Some have left their dreams behind. Some can't go back. Some can scarcely countenance even their own company.

But whatever the cause, whether from shyness or "smallness" or "greatness," or some mistake, or some misfortune—or whether it be because life has been lived long—we can be sure that no one really wants to be lonely.

And no matter how proud or shy or unapproachable a person appears, if we can find a way to approach him as a person, we shall discover the quality of humanness in his heart, and we shall discover there something of the same longing and loneliness that we have in our hearts.

And much as it may hurt to be alone and lonely, it may hurt much more to be lonely in the presence of thoughtless people.

It Works!

If you want to try an interesting experiment, pick out the most stony-eyed, tight-lipped, grim-faced person you can find. Don't cheat. Don't pick out an easy mark. Pick on someone who has really crawled inside himself—someone whom you assume is aloof, uncompromising, uncooperative, uncommunicative, or downright caustically contrary. Pick out a person whom you would ordinarily choose to avoid, and try casual and unpretentious kindness and consideration.

Don't expect to thaw him out all at once. Don't expect to crash through his outer crust with the first thrust. (You wouldn't expect one blow to break reinforced concrete. You might have to hit several times in the same place before you would reasonably expect results.) But try it with honest, unassuming sincerity, and see what can be accomplished with that kind of kindness.

If you need any added evidence (evidence in a negative way), watch how other men harden when you harden—how they strike back: spark for spark, fire for fire, fist for fist, sarcasm for sarcasm.

All of us, perhaps, feel terrible at times after we have lost our tempers—terrible and embarrassed: Embarrassed because of our lack of self-control, because other men have seen us at our worst, and because our anger has aroused anger in others.

It is still and everlastingly true (and inherent in human nature) that "a soft answer turneth away wrath." And it is equally true that a hot or hard answer brings out the hotness and hardness in others.

A half-century or so ago Henry Drummond wrote a brief brochure which has since been widely read and which he called the *Greatest Thing in the World*. He was referring, of course, to "love," as paraphrased from the First Epistle of Paul the Apostle to the Corinthians, chapter 13—the chapter on charity—which all of should read much oftener than once in a while, and which begins, "Though I speak with the tongues of men and of angels, and have not charity, I am become as sounding brass, or a tinkling cymbal.

"And though I have the gift of prophecy, and understand all mysteries, and all knowledge; and though I have all faith, so that I could remove mountains, and have not charity, I am nothing.

"And though I bestow all my goods to feed the poor, and though I give my body to be burned, and have not charity, it profiteth me nothing.

"Charity suffereth long, and is kind; charity envieth not; charity vaunteth not itself, is not puffed up,

"Doth not behave itself unseemly, seeketh not her own, is not easily provoked, thinketh no evil;

"Rejoiceth not in iniquity, but rejoiceth in the truth;

"Beareth all things, believeth all things, hopeth all things, endureth all things.

"Charity never faileth: . . .

"And now abideth faith, hope, charity, these three; but the greatest of these is charity."

It is true—and it works. Kindness will melt a man when heat and hardness will only make him harder. Of course we wouldn't want to say that everyone we cultivate with kindness will immediately return kindness. Sometimes it takes a long time for the remedy to work. Sometimes, with some people, it may never seem to work. Seemingly there are some incorrigibles. There are flagrantly, obdurately, deliberately difficult people. There are those who have gone so far that they seem to be all but unreachable, untouchable and impenetrably adamant.

Lucifer must have been long and patiently labored with love. Absalom was dearly beloved by David. And other fathers who have somehow found themselves alienated from their sons—some of them at least have long and sincerely tried love.

But whether we can see it or not, kindness cannot help but cause some softening inside. And if we persist sincerely enough, even the most difficult cases are likely to show results after long labor. I wouldn't want to guarantee that it would always work at once. But this I would be willing to guarantee: that kindness will work oftener than anything else in the world will work.

And when the final score is in and the results are recorded, we shall find that kindness (and the love from which it comes) is still "the greatest thing in the world."

Ten for Temper

Anger is like those ruins which smash themselves on what they fall.

—Seneca

In his nineteenth-century *Handbook of Proverbs,* H. G. Bohn includes this axiom on anger: "Anger begins with folly, and ends with repentance."

The influence of mind over matter—and over health and happiness—has been much talked of lately, almost as if psychosomatic symptoms were something new. But one of the greatest experiments concerning this subject was conducted more than a century ago by William Beaumont, a frontier army surgeon who, through an unusual set of circumstances, discovered how mental and emotional factors affect the ability of the stomach to handle food.

Most of you may remember the story of how a young half-caste Indian of French-Canadian descent, Alexis St. Martin by name, had a hole opened up into his stomach by an accidental gunshot, back in 1822, and how, through this opening, Dr. Beaumont observed digestive reactions for a long time. Among his many significant findings, published in a pamphlet in 1833, Dr. Beaumont discovered that when Alexis was angry the flow of the digestive juices was retarded and the stomach failed to do its normal work in many ways.

This is just one of many things that anger does as it impedes normal processes and pours poisons into the physical and mental systems of man. It is still true, as it was when it was anciently written: "Whom the gods would destroy they first make mad."

"Anger," said Horace, "is a brief lunacy." An uncontrolled temper does indeed seem to be akin to temporary insanity, because men do things in anger that they would never do in their right minds—things they may regret for the rest of their lives. They strike bitter blows with words and with weapons in a way that they would never do if they had controlled their tempers.

Of course there are occasions that call for righteous anger. As Aristotle observed, "We praise the man who is angry on the right grounds, against the right persons, in the right manner, at the right moment, and for the right length of time." We don't have much respect for a person who doesn't have a "temper" at the right time. Neither, on the converse, can we impose complete confidence in any person who hasn't learned to control his temper.

One of the greatest personal conquests I have ever observed was the conquest by a man who in his younger years had a violent, volatile temper and who heroically learned to control it later in life. On the other hand, I know an able man who almost has the unqualified affection of countless friends—except for one flagrant fault. He hasn't learned to control his temper. Literally, he is likely on small provocation to throw his bag or break his clubs on the golf course and utter a volley of violent oaths when he or his partner makes a poor play. With him, tantrums of temper seem like drink to some men. He goes for a while without letting loose, but when he lets loose he lets loose all the way, to the hurt and embarrassment of himself and everyone around him. This man pays a high price for his tempestuous temper.

While there may be grounds for righteous, reasoning anger, there are never justifiable grounds for uncontrolled anger. A man whose anger is out of control is no more capable of acting for himself intelligently than a man under the influence of intoxicants. Indeed, the odds are all against the person who loses his temper. As Thomas Fuller expressed it: "It's two to one in all things against the angry man." And, "How much more grievous," wrote Marcus Aurelius, "are the consequences of anger than the causes of it."

In his *Crusade in Europe,* General Eisenhower tells of the great qualities of character that contributed to the remarkable leadership of the late General George Patton—but whose high-tension temper could, on occasion, have cost him his command.

I don't suppose there is any universal cure for trigger tempers any more than there is a universal cure for anything else. But one of the safest tonics for temper is time. Many centuries ago Seneca said, "The best cure for anger is delay." And the idea of the "ten count" has been traced back at least as far as Thomas Jefferson, who wrote, "When angry, count ten before you speak; if very angry, an hundred."

Many a man has been saved from many a mistake by counting ten—and I am sure that many more men have been saved by the "ten count" than have ever been counted out by the count of ten.

The "Oil" of Understanding

It is often easy to be right in what we do, but wrong in how we do it. A multimillion illustrations could be given, but take just this one for example:

Often it is necessary to relieve people of their positions—to alter their assignments, to change their titles, their offices and their activities, or even to dispense with their services altogether. For many real reasons, such action may be unavoidable—because of age, because of progress, because of rules and regulations, and because of changing circumstances and economic necessity.

Let's admit that what is done in such circumstances often has to be done even if it unfavorably affects some people. Let's admit that moving men around or hiring and firing or shifting assignments is essential and right in many situations.

But *how* it is done may be another matter. It may be done cruelly and curtly; it may be done evasively and cowardly. Or it may be done by calling a person in, and taking him into our confidence and giving him honest answers, and allowing him time to adjust to the new situation—and telling him first, so that he won't be shocked and embarrassed by hearing it from outside sources, through gossip or the "grapevine."

It's the way things are done, the way things are said— the deceptive means, the shady methods, the aggravating attitudes and inconsideration, the cruelty and unkindness—that cause so much resentment and resistance and friction in human affairs, and that wear away at human hearts.

It isn't enough to be sincere—it is also necessary to be right. (A man can be sincerely wrong.) And it isn't enough to be right—it is also necessary to have an understanding heart—to be correct without being cruel—to be right without being bigoted. Frequently we may feel sure we are right in principle. But it isn't a question of compromising principles. A man must stay with his principles until he is honestly convinced otherwise. But it is possible to be right in what we think and wrong in how we present a proposal, wrong in our attitudes, wrong in the caustic curtness of our answers, wrong in unkindness and discourtesy.

Two acquaintances were heatedly arguing the other day. They both had a point, and basically their opinions were not far apart. Their difficulties were not so much a matter of principle as of personality. But they were contentious and caustic. They were generating "heat" instead of "light."

And as the friction increased, a third man entered, and made an understanding observation: In the engine of an automobile, he said, all the moving parts are fitted closely and smoothly together. The pistons and the rings around them are smoothly and accurately set against the cylinder walls. And the bearings and the gears and the valves and all the other moving parts are accurately engineered and fitted.

But no matter just how right the machine may be— how rightly designed, how accurately engineered, how smooth the surface of its moving parts—they are crowded so closely and move so quickly that friction and high heat would wear them away if it weren't for the oil that is added—the oil that puts a fine film on the surface.

And like the pistons that are fitted into the motor block, like the rings that are crowded closely to the sides of the cylinders, in the society we live in we are often crowded closely. We often live in close quarters. We work in close quarters. Our ideas and interests often clash. And if there isn't a film of "oil" of understanding in all this rubbing we do, physically and mentally and emotionally, we'll generate high heat and break down the social machinery and wear away at one another.

•

Very Important Person

Added to all the other endless alphabetical abbreviations is one that has become common in news parlance and in social and political protocol—VIP, which, as you wise readers already know, stands for Very Important Person.

It has been a long time since the world at large believed that "the king can do no wrong." But we have become accustomed to what someone has called a "shortage of copper and a surplus of 'brass.' " We have become accustomed to the parade of VIPs with their publicity and patronage, their fanfare and followers. And often (even if we may think the individual doesn't deserve it) there is a certain respect and deference due the office itself.

Some men are loved for themselves, and some men are waited upon because of their positions. (Some, fortunately, are sincerely accepted for both.) But perhaps one of the "unkindest cuts" that can come to men accustomed to patronage and position is to learn that people have been paying respect to their position and not to them personally. One thing that none of us should ever forget, if we were ever to hold an office, is this: Strip us of our office and authority and we would perhaps swiftly see that we are not personally very important in the eyes of some people.

But what really started us on this subject (and all that has gone before is purely preface) is this conviction: We know of no one in life who isn't an Important Person. We know of no man on the street (or in the gutter, for that matter) who isn't a child of God with the same rights and with the same relationship to his Father in heaven as all the rest of us have.

We know of no one, young or old, from infants to elderly individuals, whose past or whose potential we would want to appraise as being unimportant. We know of no one we might see in any public place—on subways or busses, or walking in shabby shoes—or any boy selling papers, or any abandoned urchin, who doesn't have an inestimable, unknown potential, here and hereafter.

We could go down the list of all of them: immigrants; nameless, unknown lads (some of whom have come to this country and have been its benefactors), not all of them physically prepossessing, some of them pitifully underprivileged—but within each is an immortal spirit, an immortal personality and potential, and an eternal God-given intelligence.

Sometimes it seems to be assumed that anyone without influence is unimportant. But we have a feeling that before the bar of the Great Judge, the tables of influence may frequently be turned, and that "many that are first shall be last; and the last shall be first." (Matthew 19:30.)

(And frankly, we see no reason why children should be bypassed in public places or made to wait beyond "their turn." Do a few years make so much difference in the right to courtesy and consideration?)

Every man's feelings, every man's struggles, every man's sorrows, every man's hopes, every man's opportunity in life is important to all of us. And we wouldn't want to eliminate from our list of Important Persons anyone who has been given the privilege of living life, and whose brother and "keeper" we are, because the Lord God has said that it is so.

All the people who live behind all the doors we pass (and don't pass) are important. This was the message of the Man of Galilee: the message of the dignity and freedom and eternal importance of every individual child of God.

Furthermore, we are not the final judges of our fellow men. Of course, there are laws that we must enforce if we are to live in the same society. But we don't know enough about the makings of a man, about the eternal complexities, to give final appraisal. Fortunately, final judgment is in hands higher than ours.

We have heard of a father who was living alone and suffering from an incurable illness. Christmas came and went without his seeing his children, some of whom (who were able and available) lived in the same city. They presumed much in bypassing him—despite misunderstandings they may have had (as who of us hasn't) and despite misfortunes he may have met (as who of us couldn't?). He was an Important Person (as we earnestly believe his family would some day discover— sooner than too late, we hope).

There is much false pride in the world, as well as false humility. There are those who falsely efface themselves. Dickens' fans will never forget Humble Uriah Heep. ('E was 'umble all right—like a snake in the grass.) May heaven spare us from self-seeking "humility!" But there is a kind of humility which is an indispensable component of greatness in people —the kind that recognizes in all other men a divine dignity and an immortal potential beyond our power to appraise— and that recognizes in all others the same rights and the same relationship to God as we see in ourselves.

Literally, there is no such thing as an unimportant person.

Rebellion

No man ever lived his life exactly as he planned it. And no man ever lived life exactly as anyone else planned it. There are things all of us want that we don't get. There are plans all of us make that never move beyond the hopes in our hearts. There are reverses which upset our fondest dreams and most cherished desires.

Unforeseen events are always in the offing. And when events take a turn we didn't anticipate, and thwart our plans and purposes, resentment, and even bitter rebellion, are often our first reactions—rebellion against life, and against our inability to control it according to our own ideas.

But even though it is sometimes difficult to see or to accept, many of the things we don't plan add a richness to life and a breadth to experience that we never would have known if we had been permitted to call every play and to shape every event. And yet, often we persist in railing against irrevocable realities. We fight facts that cannot be refuted, and rebelliously beat our heads and bruise our hearts because life isn't always what we think it should be.

Countless people who have had their careers carefully planned have had them swept away by a single sudden circumstance. Accidents, sickness, misfortune in money matters, the loss of loved ones, the faithlessness of friends, the perfidy of people, the missing of time and tide, and many other such circumstances can, in a moment, take from any of us the plans and purposes and pleasures we have long pursued.

When such misfortunes come to others, it sometimes seems easy to advise them how to salvage the wreckage of their plans and purposes. It is often easy to be philosophical about other people's troubles. We may even cite them some classic examples: Beethoven making music in his deafness; Pope composing flawless poetry despite his misshapen form; Milton making immortal verse with sightless eyes.

But Milton and Pope and Beethoven, and many more like them, offer little personal comfort when misfortune makes its home with us—with us personally, not with some historical hero; not even with our next-door neighbor. And, in truth, the classic examples to which we often refer are not more dramatic nor more heroic than what many men do despite heartbreaking difficulties, in almost every town, and in many, many families.

But what else is there to do when life rides roughly over our best-laid plans? When some unlooked-for accident, or some unwanted circumstance becomes an irrevocable reality, when we are faced with unchangeable facts, there is no peace or purpose in letting rebellion rankle within us. Rebellion isn't the answer.

Neither is passive resignation. Resignation may retreat too far, may lie down and give up in unconditional surrender. Abject resignation smacks too much of the once-proud Napoleon who wrote from the shadows of his later life: "O, well, no matter what happens, there is always death."

But somewhere between rebellion and beaten resignation, there is a glorious fighting ground where a man can make the most of whatever there is left of life. Shall we call it reconciliation?—the reconcilation that still faces the day and does with it what can yet be done.

There are many things seemingly unjust that are imposed upon men by a seemingly cruel fate. There are many things in life beyond the present power of anyone to answer or to understand. But what we cannot understand we shall have to accept on faith, because it is the thing to do and also because there doesn't appear to be anything else to do. In any case, rebellion isn't the answer. To fight facts is futile.

But neither is hopelessness the answer. The way to personal peace, the way to effectiveness, the way to happiness is to change what should be changed, if we can, and to make the most of what we cannot change, without giving way to the bitterness of rebellion.

Going Places

Sometimes young people who are working their way up become discouraged by the long look ahead. They see those who have "arrived," and they sometimes suppose that the only real satisfaction in life comes with having gotten where one is going. But if they suppose this, they have made a mistake, for going places can be as thrilling, and often more so, as merely to have gone places.

It is often said that "anticipation is greater than realization." And moving in the right direction is often more satisfying than having "arrived." For example, with children (and with most of us), actually to be on our way to a picnic can be a greater thrill than already to have gone as far as we're going. When we have had our fun and spent our time, there may be many satisfactions and happy memories—but not like the thrill of going places.

To have eaten is also a satisfaction. But to be hungry and actually to be eating is one of life's most genuinely enjoyed experiences. And playing in today's game is much more exciting than the memory of a game we once won. And the pleasure in travel, or much of it at least, is in the actual going and not merely in having arrived.

To have gotten where one wants to go and to sit down and say, "Here I am" would seem to give much satisfaction. And no doubt it does—for a time. But not to be going any farther must be an awful anticlimax in any man's life—for men are creatures of movement. And he who has his eyes on the future begins to look for other places to go as soon as he has gotten where he was going.

Indeed, if having "arrived" were to mean that we've gone as far as we're going, and that here's where we stop, it would also mean that much of the best of life has already gone by. This is one reason why many men don't quit working even after they have reached a place of eminence, and have acquired all the money that anyone could ever reasonably want. They like to be in the game, to be doing things, to be on their way.

Many who have sacrificed much to "arrive" find that the happiest years were lived while they were moving up. No matter who they are or how far they have gone, they often find that getting there was much more interesting than merely having gotten there. And they often find less pleasure in the things they have than there was in getting them.

Of course, a hard climb is a good thing to have over— but not if it's the last climb!

But, in a final sense, men will never "arrive," for to arrive finally would mean that there are no more worlds to conquer, no more places to see, no more lesson to learn, no more work to do. There will always be work to do, and men will always be moving into an illimitable future. If this weren't so, the present and the past wouldn't mean much.

And so we would say to those who are looking at the hill ahead: Be grateful for a goal that keeps you going, for an unsolved problem that keeps you learning, for interests and obligations that keep you working and moving—because whatever satisfaction there is in having "arrived," it will lack something of the thrill of getting there. Ask anyone who has "arrived" if it isn't so.

And remember this: You don't have to have "arrived" to be happy. You just have to know that you are on your way, and that you're moving in the right direction. If you know this, you can enjoy the journey, even if you're far from where you want to go.

"I" Trouble

Let another man praise thee, and not thine own mouth; a stranger and not thine own lips.

—Proverbs 27:2

One reader writes: "One of our neighbors is always showing off, always tells us where she's going, where she's been, what she has . . . what she does . . . Whenever she talks to any of us it's only to brag—and it's so tiresome. If you could please, please, write an article about braggers . . ."

No doubt we all know people who have an acute case of "I" trouble. Some of them are good, and they know it. Some of them are not so good, and they don't know it.

Let's look a moment at two sides of the subject: In the first place, there is something wrong with a person who doesn't have a reasonably good opinion of himself and reasonable pride in his possessions. But there is also something wrong with the person who lets his ego get beyond reasonable bounds —and who becomes, as Shakespeare said, in *Much Ado About Nothing,* "the trumpet of his own virtues."

Whenever a man has to be his own publicity agent he penalizes himself in the opinion of other people. He may be good, but he ought to let others say so rather than exhaust the subject himself. He should have learned, as Pliny the Younger put it, "What would have been a great source of honor if another had related it, becomes nothing when the doer relates it himself."

A talented young man some time ago calmly conceded that he was a better sculptor than Michelangelo. Maybe he was. It isn't impossible. But to hear it come unblushingly from his own lips was embarrassing—embarrassing to his listeners, at least. But he didn't seem to be the least bit embarrassed. Even if it were true, it would have been so much better if someone else had said it. And we could not help but hear again the words of Horace: "What will this boaster produce worthy of such inflated language?"

It is quite natural that we should be very much wrapped up in ourselves, because after all we are ourselves. And, since self-preservation is the first law of nature, self-praise is easy to understand. Nevertheless, an acute case of "I" trouble is and will continue to be socially unacceptable. And to hear a person openly become the object of his own adoration soon turns his auditors sour on the subject.

Bragging comes natural to youngsters. But some of them soon learn, because their frank young friends don't hesitate to tell them, that:

> If you would keep your ears from jeers,
> These things keep meekly hid:
> Myself and me, or my and mine,
> And how I do or did.
>
> (W. E. Norris)

And yet many people grow old with the fault: people who have the brightest children in the world, the worst operation in the world, who have been through the worst experiences in the world, and, who are the best of whatever they are, and have the best of whatever there is—all of course according to their own admission.

Somehow they remind us of Emerson's comment on cunning egotism, "If I cannot brag of knowing something, then I brag of not knowing." Some boasting is no doubt innocent enough, and some of it is done to make other people envious. But almost all of it is in bad taste unless it is done very deftly.

And so may we offer a few obvious observations, to whom it may concern. Other people also have doctors who thought their operations were the worst they had ever seen. Other people also have children who are very unusual for their age. Other people also have the most amazing experiences.

We could add interminably to the list. But the point is apparent—that is, to all except those who really have "I" trouble. And they will continue incessantly to talk about them and theirs. And there really isn't very much that anyone can do about it, except be bored.

> If you stop to consider the work you have done
> And to boast what your labor is worth, dear,
> Angels may come for you, Willie my son,
> But you'll never be wanted on Earth, dear.
>
> (Rudyard Kipling)

Exit Lines

Let men decide firmly what they will not do, and they will be free to do vigorously what they ought to do.

—Mencius

In drama, "exit lines" save many situations. In fact, without an exit line the playwright would often be perplexed as to how to end an impasse. It is relatively easy to bring an actor on stage and begin an argument—but how to get him off and end it!

Theoretically, a dogged discussion between two persistent people could continue until one of them faints or falls—which eventuality neither the author nor the audience can well wait for. But if the heroine can turn on her heel and cast her last withering retort over her disappearing shoulder as she slams the door (and shakes the set), or as the lights black out and the curtain falls, we can keep the play from going on and on, far (or farther) into the night. Thank goodness (we have often thought) for exit lines!

But the uses of exit lines are by no means limited to the theatre. In life, also, a reliable stock of them may save many situations.

For example, a good exit line is needed for those who telephone a busy household to pass the time of day, and assume that their leisure is everyone's leisure. Not infrequently the urgent exit line for such a situation is voiced in flustered feminine phrases: "Excuse me! I smell something burning!" (Exit running, as Shakespeare would say.)

There should also be some safe and sure exit line for the remotely remembered acquaintance who strolls through your office door on your busiest morning, and prolongs pleasantries while your deadline is getting deader and your blood pressure is rising higher. "Yes, the family is well." "Yes, I remember George." "Yes, Hickory High was a grand old school." "Yes, the years do pass!" (It's astounding that apoplexy doesn't have a higher incidence!)

We could often use an inoffensive but infallible exit line for the person who has time to waste, and promptly proves it, and for the visitor who supposes that his vacation is everyone's vacation.

But there are also numerous needs for exit lines in more serious circumstances. There is a line in *The Hucksters* that is worth preserving and pondering. After the chief character has permitted himself to be maneuvered through many reversals of principle and opinion to keep the patronage of a pampered client, he finally reaches his limit, renounces his high-paying position, and walks out a free man, with this line: "There isn't enough money in the world!"

There isn't enough money in the world to justify any of us in doing many things we might be doing for a share of it. Affluence that can't live with conscience and conviction is always a bad bargain. And whoever may have bought it at so high a price should have thought of a good exit line before he got himself into that unenviable position.

An unforgettable exit line of sacred history is the one that terminated the temptation of Jesus the Christ by Lucifer, his fallen brother, when "the devil taketh him up into an exceeding high mountain, and sheweth him all the kingdoms of the world, and the glory of them; And saith unto him, All these things will I give thee, if thou wilt fall down and worship me. Then saith Jesus unto him, Get thee hence, Satan." (Matthew 4:8-10.)

Ofttimes people—especially perhaps young people—are persuaded with promises of preferment on the one hand, or implied threats of unpopularity on the other. Ofttimes such alternatives as these are offered: Follow the crowd, or be an oddity. Do what we do, or be strangely different. Take your choice between prudence and popularity!

Discreet and definite withdrawal from those who urge such alternatives is always in order—and often the only adequate exit line is an emphatic "No."

Indeed, a definite and determined "No" is one of the best exit lines ever spoken, because many people don't understand any other language. There are times when a polite "No," with explanations offered, would be utterly inadequate. And so, all of us should keep on hand an unequivocal "No" as part of our rough and ready stock of exit lines, for any situation that calls for language that can be understood even by people who don't want to understand. And where action is called for, slamming the door and setting out on a determined run may do just as well—or better. Doing just that has saved many a person from many a mistake—and Joseph in Egypt was one of them.

In social situations, in business bargaining, and in many other matters, all of us are placed in the position of meeting many proposals. We must be open-minded and listen to a variety of views. But when what is being proposed transcends the limits of propriety and principle, of conviction and conscience, there is no point in continuing consideration.

Safety and sanity suggest that we adopt principles within which we will conduct our lives and beyond which we will not be moved—principles by which we can immediately decide what will be our final answer—our exit line—to any proposal. To quote again: "Let men decide firmly what they will not do, and they will be free to do vigorously what they ought to do." —which, in itself, is an excellent line. Exeunt Omnes.

Index